MINUS ~~THE~~

JOURNEY

A Journal through Europe—
a Redemption in Serbia

Michael N. Sever

To contact the author, please go to: michaelnseverauthor.com

Book design and publishing management:
Bryan Tomasovich, The Publishing World

Sever, Michael N.
Minus the Journey: A Journal through Europe—a Redemption in Serbia

ISBN: 978-0-578-31158-6

1. Biography & Autobiography/ Memoir. 2. Travel/ Eastern Europe. 3. Humor/ Travel.

AMMS Publishing

Distributed by Ingram

Printed in the U.S.A.

MINUS THE JOURNEY

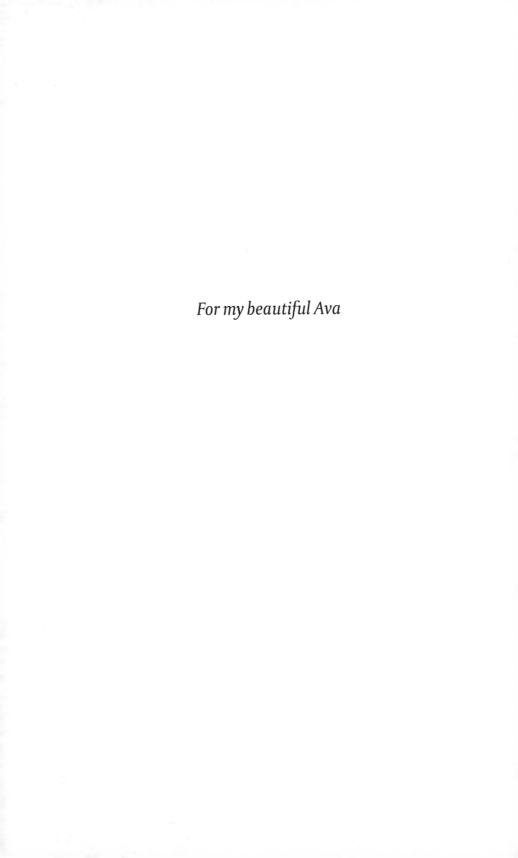

For my beautiful Ava

Preface

O ne of the border guards directed us away from the line and into a parking space. Jovo then let me know I needed a visa to enter Yugoslavia.

This I did not have. The American embassy in Dublin had said I did not need one. Goddamn bureaucracy. I remembered that the informational documents they gave to me were quite old, but I had been assured that they were accurate.

You would think the most powerful country on Earth—the winners of the Cold War, the defenders of democracy—would have up-to-date information for its citizens, especially about entering one of the most dangerous places in the world.

Fuck. I had bet my life and ten thousand dollars on that old information!

I quickly forgot about the inadequacies of the American State Department; the sequence of events that happened next would stay in my mind forever.

The three guards that had held their guns on us returned and again took position, now aiming their rifles at our heads.

They allowed Jovo to get out of the tiny car with all four of our passports. He headed into the small building—the defending fortress at the Yugoslavian/Hungarian frontier. As he walked in, I saw Jovo wave at a smallish, bespectacled woman dressed in military fatigues.

She did not wave back.

He entered the building and headed directly to her. She displayed no affection; she seemed as stern as a dominatrix. It was hard to discern what was transpiring, but I saw him wildly gesticulating and pointing to the car, speaking not just to her but to all the guards.

The woman, obviously the boss, stood there, still, listening intently as this crazy man nearly hyperventilated.

Jovo and the woman disappeared from my sight. It ran through my mind that they had had enough of him: time for torture at the Yugoslav border.

Prologue

On March 11, 1993, my father died at fifty-six from ALS (Lou Gehrig's disease). He had suffered through this crippling, fucked-up disease for less than two years. When the end of the line came that late winter morning, I knew I needed a fresh start—I needed a new experience to get me through my grief. I also wanted to do something to honor my dad's memory. But I wanted to complete my graduate program at Valparaiso University, so I had to bide my time.

Before I started my final semester at school that summer, I took a preliminary road trip from Crown Point, Indiana, to the East Coast. I drove with my high school friend Jason, who had booked a couple of fashion modeling jobs in New York City. My mother, sister, and maternal aunt came along in another car; they were off to visit my aunt's newly discovered granddaughter in New Jersey. We would be with them for the first two days and then take off on our own.

After some adventures in New York, Baltimore, and Washington (where an old college friend lived), Jason and I hit the road back to Northwest Indiana after about ten days. My main memory from that ride back was our agreement to listen to one song, Pink Floyd's "The Final Cut," for six and a half hours straight. It was on cassette tape, so we had to rewind it every time. Despite our best efforts, our sanity was damaged but remained intact.

I completed the requirements to earn my master's degree and then hit the road. I left Indiana on August 11, 1993, exactly five months to the day after my father's death. I was ostensibly moving to Seattle, one of the trendiest and coolest cities in the world at the time, due to the nascent "grunge" scene. One of my closest friends from high school had moved there nine months before, which made it a bit easier.

Once I got there, I was still restless. I hadn't accomplished all that I wanted. I stuck around the city for three weeks, and then I made plans to go to Europe on the cheap.

I had been to Europe once before—Yugoslavia in 1985, with my father, mother, sister, and a close cousin. We had visited my older first cousin Jovo and his family, wife Anja and children Dusan and Mirjana. It had been a memorable trip meeting those truly wonderful people.

As I was kicking around Seattle one day, it hit me—a war had been raging for about a year and a half between separatists and the federal government of Yugoslavia. An embargo had been issued by the United States and its allies against the Serbs, so food and everyday goods were scarce.

It was a revelation. That would be my mission. That would be my calling; my covenant to myself. That is how I would pay my respects to the memory of my father. I would travel to Europe and do something for his, and my, extended family. What I would do, I did not yet know. How I would get into a war-torn country, I had not yet figured out. It was an impulsive decision, but something that I felt compelled to do.

Grief is love with nowhere to go.

So, without any planning, and my girlfriend Carly having her doubts, I bought a plane ticket to Amsterdam. My return ticket was to depart from Amsterdam exactly two months later. I would spend that time in Europe traveling and planning my trip into Yugoslavia.

1

The Netherlands (part I)
Germany (part I)

Amsterdam, Cologne, Dresden, Berlin

September 8 and 9

I boarded the plane from Seattle to London expecting a long and tedious flight. The nine-and-a-half-hour journey precisely met those expectations.

I only brought two magazines, a *New Yorker* and a *Newsweek*, as I planned to catch the in-flight entertainment for most of the flight. That was a big mistake, as the programming included *Made in America* and a *Family Ties* marathon. Watching those made the experience nearly interminable.

On top of that, my earphones, did not work well, which added to my frustration as I couldn't fully enjoy hating the entertainment. On my fourth pair, I was able to get them to function by wrapping a rubber band around them.

I am told that is the same procedure United Airlines uses to access and repair their engines.

I chatted with a couple of older fellows, Alan and Steve, from Leeds, England. They regaled me with their stories of their old-man travel adventures in the Rockies.

We also discussed beer. They assured me that, if I were to drink in London, I would find no quality beer. The only beer that was worth anything was from Leeds.

I began to note that, but then I remembered where they were from. Yes, boys, the beer out of Leeds is legendary. Thank you for your honest critique.

The lights went out soon after our talk and I tried to get some sleep.

Not a wink. Perhaps it was nerves. Maybe it was the uncertainty of what I would do to fulfill my promise. I only knew that when our pending landing was announced, I was exhausted, mind and body.

An additional announcement was made for those scheduled for the connection to Amsterdam. That was my flight, so I listened intently. We were to meet at the UA terminal room. These instructions were useless to me, as I had no fucking idea where that was. So, when I deplaned, I went the wrong way and almost missed the meet-up. After frantically asking numerous airport employees, I finally found the goddamn UA terminal room. It was, of course, just next door (but in the opposite direction) to the gate where we'd landed.

There, along with me, were five Seattle businessmen from a computer firm. The United crew led us outside, and we were whisked all around the enormous airport tarmac in a small van.

Getting used to the left-side driving was tough enough; getting used to it on an airport runway with blind turns was a completely different matter. I thought the lady driving was laughing maniacally, but I could not be sure. We finally made it to the British Airways plane and climbed up the airstairs (like in the movies) on an open tarmac.

On the flight I was seated next to a sweet and very pretty English girl named O'Dean. She told me that she lived in Portsmouth and was visiting her grandmother ("Dame") in Holland. We talked most of the way and parted in the airport.

I have a girlfriend who I love, I repeated over and over in my head like a mantra.

Once I got off the plane, I went to find my backpack, but I got lost once again. Eventually I found my bag sitting by itself on a conveyor in a quiet corner of the Amsterdam airport.

After passing through customs—and making a stop at a bathroom—I started to walk to the airport Metro stop. On the way I was approached by three Dutch girls, all of whom spoke English very well. So, after some flirtatious chatting, I reminded myself of my mantra and then went on my way.

I then embarked into The Netherlands; into Europe; into my adventure.

Still without any sleep.

I got on the city train with my Eurail pass validated and sat next to a quiet old Dutch businessman. No need for the mantra there.

After a fifteen-minute ride, I was in Central Station in downtown Amsterdam. I didn't know where to go or how to get there; I knew no one and didn't speak the language. Thankfully, I learned pretty quickly that most Dutch people spoke English.

While most Americans think Dutch is just a cheap date.

I first went to the tourist info desk but turned around after I saw the line. After I did that, I was approached by a junkie who wanted to take me to his hostel. No thanks.

Then I looked in my Frommer's travel guide and chose a decent sounding CYH (Christian Youth Hostel). It was on the other side of the city, so I got on my desired streetcar, according to the book. Before I got on the tram, the driver looked at my pass and did not think it was acceptable. A girl interrupted us and told the driver she would check it out and make sure it was kosher. I retreated with the girl on the crowded tram where she briefly looked at the pass. She quickly concluded it wasn't valid, but she didn't seem to mind, as she immediately changed the subject to smoking hashish. Next, she suggested that I get off at her stop since it was close to the youth hostel. I did, she pointed me the right way, and we parted, chaste. Have a grateful day.

The CYH was full. Shit! What could I do now? It was late, raining, and I hadn't slept in over a day.

The Christian girl working the hostel desk (wearing a "God is Incredible" T-shirt) wrote down a few other hostel numbers for me and allowed me to call them on their phone. Success, as the Anna Hostel had a bed—yeah! Some sleep. I did make sure to keep the sheet with the other hostel phone numbers though.

I set off, this time walking back toward the city center. After about a half hour in the cold rain (I only had on a T-shirt, shorts, and Teva sandals), I decided to go to a café and call another hostel that I was told was much closer.

Another success: they also had room. I got directions and walked another fifteen minutes. This walk was through a seedy part of town where the business "day" was just about to begin. Prostitutes were opening the curtains of the windows where they would stand to show off their wares to prospective clients.

I made it through the gauntlet of johns and junkies and found the hostel. It was an abysmal place—all concrete. As I was so tired, I paid the full twenty-five guilders and walked into the front area.

But, alas, there were no beds left. The clerk unfolded a cheap plastic lawn chaise for me. He then generously covered the monstrosity in filthy hostel sheets. But then—oops—he didn't have a pillow. I gave him a sneer, and he said he may have one in the back. He ventured to his office and found me a goofy, pink, small children's pillow to use.

Fuck it. I needed sleep.

Finally, with dazed, half-shut eyes, I entered the cold cement back room of this warehouse hostel and claimed a small open space among the fifteen or so cots to place my lawn chair. I talked with a guy and girl from southern France who were painting on cardboard. Just as I was getting ready to close my eyes (at seven o'clock), Natalie, the French girl, handed me her huge pillow, saying she would be sleeping with her man and wouldn't need it.

A French angel.

I did sleep, but only for three hours. I then got up and read. Eventually people began to return from their evening debacles. After the place calmed down a bit, my earplugs went in, but the lights did not go out until one in the morning. After the long day (days?), I fell fast asleep.

September 10

I have to catch up and finish this story. I wrote yesterday's story in a room in Amsterdam (I'll explain that later), and now I am finishing it on a train to Germany.

I woke up in the hostel on Friday morning after a surprisingly good sleep. I didn't shower, only washed my face, as it was all co-ed and I was not quite ready to share my nakedness with everyone. While I was changing, the fellow next to me woke up and asked if I was an American. (He obviously was.)

The artist-type guy (read: junkie) and I began to talk and eventually decided to get breakfast and contemplate what to do that day. He was really excited about the hashish in Amsterdam, telling me he'd spent seventy-five guilders on it his first two days there. He then showed me a bag of the "great weed," that was equal in size to an American dime bag. Looking me over he decided that I would be a great person to get high with, even asking me if I had been to the (Grateful Dead) "show" in Seattle.

No, I was not at the Seattle show, but yes, to the Eugene, Oregon, show last month.

I left with the junkie into the rainy, dark, seedy neighborhood and began to move through the city. But, while I was concerned with food (I hadn't eaten since the flight), he only wanted to get high. My side prevailed as we went to a small café and I got a croissant and a Coke. The guy was out of money and didn't eat. I thought, sorry, but fuck this junkie. I didn't know if Tennessee Jed would need a miracle every day, but he sure would today as I wouldn't buy him a thing.

I told him it was a quarter to ten as I remembered that he had to meet someone to go to a cheese fest in the country, (he had asked me to come along), at nine thirty. We parted and finally exchanged names. (His was Danny, not Jed, to my surprise.) We also made plans to meet at the Central Station under the "C" at six that evening.

Spoiler: I did not meet him.

Bye.

Now I had to find a room so I could lose the backpack and relax and see the city. I hit a phone, and the second place I called, the Van Oona, had a room—peace of mind.

I got there, walking, in half an hour. The hotel's very pleasant owner told me to relax as I was still hyped up from the walk.

"I'm not high," I thought I needed to say, but did not.

Was everyone under twenty-five high in this city?

I did begin to relax as soon he gave me the key to room 12. It would not be ready for a few hours, but he allowed me to stow my pack. I set off to see the city.

One block away was my first stop, the Anne Frank House. There was a very small line, so I got right in.

Up a narrow flight of stairs.

At the top I stopped and imagined her era. An era of fascism and intolerance; a time of hatred and bigotry; death and destruction.

Not much had changed except the scale.

I was then led to an exhibit area with a few video monitors. While I was in there, I looked into the adjoining room and I saw a half-opened bookcase.

Forget the video.

Walking through the porthole, I was overcome with a strange feeling of what had occurred there nearly fifty years earlier. It was an eerie feeling as I entered the annex I had read so much about. Strange to be in the same rooms where Anne had so delicately detailed human drama.

She was twelve when she walked through the same door.

Twelve.

I never thought I would be in Amsterdam to enter this strange looking glass into history.

As I walked through the numerous rooms, I was struck by their size. They were all larger than I had imagined. Despite that, I could not imagine spending twenty-some months in those benevolent cells.

One part that struck me was the door frame where Mr. Frank had kept the height measurements of his daughters as they grew. With simple pencil marks on a door frame, I saw the passage of time and the growth of two young girls.

Heartbreaking.

I did my best to hide the tears that were welling in my often-cynical eyes.

Many others there could not.

I gathered myself and moved on.

From there, I entered Anne's bedroom and was pulled into her world.

I was pulled into the war-torn world of 1940's Europe as seen through the eyes of a little girl.

The pictures of Hollywood and German movie stars that Anne herself posted to her walls were still there, protected behind plexiglass.

Just before the end of the tour (which included exhibits of past and present examples of racial intolerance), I entered a room with a glass display case. In the middle was Anne's first diary. It was plaid orange and brown, still in excellent condition, with only the lock cut off and what appeared to be a small stain on the cover. To its left was Anne's second diary, a larger one that was black-striped. On the far right was a third diary with its pages open to Anne Frank's last entry before she was murdered at Auschwitz.

After seeing those, I went back to the previous room and read the inscription underneath a photo of Anne. In the middle of the paragraph was a quote from one of her later diaries, "Despite everything that has happened, I still believe that people are good at heart."

After that heavy-duty dose of reality, I began to feel a bit guilty. My troubles of yesterday felt like a rich pageant.

Next door to the Anne Frank House, a coffee shop sold city tours. I needed some time to decompress, so I purchased a tour ticket for nineteen guilders. With it, I was able to see the whole city through a tour of its canals. I also received a discounted day rate for several museums.

On the boat, I heard two girls behind me who sounded American. We introduced ourselves and I saw that I was mistaken as they were not girls but two businesswomen in their late thirties. We talked until we reached the Rijksmuseum, where all three of us exited the boat together. We took some pictures and then went our separate ways. They headed to the Rijksmuseum, and I went to the Van Gogh Museum.

The Van Gogh Museum was very well done. But if one does not appreciate his work or his influences, it should be avoided like the plague. Of five floors, three are all Vincent's work. One floor is nineteenth-century Japanese geisha paintings; the last is nineteenth-century impressionist works. I love Van Gogh and fully enjoyed the entire museum. Especially his oils of his bedroom, Gauguin's chair and his self-portrait.

I left after two hours and walked two blocks to the Heineken Brewery for a tour and some free beer. But the tours were sold out, so I made my way back to the boat for the next series of museums. While I was waiting for the tour boat, I saw a beautiful Italian-speaking girl (who I had earlier asked for the time). We boarded the boat and attempted to communicate through smiles and gestures. I was able to learn that she was not Italian but Swiss and her name was Lorraina.

I repeated my mantra from earlier. "I have a girlfriend who I love."

Together, we got off the boat at the next stop and headed for the Amsterdam City Museum. Not a bad place, but there was nothing in English. As we were made our way through the exhibits, Lorraina got excited and started to point at her watch.

"We're going to miss the boat!"

We took off running through the streets of Amsterdam trying to find our canal. We made it with two minutes to spare. We again communicated in the most minimal terms until her stop.

She got off on the north side of the city. We said good-bye, and I, and the boat, departed. I kicked back and tried to decide what I was going to do that night. As I was considering that, I felt a tap on my shoulder. It was the two American businesswomen I had met earlier. I took a seat at their table (filled with Heineken cans), and we began to talk.

Melissa and Susan, both from Boston (though Melissa was originally from Chicago), had been on their working trip for two weeks—first in London, now in Amsterdam, and next in Paris. They confessed they were disappointed when the "beautiful" girl got off the boat without me.

I thought about Carly and cursed my honest chastity.

Anyway, the ladies and I talked for the last half hour as we returned to our original stop.

We got off the boat together and made our way to a café for more Heineken. At the outdoor café, three blocks from the Anne Frank House, I ate for the first time since breakfast. And we all drank, quite a bit.

We stayed there for about an hour. As the sun began to set, we made plans for that evening. It was six when we parted, planning on meeting back at their hotel (Pulitzer) at half past seven.

I went back to my small room (where I began to write yesterday) and cleaned up.

I walked to their five-star hotel in five minutes. They were not ready of course, so I made my way to the lobby bar. I turned a corner into the dark, high-end lounge where I almost literally ran into Melissa.

At the bar, I joined Melissa and Stuart, a bearded, burly American friend of hers who was also working in Amsterdam. We ordered drinks and waited for Susan.

When she came down, all four of us had one more drink and then headed into the early-evening Friday air of Amsterdam. Stuart was very familiar with the city and led us to an area with an astonishing array of food choices. After we examined the menus for an hour, we finally decided to eat at an Indonesian restaurant.

The tiny place had no other customers, so we sat at a front table by the window, the best in the house, to watch the strangeness of Amsterdam pass by. After a few more beers, we finally ordered our meal.

Stuart told stories of traveling through Europe and Africa until our dinner arrived.

The first course was great, a full array of flavors. The next course was huge, with twenty-one different bowls to choose from: peanut sauce, goat, chicken, beef, dried fish, etc. I tried it all, including some incredibly spicy goat. Susan and Melissa did too, and we all suffered the mouth heat together.

We stayed at this dimly lit place with Indonesian music quietly playing in the background for two hours, drinking Heineken and chatting the whole time. When the check came, Melissa took it and charged it all to her company—incredible. Great food, beer and company!

We left the restaurant and beelined to the seedy Red-Light District. I wasn't too surprised to see that this was the same part of town I'd slept in last night. But I did not notice the details of it yesterday as I was so tired.

The neighborhood was really lit with red lights, illuminated advertising for the working ladies.

Susan and I ventured down a side street where, quite beautiful young (usually Asian) girls stood half-naked, "for rent."

We then saw a young man cut a transaction with one of the girls. She led him to a side passage into her building, closed the curtain to her pinkish-red room, and then, I assume, finished the deal—depressingly strange.

There were also sex shows with guys hustling outside to bring in customers. "It's a family show—bring in your wife," a hawker said to me as I was walking with Susan.

Along with sex, there were drugs everywhere, and everyone seemed to be a dealer. I lost count of how many times I was offered a taste.

"Want acid?"

"Heroin?"

"Coke?"

It was an open, bizarre sex and drug bazaar filled with well dressed women and men, addicts, and "Fuck-Fuck" joints.

We worked our way to Central Station, where we parted ways with Stuart (a plane to the States awaited him).

Melissa, Susan, and I, depressed from the Red-Light District, hailed a cab to take us back to our respective hotels (their 5-star, my ½-star).

We were dropped off at the Pulitzer, and the two amazing women paid the entire fare. When I insisted on paying, they flatly refused, telling me to save my money. They gave me their cards, and I promised to write. We shook hands and parted.

I know that that will not be the last time I see them because I intend to do all I can to visit, or at the least write to them. Two great people that let me use their guide (Stuart) and paid for an entire evening out—what a start to this adventure.

I tossed and turned until six o'clock before I really dozed off. I slept so well, in fact, that at ten thirty a man knocked on my door thinking that I had already left. I got up quickly and showered. After that, looking for food, I climbed (and photographed) the steep stairs to the dining room.

Breakfast was over, but, as I was quite hungry, I took some bread and jam from a plate on an un-bussed table (not so gross). Just after I did that, the owner came into the dining room and surprised me with my own breakfast—ham, cheese, eggs, coffee, and water—despite their breakfast service ending. I ate, paid him (fifty-five guilders), thanked him and said good-bye. If I can, I will stay here again when I return to Amsterdam in November.

I ventured toward Central Station (and made it without getting lost). It was eleven thirty, and (after checking at a counter), I found out that the first train to Cologne was at 1:00 p.m. No problem. I sat on some stairs, ate a ham broodjie (lots of ham), and began reading Hemingway's *For Whom the Bell Tolls*.

Before I got on my first train to another European city, I was a bit anxious, so I made sure to check that it was the correct one a few times. Once my paranoia was sated, I hopped on.

As I wrote this, I sat in the second car from the front, fourth row from the back, right side, window seat. I heard a German voice announce that the restaurant could be found at the back of the train. After the visit to the Anne Frank House earlier, it was not a welcome language to hear.

I've caught up on my writing, and I have one hour left before I arrive in Cologne. I will spend that time resting my writing hand and appreciating the French and German countryside. By the way, the train is cooking, traveling at maybe 75 to 85 miles an hour.

September 11

I am writing this in the morning in Berlin, so I have to quickly catch up.

After the train stopped Saturday in Cologne, the first thing I did was head to the ticket window to check out the sleeping car situation to Berlin. My plan was to spend all day in Cologne (from four in the afternoon until ten thirty), and then sleep on the night train during the eight-hour ride to Berlin.

The first agent I reached did not speak English. I tried to use my phrasebook but to no avail. However, she did understand that she didn't understand, so she found another agent who did understand (English).

This agent told me that I needed marks to pay for the sleeping car, as they did not accept credit cards. So, I exchanged a hundred dollars and returned to pay her twenty-six marks for what I hoped would be a comfy night.

I then put my pack in a locker, bought a map, and headed out into the streets of Cologne. I figured that I would go into shops and cafés all day to kill time.

As soon I left the train station, the first thing that came into view was the cathedral. It was spectacular—as tall as an American skyscraper but built (beginning) in the thirteenth century. It completely dominated the area; it made everything around it look insignificant as it towered over the city. An ancient city, that is, as I soon passed an old Roman gate and sentry tower that were erected in the first century AD.

As I walked through the town though, the people seemed to be brooding and silent. It was a distinctive but dichotomous old town, filled with historical and colorful character but also doleful and dismal citizenry.

As I continued through Cologne, I window-shopped and passed theaters showing mostly American movies. I continued to walk all over town, since I really couldn't get lost. To reorient myself, I simply pointed to a picture of the cathedral with an inquisitive look to any dour passersby.

It started to rain, but I had my umbrella. As I walked down a side street looking for a place to eat, I passed a small café that seemed to have a strange, but positive, feel. After I passed it and walked about fifty feet, I turned around in the now driving rainstorm and returned to the bar. Something seemed to be pulling me there.

I asked the bartender if he spoke English—he did! I asked about the food, and he told me it was authentic Yugoslavian.

What? Yes. Authentic Yugoslavian soup that his friend had just finished making (there were about ten guys inside).

He said he was Serbian. I told him my family was as well and that I still had relatives in Sombor. We shook hands as I grabbed a seat at the bar.

As I drank my strong German beer, I chatted with the bartender, whose name was Mike(!). He wore a blue kerchief and sported a tiny beard. I laughed when he asked if Chicago was as dangerous and crime-riddled as the movies made it seem.

The conversation then moved to politics, especially the situation in Yugoslavia. He told me the issues regarding nationalities were foolish, short-sighted in the modern world. In fact, the regulars in the bar, both Serbs and Croats, were drinking and playing cards—having a good time together despite the war. The bar patrons (all younger than 40) didn't care about rivalries, Mike told me. They just wanted to get back to living their lives as they had before the hostilities began.

So much for the misguided opinion of American media who were so far removed from what was truly going on.

Mike then explained that he was Yugoslavian, not Serbian. He said that the embargo was hurting his entire country more than it was helping one or two regions of it. The country was being destroyed not only through internal violent aggression but from external economic and social pressures. A victorious side was moot—the only thing he genuinely wanted was for the war to come to a quick end so all Yugoslavs could return to a life of quiet contentment.

With those words, an alarm went off in my head. I now knew what I had to do to ease my grief.

I was helpless against the internal aggressions of war, but I was not helpless against external social and economic adversities. I would help my father's family—*my* family—cope with this external pressure. I would collect money from American relatives and bring them the hard currency. Jovo, his wife Anja, whomever, could decide how they would, and if they would, distribute it. In memory of my father, I would bring them some semblance of contentment.

After this, the conversation lightened as Mike told tales of his travels from London to Moscow as I ate and enjoyed a few more German beers. We kept talking about nothing of real consequence— girls and sports seemed to dominate the rest of our chat.

As we were talking, a man, completely drunk, walked in and took a seat next to me at the bar. He knew English and joined our conversation although he slurred his words so god-awfully he could have been speaking Klingon for all I knew.

He told us that he was an Ethiopian foreign affairs agent stationed in Cologne. He was a registered troubleshooter with a license to kill. No, wait, that's James Bond, not this dope.

After some time, Mike and I began to ignore the drunk and kept talking. Soon though, Ethiopia's 007 interrupted us again to tell us he was Orthodox Christian. He showed us his ID and made a big deal that he told us his religion, but we simply didn't care. Eventually, after being ignored by everyone in the bar, the not-too-secretive agent loudly left.

Soon it was half past eight. With John Denver's "Country Roads" playing on the stereo, I said good-bye to Mike. I paid him sixteen marks and ventured into Cologne once more.

As I made my way back to the station, I sat at various benches, all the while taking in more of that beautiful city.

European cities smell different from American cities. I don't mean that there is a difference in body odor chemistry or personal bathing habits, but in the redolence of the pollution. I think it is the smell of all of the diesel engines, especially the trains that have been filling my nose since I arrived on this continent. I am sure that this will be an olfactory memory that will stick with me for quite a while.

I got back to the cathedral, found a seat, and listened to a classical music concert under the shadow of the great church. Soon I made it back to the train platform, where I heard the chatter of three American girls. I walked over to them, and we all began to talk.

The girls were Kim, Sarah, and Samantha, originally from Cincinnati, all my age (one was one year younger) and all now scattered across the United States.

Eventually we got on the train, they headed for their seats, and I made my way to my sleeping car.

On the train I met a French Canadian guy named Yves. We looked for the sleeping cars but had a lot of trouble finding exactly where to go. After I lost Yves, I got into an argument with a conductor since he did not believe that I had purchased a sleeping car. I dug out my receipt and showed it to him. All was settled as he showed me the correct place to go.

In the car, I joined a young man, his mother, and another man in a sleeping car that had six beds. I did not sleep very well, but I did sleep.

I was woken at six thirty in the morning by a new conductor. This dickhead quickly grabbed, checked, and then threw my Eurail pass back at me.

Then, not five minutes after that dick left, I got a terrible nosebleed. So, I went to the WC to check on what condition my condition was in. My right nostril was oozing a steady stream, and my left began to seep as well.

Great.

Eventually it stopped, and I headed back to the car with a throat full of congealing bilirubin. The guy and his mother checked to see if I was OK—in German. Nice people.

I was fine, I told them. *Danke.*

Alright, by the time the overnight ride was complete, my throat was clearing.

I left the sleeping compartment and found myself in the Berlin train station (later I discovered that I was in East Berlin, only fifty feet or so from where the Berlin Wall recently stood) with no real plans.

I saw Yves in the station's tourist information booth, and I joined him in line to find accommodations. However, the clerks were quite uninformed information peddlers; they really had no clear direction on what to recommend.

Disappointed and with no rooms, Yves and I left the tourist office. But we ran into the three girls who I had met the night before in Cologne. All five of us decided to venture to a place listed in my Frommer's book. We hopped on the Berlin U-Bahn lines (without paying) and began a journey of desperation through a very complex city.

We soon realized that Berlin had no central hub, no Times Square as it were. On top of that, the city was expansive, with inconvenient subway stops. We got lost a few times and had to ask Berliner after Berliner where we were.

Ich bin not *ein Berliner.*

After some time, Kim did begin to grasp the subway system, and we were able to find the correct station where we could walk to the hotel. But, once we exited the subway onto the street, we got lost again. After asking a few more people for help, we found the rundown youth hostel.

Inside, Yves and I got one room with four extra beds and the girls got another. We locked up our packs and went out into the dreary early afternoon streets of Berlin.

The first place we hit was the Berlin Wall: Checkpoint Charlie, the legendary crossing point between the Communist East and the

Capitalist West. It was so bizarre to imagine this place, less than four years ago, being one of the most heavily guarded sites on earth. Today, it seemed so natural to cross over to the other side, through the empty spaces of the now living art gallery that the wall had become.

The art on the wall was thought-provoking. Most appeared on the Eastern side—some political, some humorous, some uplifting, some somber. All inspiring, completed by a damaged but now recovering populace who lived in the epicenter of the Cold War for thirty years. We took pictures and small portions of the wall.

We then began our journey diagonally across town to the Egyptian Museum to see the bust of Nefertiti.

After a tortuous journey (my feet began to sprout a few blisters), we made it to the section of Berlin called Dahlem, where we met a nice Aussie couple and their two children. The (now) nine of us beelined to the Egyptian Museum.

It was alright. I had seen so much of this art in other cities (Chicago and New York) that I was more concerned with resting my feet than seeing much. But the bust of Nefertiti was cool. Beautiful chick.

The original five of us—Kim, Sarah, Samantha, Yves, and I—got back on the U-Bahn and headed to the middle area of Berlin. We were on the hunt for a cheap place to eat that was listed in the Frommer book. However, once we found it, we saw that it had recently closed.

Shit.

I was beginning to think the Frommer book may have been a bad investment. It had been pretty consistent in providing inaccurate information.

Oh yeah: throughout the day, Yves kept passing out, falling asleep. Once, he fell and hit the ground hard in the subway. On top of that, as we walked through the city, he lagged about twenty feet behind us all day, struggling to keep up (and struggling to keep his cigarette lit). He was like a narcoleptic, nicotine-addicted toddler. He was a blast to keep an eye on.

We did end up finding an Italian restaurant where we sat, ate, and drank for an hour and a half. We stuck around the restaurant, where we had a great time, even ordering dessert. Eventually we left, saying good-bye to the fantastic, good-natured Turkish server (who sported a Bugs Bunny tie), and headed out into the dusk of Berlin. We made it back to the hostel relatively easily and planned to take a short nap before hitting some clubs.

In the lobby, we didn't say good night, as we were sure we would be meeting up soon to go out for the evening. Yves and I headed to the male section and the girls to theirs. I hopped into bed to take a quick nap; I didn't even take out my contacts.

Uh-oh. I did not wake up until eleven o'clock at night. I saw (and heard) Yves was still sleeping, so I got up, headed down the hall to the WC, took my contacts out and then lethargically returned to bed.

I slept until six thirty. Thirteen hours of sleep! I achieved this masterpiece of slumber despite the tremendous snoring of Yves.

His snoring was incredible—loud even through my much-appreciated earplugs. It was ground-moving as it shook the entire building. Around seven that morning, another hosteler (who must have arrived to share the room after we passed out) began to shush Yves. As Yves only responded with louder snores, the man started to get pissed. I finally helped the guy and we got Yves to shift a bit, which lowered his volume.

I showered, shaved, etc.

Yves woke up around eight and promptly lit a smoke.

We headed down to the dining room for breakfast, where we met Kim. She told us that she got into a bit of an argument with the desk clerk over some passport issue. As she was telling us the story, the other two girls came down to our table. Yves and I found out that the girls fell asleep just like us, so we all missed our only night in Berlin.

After breakfast we went back to our rooms and grabbed our backpacks. Then, just before we checked out, we stole a couple of sandwiches from "Groucho" (the desk clerk who had been giving Kim a hard time) and headed off to briefly sightsee before leaving the city.

We hopped on a subway bound for Potsdamer Platz. We were looking for the area purported to be Hitler's death bunker. But, when we got off the train and climbed the stairs to Potsdamer, we saw, in a large open field, that the German circus was in town.

Thank God it was so early, as there were no clowns mindlessly shuffling about. I couldn't imagine a German clown's horrible, spirit-numbing angst. Or a sullen ringmaster, dressed in varying shades of grey, marching us through his distressing Deutsch dystopia.

After carefully avoiding the tents and the disconsolate caged animals, we realized that we were heading the wrong way. We consulted a few confused passersby to point us in the correct direction for Hitler's bunker, and they shockingly obliged. But, after making a few turns, the five of us literally staggered into the Brandenburg Gate. Whoa!

Again, the same feelings I had yesterday at the Wall—Berlin was such a different city than it had been just four years ago.

Pictures were taken (I hoped that my cheap camera worked properly), and we headed across the street to the Reichstag. I hesitantly gave a quick history lesson to the group as we made our way around the immense, square building. (By the way, they wanted the lesson, as they were asking numerous questions about the Reichstag, World War II, and the Cold War).

On the east side of the Reichstag was a memorial (about ten feet long and three feet wide) to those who died trying to cross the Wall.

We continued around the building looking for an entrance. When we reached the north side, we found out that the Reichstag was closed on Sunday. Yep, it was Sunday. That was fine, as we were set on leaving Berlin anyway.

We continued around, making it to the western section of the building, the side that became a sad part of history. It was that perspective that was shown on all the films and newsreels—the side that became a symbol of Nazi Germany. The swastika flew over that part of the Reichstag for twelve agonizing years. Finally, in a famous newsreel, that symbol of hate was blown up after the Soviet Red Army took the city in 1945.

Right below that western section, there was a huge, open tract of land where, I assume, crowds of people would gather during the 1930s to catch a glimpse of the raving, maniacal Hitler.

All in all, it was an incredibly heavy and sad place.

We crossed through the Brandenburg Gate and made it to the hawkers in former East Berlin. There were all types of goods for sale—authentic military hats, uniforms, and medals from East and West Germany and the former Soviet Union. I noticed that some of the heavy woolen military coats were from former three-star Soviet generals.

I ended up exploiting this nascent capitalism by buying a pair of West German and Soviet military caps.

We never did find the actual spot of Hitler's bunker. Happily, there is no marker of the place where that beast took his last breath.

After that, the five of us made it back to the station. There we said good-bye to Yves (we did not get his address or his last name), as he was making his way to Amsterdam (and probably a lot of porn shops). I felt I should remind him that every sperm is sacred, but I let him leave without that dire warning.

The three girls and I were now headed to Prague. We bought five bottles of cheap Bulgarian wine and waited outside on the platform. The train finally came—thirty-five minutes late and crowded. We didn't have a seat, so we stood by the WC, where I reminded everyone that we didn't have any Czech currency; we didn't even know what it was called. So, in a panic, we jumped off the train right before it was ready to leave the station.

Back on the platform at the edge of a Berlin train station, we took a seat, opened the food we stole from the hostel that morning, and had a picnic. Four in the afternoon, relaxing with food and wine.

After downing a few bottles of the bargain-basement wine, we decided to take a train to Dresden. What the hell; we'd get to Prague later, we figured. So, we stumbled back to the main terminal, found the correct track, and got on board. Off to eastern Germany in a private car, just the four of us and a few more bottles of wine.

We arrived in Dresden (out of wine) and found out through the tourist desk that the city was pretty booked up. Although they were able to send us to one hotel that might have rooms. We walked there, but they were full.

Shit.

We headed back to the station and decided to try our luck with Prague once again. There was a train that left Dresden in two hours, so we would arrive in the Czech capital at midnight.

We began to walk through Dresden, a city completely burned to the ground by Allied incendiary bombs during the last days of World War II, and made it to a café in the main square. After more food and a few bottles of beer, we headed back to the station. Incredibly, we bought more cheap wine before we boarded the train.

In another car, again, all to ourselves, we got drunk, played cards, and relaxed for the three-hour ride. Our discussion inevitably turned sexual as we got increasingly more inebriated.

The girls related their Amsterdam experience, which was a bit different from mine. My journey with the ladies from Boston missed the five-dollar sex show my new travel companions attended. That was a show filled with bananas, dildos, whips, and lesbianism—relief, as romance was apparently not dead in Holland.

2

Czech Republic, Poland

Prague, Kraków, Oświęcim

Well, after that, we made it to Prague— "We're not going to Moscow. It's Czechoslovakia. It's like going into Wisconsin!"

We got off and had nowhere to run and nowhere to hide. We only hoped to find a place to sleep other than the train station. But almost as soon as we got into the main terminal, a girl approached us and offered us four beds in her flat. After questioning her (all four of us were quite drunk) and seeing pictures of her place, we decided it would be the best call for tonight as the hostel, which was quite far, was not a sure thing for accommodations.

We got in two cabs, and the girl, Jana (we called her "Yanni," although she was not a new age musician), paid for the five-minute ride to her flat. We got out of the taxis into a great neighborhood filled with old brick buildings. She led us to a beautiful old apartment complex, where we climbed the stairs to her flat. Once inside we stowed our packs and told Jana we wanted to party.

After Jana gave us some insight about the sites of the city, she led us to a bar less than a quarter of a mile from her place. Inside was one older man (who spoke a little English), a bartender (a woman), and another younger man. Later, a few more people arrived.

The five of us sat at a table in the back, drinking, talking and watching MTV (the Blind Melon Bee Girl video was on). At different points through the night (and at different levels of inebriation), everyone in the place took the time to introduce themselves to us, strangers in their paradise.

We ate four plates of food, family style, and ordered drink after drink. Jana also had a good time, as we bought her four rum and Cokes.

In between drinks, Jana grabbed a cue and started to play pool. Soon, with the extra bravado that four rum and Cokes inevitably brought, she challenged me to a game. First, I refused, and she mocked me.

"Weak," she said, with a sly smile.

I ended up playing her and found out quickly why she challenged me—she won quite handily. But in the second game, I staged a miraculous comeback to beat her. After some more fun, we headed back to her place for the night. All in all, it was a great time.

September 14

The next morning all of us slept quite late. I woke up around two in the afternoon and proceeded to do all of my laundry by hand, getting a blister on my left thumb in the process. While I was doing that, the girls went to the local market and picked up food.

We all showered and headed out the door to see the sights of Prague. First stop, via cab, was the old part of town, Wenceslas Square. Lots of street vendors, hawkers, etc. We made our way through all of the people, stopping and looking at various shops (mostly at CDs). We wound our way through the narrow, beautiful side streets of old Prague and came upon the nexus of the medieval square, with the fourteenth-century astronomical clock dominating the view.

It was an extraordinary place—Disneyland for real. I cannot put into words what this place looked and felt like. It was like going back in time and experiencing a place, a real place, that has existed and stood firm through centuries of tumultuous historical change. The square has existed from before the Black Death to after the fall of communism and beyond.

The four of us paid the ten thousand korunas (Czech currency) to go up the steep stairs of the bell tower. We viewed sunny Prague in all its medieval and modern splendor.

We returned to the town square and decided that we wanted to see a show. We wouldn't be picky—any show would be fine. In the process of finding one, we explored more of the old part of the city, stopping at various cafés throughout. We finally stumbled into a café we all liked right on the banks of the Vltava, directly under a bridge. (In fact, we are there again today, two days later, as I am writing this, trying to catch up.)

We never did find a show that day but did get a glimpse of the medieval Charles Bridge around sundown—a wonderous stone arch bridge that was begun in the fourteenth century.

As the sun began to set, we strolled the residential streets and witnessed the quiet parts of this beautiful, grand city.

Back in the square just after sundown, we found ourselves staring at a sign that simply yelled "DISCO." We had to go in. On top of that, the sign said it was free, no cover. Well, it wasn't exactly a show, but we were all in for the experience.

We ventured down a set of old cement steps and into the disco, which was probably an old wine or root cellar. It was a venerable old place, smelling of smoky oak and stale beer—a monumental amount of atmosphere.

It was still early, so we sat near the bar at an old wooden table for four. Beer was cheap, about one American dollar for a 22-ounce bottle of strong Czech ale. The drink special was a 5-ounce plastic glass of vermouth topped with a thin slice of lemon. We did the math and figured those were around a dime each.

As we waited for the DJ to start, a woman on the small stage sang Elvis songs accompanied by young fella on guitar. An Elvis cover duo for the opening act? I couldn't wait to see what was next!

Soon, and after a few more beers, the crowd thickened, the disco ball lit up, and the DJ began to spin. We didn't know any of the songs, but we really wanted to hear ABBA's "Dancing Queen." Sarah and I decided to grease the palm of the DJ and request the Swedish foursome's hit. We slipped him a dollar bill and our request. The next song he played was "Dancing Queen!"

The four of us were on top of the world as we hit the wooden dance floor. We began to sing and dance like mad. But, when the song ended, uh-oh, he started spinning "Dancing Queen" again. We stayed out on the floor, drunk and dancing like fools.

When he played it a third time in a row, we decided that we'd had enough and returned to our table. As the night developed, the DJ, I guess quite happy for the dollar, played the song repeatedly. Sometimes we danced, sometimes we didn't.

As we continued to drink (and reluctantly dance), we also watched the crowd—and saw a couple of punks throw up as well. Eventually, a Londoner began to hit on Samantha (who did look particularly suave in the dark club sporting her pink John Lennon sunglasses). While he was hitting on her, his mate talked at me. I think he was pontificating on about his favorite football (soccer) team.

Soon the night at the Bohemian disco (filled with drunks, punks, and dancing queens) wound to an end.

We headed out and found a group of cabs in the square. I offered one driver a dollar to take us to Jana's flat. I figured a dollar had worked wonders in the club, so why not now? He laughingly refused.

Oh well, at least it was enough for ABBA.

We soon found a nice older cab driver who got us to Jana's quickly. We happily paid the cool old guy five dollars American.

Sarah and Samantha immediately went to bed as it was about one o'clock in the morning. But Kim and I were not done, so we went to look for a local bar. We found a different one from the other night and hesitantly went in.

Inside, we started out on burgundy but soon hit the harder stuff. We found one of the six people in there, Vera, could speak a little English. The chubby, blonde, fortyish Vera was a great find. We told her we were staying at Jana's flat, and she got excited. They were good friends, so she took to Kim and me immediately.

We talked about such things as her son in Sweden and the war in Yugoslavia. As we were chatting, a man at the end of the bar gave Kim a porcelain cup that he made. As he was autographing it, another man fell out of his bar stool, drunk.

Kim now had men falling at her feet.

After a couple of drinks, Kim and I returned to Jana's place. We took a seat outside on the stoop. Kim and I chatted about a number of things, with the talk eventually moving to philosophy.

With fresh booze and disco in my system, I considered a go at Kim. But again—fuck—the better angels of my nature took over, and Carly filled my head.

At four in the morning, Jana came outside and told us that we needed to move inside as we were going to wake the neighbors or at least the area golem.

Good night.

September 15

The next day was a now-usual day in Prague. My feet continued to hurt with my awful "cross-training" Nikes ripping them apart.

Since my feet were covered in blisters, the four of us headed to Wenceslas Square once more via cab. This time we made it across the Charles Bridge to the palace. That section of Prague was just like the other, graceful and exquisite.

We walked around, taking time to stop at various cafés, including our favorite one by the river and under the bridge. Also, since we never found one yesterday, we were still on the hunt for a show.

Today though, we were in luck, as we found a performance. We saw posters for an inexpensive classical music festival and concert being held in the city. After a circuitous search through Prague, we found the venue and bought tickets (thank God for accurate city maps).

Before the curtains rose, we beelined to the theater café and ordered a drink. We grabbed a seat and drank in our squalid tourist clothes while everyone around us was dressed in tuxedos and evening gowns. Surprisingly, no one gave us a second look or sideways glance.

When the interior doors opened, we made our way up the stairs to our cheap balcony seats and got a great view of the sparse crowd. There were not a lot of people there to watch the seventeen-piece orchestra doing selected Germanic and Italian compositions.

The four of us got the chance to rest for two hours.

The heavenly music, the elegant hall (the largest in the city), and the glory of Prague tallied up to a great night.

We headed home early; my feet were now a bloody mess. A nice old cab driver gave us a ride and even stopped the meter, for good, after he made a wrong turn.

September 16

The next day began as usual as we woke up late. We then bid farewell to Jana (an incredible host) and ventured out for breakfast (today in a hotel restaurant).

We headed into the square once again, and then to the café under the bridge. Next, we hit a bookstore where we loitered for 45 minutes. Finally, we began our trek to the train station to buy tickets. (Our Eurail passes were not valid for travel in Eastern Europe.) I needed a ticket to Poland, as I was going to Auschwitz. The three girls, to Budapest. But, as we were deciding how to do that, the girls (mainly Kim and Sarah) decided that they wanted to go to Poland, Auschwitz, as well.

Together again.

We bought the tickets and checked the itinerary. There would be a stop and train change in Katowice, where we were to get on a train going to Warsaw via Kraków, our final destination.

We got onto the train and took our seats—Kim and I on one side of the second-class car and Sarah across from me, with Samantha in the final seat. We stored our seven large bottles of water and an enormous amount of food (we wanted to be prepared with supplies in case there were shortages in Poland). We killed the lights immediately and tried to get some sleep. After some time, Kim and Sarah sprawled out on the floor where there was just enough room for both of them.

Soon the border patrol came in and checked our tickets and passports. This was the first truly intense passport or border check of the whole trip.

All in order, the lights went off again.

On the train platform, changing trains in Katowice at four in the morning, we met up with three more people—a baker from Seattle, a Japanese student, and a guy from Little Rock. We all split up, since there were no cars completely empty. Kim and I headed to one that had one lonely, sleeping Pole already occupying it.

The lights went off, and I finally got some decent sleep, on the side all by myself.

September 17

After being rudely awakened by another border guard and then falling briefly back to sleep, we arrived at Kraków at 5:45 a.m.

In the cold early morning, we added a fifth person to our party: Dave, the guy we met last night from Little Rock. We stored our backpacks in some luggage storage units on the train platform and headed down the street to the bus terminal. There we planned on waiting three hours for the 8:30 a.m. bus to take us to Oświęcim.

However, as soon as we entered the building, a man approached me and asked if I wanted to go to Auschwitz. (Ask is too strong; he merely said, inquisitively, "Auschwitz."). I asked him how much and for how long a duration. After some rudimentary haggling, using my elementary Serbo-Croatian, I got the price for an all-day trip to forty American dollars for all five of us. He would drive us there, about forty miles, stay with us, and then drive us back. But the majority of the group vetoed my work. They would rather pay the $1.25 for the bus.

After some time waiting in the smoky, cramped, depressive bus station (and numerous bad-taste Polish jokes by Kim), the entire group came to their senses and decided to get a cab. The first driver we approached said "No—too many people." The next potential driver approached us. This man had been standing in the bus terminal since we arrived. I made eye contact and we approached each other. I got the same deal that I negotiated with the earlier driver, forty dollars all day. No veto this time.

We piled into his car and headed to quite possibly the most horrible place on earth. It was Friday, September 17, 1993.

I have caught up on my writing.

The driver insisted that I sit in the front seat since I was able to rudimentarily communicate with him with very basic, childlike Serbo-Croatian. The other four piled into the back seat of his tiny car.

The ride to the camp took about forty-five minutes. In that time, we passed countless children with brightly colored backpacks heading off to school. The countryside from Kraków was beautiful: rolling hills, quiet towns, silent people. We passed churches and factories, new homes and ancient cottages as we wound our way down the modern road through southern Poland.

There was absolutely nothing sinister about the area. Honestly, I thought it would be dreary and oppressive, like a black and white photo gone terribly wrong. It was not. It was serene and colorful, promising nothing of what lay ahead.

I could only imagine the region just fifty years ago. I was sure it looked the same. The same cultural makeup, the same climate, the same vegetation.

The era of WWII is not long removed from our time, which made seeing this countryside all the more surreal.

As we entered a town, Oświęcim, there was a sign for the Auschwitz Museum. (Oświęcim is the Polish name for Auschwitz.) Well, this was it: the actual town.

I figured that the camp(s) were on the outskirts. But no, the first camp, the place where Höss and his officers resided, was in the actual middle of the city! Maybe this was a result of late-twentieth century sprawl, but that was beside the point. Auschwitz's main offices, its barracks, its first punishment cells, its first gas chamber and execution yard were in the city!

We parked at an adjacent lot, and the five of us exited the car as our driver stayed behind. We entered the red brick, architecturally pleasing main building. Inside were posters and photographs, paintings and sculptures of the horrors of Auschwitz.

After we told the women working the front desk our nationalities, we headed outside, through another door, and into the interior of the camp. We walked past a former barracks and then saw the barbed wire gate. Two fifteen-foot-high electrically charged fences separated by about five feet of space closed the outside world off from the horrors of the Holocaust.

We entered under a gate that read, in German, *"Arbeit macht frei,"* ("Let work make you free") and were surrounded by numerous red-brick buildings that looked like the small dormitories of a mid-sized university.

The tour (picked up on pamphlets as we entered) led us into about six or seven of those red buildings. Inside each were different displays of the atrocities of the Holocaust.

There was no desire to soothe the feelings of the late-twentieth century visitors. The true terror of the Third Reich was there in all of its diabolical detail.

There were huge rooms filled to the top with human hair. There were other rooms filled with spent cans of Zyklon B (there were also some actual unused white cyanide pellets, safely tucked behind glass). Others were filled with everyday property: suitcases, pots and pans, shoes, brushes, eyeglasses, and countless other objects.

These displays, especially of the personal possessions, were almost impossible to come to terms with. As I stood in front of the enormous piles, I began to reflect that each had a story, each had an owner that died a horrible death there.

It was all the more difficult to contemplate the objects that had belonged to the children. Little dresses, pacifiers, and dolls filled some of the sealed cases. Those truly depicted the depravity of the Nazis and their belief in a second-class race.

(Tonight, one of my travel companions, the usually lighthearted Kim, confessed to me that every time she approached a children's property display, she began to cry.)

As we ventured through this vileness, there were a few children's school tours going through the camp, hopefully so future generations will never forget.

As we wound our way through the tour, there were also various written documents in display cases. There were no translations. The displays are not for tourists; they are a testament to the destruction of humanity that occurred there. There were a few names that were discernible however, such as the camp commandant's name, Höss.

A huge urn on display contained the ashes of untold numbers of Holocaust victims.

Throughout the corridors of these buildings were thousands of pictures of the victims of the Holocaust. I saw shaved heads and somber faces (strangely, though, one woman was smiling).

Why did the Nazis order such record keeping of a people that they had deemed so worthless?

Eventually we made it to the basement of one of the buildings and came to the punishment cells. They were tiny, four feet wide and ten feet high. These were to accommodate four prisoners. To get in they would have had to crawl through a very small (six-inch by six-inch) iron-gated hole and into the solid brick and concrete rectangular box.

In addition to those actual cells, there were displays of the sleeping arrangements for this part of the camp—straw on the floor made the human sleeping quarters resemble barns.

The next stop, outside of the buildings but still inside of the camp's barbed wire gates, was the gallows and the execution wall, where prisoners were hanged or shot, respectively.

At the end of the pamphlet tour, we exited through the barbed wire gate and found ourselves in front of the last few exhibits. The first place we came to was where camp commandant Höss was hanged for his crimes against humanity.

To the left of that was the first gas chamber and crematorium of Auschwitz. It was the only one still standing. I climbed down the six stone steps and entered the chamber into a room about thirty yards long and fifteen yards wide. All cement. In the ceiling there were a few one-foot-square holes where the Zyklon B was dropped.

About halfway through the darkened chamber and to the left was the crematoria. Four huge furnaces with rollers inside that lead to four tiny openings on the other end. Human remains would go in one side, and ashes would come out the other.

The five of us left this rear area and returned to the main building, where we began the tour. I erroneously assured the group that this was the main and central part of Auschwitz.

I was grossly mistaken.

We returned to the cab driver who then began the three-kilometer drive through the small, idyllic town. After taking us through a serene landscape, we arrived at a place that cannot come from one's imagination; it was too gruesome.

But, there, it exists.

The immense camp at Birkenau has not changed. The huge brick gated entrance was exactly the same fifty-plus years after its unholy construction. It was amazing to see how far the seemingly perpetual fence (the exact same design as the first camp) stretched behind it.

The five of us walked into the entrance. There was no office, no tourist counter. There was just a small room with a few stacks of takeaway sheets containing a bit of history. I assumed the keepers of this place wanted people to visit there and pay homage in any way they pleased.

We were the only people there.

It was us and Auschwitz-Birkenau.

We entered the camp itself through the ghastly gate, into the odious land that became a hell for millions of innocent people.

It was sprawling—easily over one-and-a-half miles long and wide. It was so disturbing that such a complex would be built for the sole purpose of killing.

There were not many structures standing. Most of the prisoners' barracks were gone, with only brick chimneys remaining. The liberating Soviet Red Army had apparently set fire to most of this huge complex, too disgusted with its purpose to let it remain standing. (This is just the opposite of the American liberating armies, who decided to leave the camps they discovered intact for fear that later generations would deny their existence.) Today, there were only forty brick and about ten or so wood buildings left standing.

Once inside we saw a sign with an arrow pointing us toward an "exhibit." We slowly walked the path toward it for about twenty minutes (not even reaching halfway through the length of the camp).

It was about forty degrees Fahrenheit with a cold, brisk, late summer breeze, which, coupled with the utter quiet and calm, added to the dreamlike setting.

We made our way through the wasteland and entered a barracks that housed the men who were assigned to do the hardest labor of the camp, such as digging ditches. Upon entering the one-story brick edifice, we saw two small rooms on the left side of the antechamber leading into the main barracks. There was no mention of what they were used for, but I assumed they were offices for the Nazi security detail.

On each end of the building there were rows of urinals and sinks, where I can only imagine the Nazi prisoners readied themselves for "rest" each night.

We entered the main chamber and saw a huge painting on the slanted ceiling of the room. It was done during the Holocaust by a Jewish captive. It was of camp workers digging an irrigation ditch as Nazi officers (both men and women) supervised their progress. This was a wonderful, strangely uplifting work of art. But it begged the question: why did the Nazis allow this to be done? Such a strange world of dichotomies.

The "beds" of the barracks next caught my glance. Three levels (wood on the top two and cement on the bottom) of bunks throughout this narrow building were all that were housed there. These were the bunks that are in so many history books and documentary films. There are countless photos and films of emaciated victims lying on these very slats as they slowly, excruciatingly withered away and died.

I hesitantly touched one of the beds, thinking of the horror that the people who "lived" there went through.

It was visceral.

It was real.

I nearly became physically ill. A hopeless feeling washed over me as I felt the disgust and sickness of the Holocaust.

I began to reflect. I could not believe that I was there; I was in the same building that I had seen in so much media. I could not believe that I was in the same building where such horrors were enacted on the innocent. I thought of how this place looked fifty years ago—the bustle of the men. The filth. The despair.

The loss of hope.

Death.

There were no words.

The five of us silently walked around and explored the barracks.

After quite a while, we walked outside and began the journey to the far end of the camp. On the way we passed a few more barracks. We looked inside of their locked windows. They all looked the same, as nothing had been done to this place since the Red Army liberated the camp in January of 1945.

The history was still alive.

The history was not clouded by ropes or glass cases. It was exactly as it was during the last days of the war.

There were no tourist information booths.

There were no street vendors inside or out.

There were no snack shops.

There were no gift shops.

Base capitalism had not affected this place. There was nothing to cloud the truth of Auschwitz-Birkenau.

Our small group of five continued walking and saw the five guard towers on either side of the fence (ten in all). As before, there were electric and barbed wire fences surrounding the entire perimeter. As we walked, we saw a clearing of the old chimneys and the beginning of a small forest. The barbed wire ended.

Then I spied large ruins that I first thought were outside of the camp. As I neared those ruins, I saw that they were indeed, still part of the camp. However, the trail to them took us directly to a few large ditches that we would first have to navigate.

Those ditches were mass graves where the ashes of many of the victims were thrown. There were no fences sealing off these three or four (not well-defined) indentations. I assumed that no one had any desire to climb down and explore those holes of human remains any closer. In addition, the holes, now fifty years old, were not covered with flowers or grass, but with an overgrowth of weeds. I guess the dumping of millions of human remains can destroy the soul of nature as it does the soul of man.

Walking to our right, we came to one of the two destroyed buildings. Approaching them seemed to be quite dangerous. But there were no safety warning signs; there were no ropes around them. You could get as close as you'd like.

This ruin and the other (about fifty yards away) were the primary gas chamber and crematorium of the Holocaust. (Hence the nearby burial pits.)

They were destroyed not by bombings or the Red Army but by the cowardice of the Nazis. As the Soviets were pushing west, the cowards blew them up to hide their complicity in the greatest crime against humanity the world had ever known.

There were schematics of the buildings posted so one could visualize their design. The section of the structure where the victims were first led and then told to undress was easily discernible even in the ruins. That was because the outline was still visible. The rubble there was much less than other sections of the building. I assumed that was because the gas chamber and crematorium had much more building material to them. This made the pile of rubble for those sections of the building much larger and thus the outline less noticeable.

We then traversed a tremendous stone memorial that had been built in 1967. This covered the fifty yards or so between the two death houses. That ruined chamber was just like the first.

As I walked across this area, I noticed poplar trees that the Nazis must have planted in rows nearby. They had actually decorated the perimeter of the gas chambers. The monsters had tried to beautify the Holocaust.

I stood on the memorial—a long pause on that cold September morning. I looked out over the complex. It was an amazing place. It was so terrible to stand with gas chambers twenty-five yards to either side, one-and-a-half miles of death barracks in front of you—and a quiet forest (with a now barking dog) behind you.

Words were truly meaningless.

The five of us took a seat on the memorial. We all sat apart, instinctively, as we needed to gather ourselves and search for our souls.

Finally, one by one, we begin to stir. A bit more walking through the memorial, and we decided to head back.

As we left, I noticed that the train tracks that ran through the complex split it in half. It was like two camps with the rail line in between. This rail line came to an abrupt end at the memorial that we were on. Literally the end of the line for millions of men, women, and children. Trains would simply dump off those that survived the journey right there. They would then be exterminated with no chance of even going through the ghastly selection process. Twenty-five yards on either side and they would be in a gas chamber. Nazi efficiency at its most horrible.

My party started down the tracks, ready to depart. I lagged behind for quite some time before I began my own journey back. I then started my trek on the first (or was it the last?) rail tie. I stepped on each individual tie for the entire one-and-a-half miles back to the front gate. The track itself divided into three at one point—I assumed because there were so many trains coming into this place that the ever-efficient Nazis had solved their traffic problem.

As I neared the end, I once again found myself sending my mind back fifty years, imagining what this place looked like. The hustle and bustle of wholesale death.

Finally, I reached the portal of Auschwitz-Birkenau once again— to the entrance that has been renamed "The Gates of Death." My four companions had been, thankfully, waiting patiently for me. We, unlike so many millions before us, were allowed to leave alive.

Back at the taxi, I told the driver that we wanted to go back to Auschwitz-I and watch the English film that was shown daily at noon.

"No problem," he said.

We arrived, bought our tickets, and took a seat in the medium-sized viewing room to watch the fifteen-minute presentation about the camp's liberation. The film, as told by a British narrator, was the story of the Soviet Red Army's liberation of the camp in January of 1945. It was a history that I was very familiar with, as I'd always been drawn to World War II and its grand scope. I had always been moved by the stories of the Holocaust but could never get a true feel of what had occurred. The revulsive scale of the terror had eluded me because of my basic concepts of humanity. But now, seeing the rooms of hair, the children's possessions, the bunks, the gas chambers—I had seen it with my own eyes. I would never look at those Holocaust documentaries and Holocaust writings the same. I had touched this living history with my own body and my own soul.

The ride back to Kraków was uneventful.

Back in Kraków, the atmosphere eased, and the five of us began to loosen-up. Jokes began again. Also talk of money and the fantastic exchange rate, "nineteen thousand zloty equals one American dollar."

We started looking for a place that cashed traveler's checks. We asked a few locals where we could get that done. We tried several of their suggestions but simply could not find a place that would cash a traveler's check or even knew where we could.

At one point, Kim said, "How many Polacks does it take to cash a traveler's check?!" As we began to laugh, a nun passed by, and Kim continued, "Oh shit, I said that in front of a Polish nun!" Bad taste, but we all laughed after the pressure of the day.

We continued down the old, cobbled streets of Kraków, Poland, finally finding a shop that would cash our checks.

Now it was up to me to find a hotel, as I was the only one who would be staying in Poland. We headed to a hotel that a travel information kiosk recommended, and I got a room there. The cost of this relatively nice hotel was only the equivalent of thirty-five dollars a night.

All five of us went up to my room and kicked back to decide what to do next. It was about five in the evening by this time, so we decided we should head back to the nearby train station to buy tickets for our next destinations (our Eurail passes were not good in Poland). I would be headed to Frankfurt, Germany, but I only needed a ticket to the border, as my pass would be good from there. The girls would be off to Budapest and Dave was headed to western Czech Republic.

But at the little station we ran into big trouble. Lines, lines, lines, and lines—it was Poland just after communism, after all.

The first line I stood in was the information queue. I got a little—information, that is. But only that I had to stand in another line. When I finally got to *that* window, the clerk did not understand a word I said. So she pointed me to another line, the information line I was just in. Needless to say, neither I nor the girls were able to get our tickets. We figured we could try again later.

The five of us now headed out for food. We walked to the city square and saw a sign for a restaurant. It was down a winding set of rock stairs. Good food, good service. After such a long day, Dave and I each ordered two dinners. The server was on top of it—he waited to bring our second after we finished our first. What a guy!

After dinner I confessed to the group that for this entire trip, the awful Nike Cross Training shoes that I had been wearing had been tearing up my feet. I finally decided that I had had enough. So the five of us left the downtown square and headed to the shopping district of Kraków. I found a shoe store and dropped one hundred thousand zlotys on a pair of generic running shoes. They felt so much better than the high-end cruel shoes I had been wearing.

Also, size 45. Who knew?

It was close to six thirty, and the sun was beginning to set. We again walked toward the train station where we experienced more of the same: lines everywhere. But I finally chose the correct one.

I bought my ticket to the German border and relaxed. The girls were also able to get theirs, for much cheaper than they expected. (Dave had managed to get his during the first go-around at the station).

At one point, when I was by myself waiting for the girls, a group of Romani children surrounded me en masse. One began to repeatedly shove a small cardboard sign into my stomach. I was told that this might happen, so I was a bit more prepared than most.

The cardboard was used to not only distract you but to hide the others' small hands as they rifled through your possessions. So, I waved my arms, yelled, and spun around in a circle as their hands began to creep onto me. I was successful; nothing was stolen. They would have only got a cheap PhD camera anyway. (PhD in this case stood for "push here, dummy.")

Now, we had another, albeit very minor, dilemma. Since we'd exchanged so much money in traveler's checks to zlotys, we had an excess of Polish currency. We had to spend it or lose it because the exchange rate for the Polish zloty was almost nonexistent in Germany and other neighboring countries.

Time for a spending spree! The girls bought a ton of food, and I bought film and a *Polish Beer Drinking Songs* cassette—whatever that was. We were big shots.

After our "spree," we traded addresses and exchanged numbers. I also noted the address where they would be during Oktoberfest in Munich. I then adjusted Sarah's sagging backpack (which had been bothering me for some time), and we went our separate ways. They were great traveling companions and would be missed.

I, now by myself, returned to my hotel and waited until ten o'clock to call my mother. No answer. I tried again at eleven, but again, no answer. Finally, after an all-night train ride, a trip to Auschwitz, a full day in Kraków, and a farewell to my seven-day traveling companions, I called it a night.

3

Germany (part II), Luxembourg, Belgium

Frankfurt, Luxembourg City, Brussels

I think it's Saturday.
I did not do much throughout the day.

I had breakfast at the hotel and talked to two Americans who were going to Katowice to photograph it. Then I headed out to spend more of the excess money I still had.

I went to the nearest auto dealer and picked up a green and orange Spider Ferrari.

Nope.

I bought a lot of food and soap.

I then headed to the train station at around four o'clock. About an hour later, onto the train bound for Frankfurt.

I got in a car by myself but forgot to close the door. Soon there were five Polish people sharing my second-class compartment. They had a ton of bags. So, to let them have more room, and for my sanity, I moved to an empty car just next door.

At that point, I heard two Americans talking nearby. I left my car (no one had since joined me) and headed next door to meet them. They had sympathy for me as they saw what happened to me in my first car—the Polish invasion, that is. I chatted with them briefly but didn't sit down. I wanted to return to my car to stake out my seat.

I left them and headed back. Back to be myself, in my own car and write. That is where I was when I wrote this. I also must admit that I was distracted with how many stops this train was making. I had definitely caught a local, so another invasion seemed imminent.

September 19

Well, I was right, the invasion came yesterday in the form of seven people in my one car. An older man (who was the first to arrive), two mothers with their children, a girl about ten, a boy about fifteen, and a young woman (who was the last).

At about 4 o'clock, I broke the stale quiet in the car by asking the young woman if we were still headed for Germany (I really was concerned, as the train had started to move in the opposite direction). She assured me that we were. Soon, she and I began to chat.

Her name was Barbara, she was a showgirl—kidding, writing that line sounded like "Copacabana" in my mind.

Barbara was a second-year medical student from Kraków who spoke decent English. She told me that she would be completing her studies in England on a scholarship the next year. We talked quite a bit and watched as everyone but the old man exited the car at around eight that evening.

As Barbara and I were chatting, the old man joined in. He was a Canadian from Calgary, born in Leipzig. He told us he owned a number of gold mines in his adopted country and had been in Katowice for a mining convention.

After some time, the old man, who was beginning to dominate the conversation, seemed to get a bit nervous. Soon, Barbara and I saw why.

As he prattled on about this and that, he dug into one of his packs and took out two shaving bags. He opened them and showed us what was inside.

Both bags were filled to the top with gold dust.

The old man encouraged Barbara and I to run our fingers through the gold, which we enthusiastically did.

Next, Doctor Barbara and I teamed up and rolled the elderly man for all of his gold. It was quite easy, as we each grabbed a shaving kit for ourselves.

Of course that did not happen.

Barbara and I just stared at the gold, ignoring the old man as he jabbered on.

Eventually we were snapped out of our dazed ogling as we arrived in Leipzig.

I decided I had had my share of the old fellow and got off the train with Barbara. Again, as we were walking to the cab stand in the near midnight gloom of Eastern Europe, my guilt of having a girl I loved in America consumed me. I decided to say good-bye to Dr. Barbara and returned to the station.

I then realized that it was too late to find a room, so if I stayed in Leipzig, I would most likely be forced to sleep on the cold concrete of the open-air station.

So, I hightailed it back to the train, which had not departed yet. I got on just as the wheels began to roll and found my old car where the old man was already laying down.

He and I surprisingly talked for only a short time as I took my contacts out. I saw that he had secured most of his bags away from the door and was sleeping on the others. Of course he slept like that—he was loaded down with fucking gold!

I secured the straps of my bag (the one filled with dirty clothing and not gold) to the metal portions of the seat and settled down to a surprisingly decent sleep.

I dreamt of showers of gold.

Gross. Just kidding.

We pulled into Frankfurt at six in the morning, and the old man knew it well. He first showed me a bank in the station where I could exchange some currency. Of course, it was closed at that early hour, but I did note it for later.

It was quite cold in early-morning Frankfurt, so the old man led the way to the station warm-room. We entered the cozy but smoke-filled room and chatted a bit more. We then shook hands and the old man parted to catch a train to a nearby small town.

And probably mindfuck a couple of other people with his gold.

I sat down in the warmth and regrouped after the eighteen-hour ride from Kraków. At that point I was able to take a better look at my surroundings. The warm-room looked like a misplaced greenhouse sitting in the train station. But nothing would ever grow in this "greenhouse." The only vegetation there was lit tobacco. It was an abundant crop.

The warm room was intended for only ticketed passengers, so a guard came by often and checked everyone's ticket. Even though I didn't have a "ticket," my Eurail pass sufficed. I was relieved that I was not booted out into the cold with the numerous homeless people who kept returning after every security walk-through.

I waited there for one-and-a-half hours, watching people argue with each other in the early morning. I was not quite sure what they were mad about—just a lot of angry Germans.

It seemed that German was a language designed for arguing.

As it was nearly a decent hour, I set off for a phone. Before I left Seattle, a friend had given me the phone number of relative of his who lived in Frankfurt. He assured me that they would be waiting for me to contact them.

I gave them a call and, as I expected, they did not answer.

After that failure, I went to the bank the old man had showed me and exchanged sixty dollars into Deutsche Marks. I left the station, looking for the poorer quarters where the ragged people go.

Lie la lie…

Out into the early morning of Frankfurt, I stopped at the first decent looking hotel I saw. It was across the street from the station, which was great because I intended to leave town early tomorrow.

The hotel was actually a nice little place. Most importantly, it was very clean.

I hopped in the small bed and slept for a bit.

I awoke and headed down the hall to take a shower in the shared shower room. After that, I realized that I was very hungry after such a long travel day, so I hit the Sunday morning sidewalks of Frankfurt to find a small restaurant for a meal and a beer for dessert.

I had a decent German meal and then strolled a bit. I noticed there were a lot of sex shops in town. Some of them were as large as department stores. I wondered if they had separate floors for individual fetishes.

After strolling through Sodom, I took a shortcut through an alley to get to my hotel. On my way, I literally nearly stumbled upon a girl shooting heroin. About five feet away from her was a pile of human shit. I must have walked in on her delicate morning toilet.

Verzeihen Sie mir, junge Dame.

Ah, Germany.

After I got back to the hotel, I found a phone and finally got in touch with my mother. I told her about my plan for Yugoslavia, and she was on board. She agreed to make some contacts in the States, mainly my Uncle Nick and Aunt (Teta) Jean. She assured me that she would fill them in on the developing plan. (Hey, I just realized that those two were Jovo's uncle and aunt as well!) I also promised her that I would call back on Wednesday from Paris to get an update on the scheme.

Then I called my girlfriend, Carly. We didn't talk for long, as the overseas connection kept cutting in and out.

Celibacy for that?

This pen I bought in Poland sucks. I got it to work but it still slips a lot.

I tried to regroup and rally after my phone calls but failed. I ended up going to bed at five in the evening, and I slept until six o'clock this morning. That eighteen-hour train ride really screwed up my body. I was now on the sleep schedule of a Florida retiree.

I'd had on the same clothes (all but the socks and underwear, which I had changed once) for eight days. I would definitely change all of my clothes tonight—everything was a bit ripe.

After all of that sleep, I arrived early to the Frankfurt station. So, I had some time to check the itinerary to Luxembourg at a ticket counter. This time waking up early paid off: I found out that I needed to change trains twice before arriving there. That was not listed on the schedule that I had, so I would have remained on a train bound for the south of France. At 7:49 a.m., I boarded the proper westbound train.

The first hour was on a train to Koblenz. It was more like a commuter train—the cars were filled with seats like a bus. I read *For Whom the Bell Tolls* most of the time.

In Koblenz, I barely made my transfer, hopping on with less than a minute to spare. This train would take me the final leg of this short trip, traveling just south of the fields of Flanders. I spent the hour in a closed car with a young German fellow who slept almost the whole trip. I did not read too much on this leg, as the scenery was fantastic.

The train traveled down a river valley (I must find out its name) with a large mountain on the left and a body of water on the right. The mountain had castles jutting out of its side every few miles. One looked like it was part of the living rock. I had never seen sights like that in America; it's just too young of a country.

After the transfer, this final leg of the forty-five-minute trip was again on a crowded commuter train. I had to stand a bit of the way, but I eventually found a seat.

After crossing the border into Luxembourg, I did a quick audit. I was in my fifth country in two weeks. That equaled all the countries I had visited in my first twenty-four years.

In that odd little country (still, an original member of NATO), there were a lot of elderly tourists. It did not seem to be a place for young people, as they tended to flock the short distance to Amsterdam. I noticed the older folks, because as soon as arrived, I helped an older American couple store their bags and boxes at the station. They had not seen (or had just ignored) the storage instructions and prices (eighty francs) for the lockers. I went through it with them (pictograph instructions, not words), and they seemed satisfied though a bit put off by the price.

Next, I headed out onto the streets of this new country and city. Luxembourg was a nice place. Not dirty like Germany (nor as sleazy). But I did stumble down a small side street that had a lot of sex shops.

So, determined not to get lost again, I went to a tourist shop and picked up a city map. There, the French-accented woman commented that this journal (the blue one) was beautiful, and she quite liked it.

Yep, those mall Walden Book Stores were known for their beautiful, aesthetic products.

There were a lot of bees in Europe, especially in Luxemburg.

I walked north and stumbled upon the castle district of town. (Oh, how often that would happen to me as I ventured through my hometown of Gary, Indiana, in my youth).

Here, a huge gorge divided the city into a northern and southern section. The city seemed to be centered around this gorge as grand buildings surrounded it on all sides.

When I wrote this, I was sitting in the northern section, having crossed the majestic bridge. I was also quite close to the primary, city-dominating castle.

I must admit, I know nothing of the history of this small country. I will most certainly have to investigate to prove or disprove my assumptions.

At the bottom of the gorge was a park with pathways and trees, no structures. None of man's intrusive influence had been allowed to penetrate the area. Luxemburg was not as beautiful as Prague, but was much more inspiring than Frankfurt.

(Just to make sure I am clear: Germany sucked.)

I ended my day trip, bought some water, and boarded the train to Brussels. It was long and boring—I slept most of the time.

Blue pen now.

September 20
(continued)

I am writing this on a train headed to Paris from Brussels, Belgium.

In Brussels I didn't do much as I was there for less than a day.

Also, it did not begin well. I got off the train at the wrong station—the north one, not the middle one as I intended. I left that station and decided to walk south to the correct one, where I would find hostel information.

Almost immediately I passed a small intersection where a prostitute stood on each of the four corners. They took turns yelling to me in German or French or Dutch or Flemish. I had no idea what they said, only that they sure liked to expose their breasts.

Neat, life in the big city.

At that point I realized that I was beginning to tire of large cities. When I began this journey, I thought I would do much more of my Yugoslavian preparation and planning in the countryside and small towns. I resolved that after Paris I'd avoid large cities and concentrate on the smaller ones, especially in southern France, Italy, and Switzerland.

I navigated through the gauntlet of propositions and continued my way south. After some time, I asked a local how far the station was. I was surprised to learn that it was still about five kilometers away, so, without paying, I jumped on the subway.

Finally, I arrived at the station. It was rush hour, so the place was packed. I did find the hotel information kiosk rather quickly. I picked up a pamphlet for the "Sleep Well" hostel but couldn't find a coin-accepting phone to call them. I walked around for about a half an hour when I finally discovered a suitable phone on the lowest level of the train station.

I called the hostel, left my name as a reservation, and then took off.

I asked a cab driver to point me in the proper direction and then, for confirmation, asked two more people from Montreal the same question. I finally found it.

It was a decent, clean place—five stories with a bar and café. But it was still a dormitory, so it was cheap, the equivalent of nine dollars a night. It wasn't much, but I didn't need much, since I would be leaving first thing in the morning.

There were four people (including myself) in an assigned room that had twelve beds to choose from. I first talked with a guy from San Diego, Remy, who was going to medical school next year. Nice guy, beard, curly black hair—kind of a bohemian-American attitude, but not a junkie.

Another roomie was an Israeli piano player. A true lounge lizard who supported himself through Europe entertaining at any bar that would hire him.

The last guy did not stick around, as he took off early to see the city on his own.

The remaining three of us talked, but I was very hungry, so I left to look for any nice, cheap restaurant nearby.

I found a Thai place, but the dolts in front of me couldn't decide what to order. After ten minutes and audible stomach growling, I lost patience and left.

I then found a place up a flight of stairs and ate a ten-dollar meal—more than my room for the night.

I got back to the hostel, and my two roommates were still there, making plans to go to a blues bar (The Blue Corner), where the lizard hoped to play that night. They asked me to come along, and I agreed. But, as they were headed for dinner first, I decided to meet them later. They gave me directions and we decided to meet at ten-thirty, which was in less than hour.

Of course, I fell asleep and never made it out. On the bright side of life(?)—I saved money. I also got an early start the next day.

4

France (part I)

Paris

Today, I showered, ate five pieces of bread with spread, and took off to the main train station. And, like yesterday, I was in the wrong place as I had to catch the Paris train at the north station (the place I mistakenly got off yesterday).

I hopped on the subway, not paying again, and arrived at track fifteen of Brussels North. I was actually forty-five minutes early and could relax a bit.

When I wrote this I was on a train in eastern France, hoping that I did not have a lot of problems locating the Hotel du Prince Eugene. My friend Jason, the same person whom I'd traveled to the East Coast of the United States with, would be staying there while he worked his modeling bookings in Paris.

September 21
(continued)

I arrived in the north station of Paris yesterday, went to the tourist office and got the Hotel du Prince Eugene's address and telephone number. I then went to the tobacco store and picked up a phone card.

I used the card to call the place to find Jason, but, alas, he had not arrived. I thought he was to have been there earlier that morning.

So, I called his parents' house in Valparaiso, Indiana, and I reached his mother. I asked her what time her son would be in Paris today.

No, he wouldn't be in Paris today, she said. He was upstairs in his room.

Uh-oh. I stopped and thought for a moment. Shit. His bookings were cancelled. I had been looking forward to seeing a friendly face.

But, as soon as I had that thought, he got on the phone (it was seven in the morning there). He told me that he would be in Paris at six o'clock the *next* morning with an entire entourage—a videographer, a photographer, and three or four female models.

My fault. I'd misunderstood and thought he was to be there today, the twenty-first.

Now, I had to find a room for tonight. I called a place from the Frommer book, a decent-sounding hostel, and reserved a bed.

I would not be able to get into the place until three in the afternoon, so I left the station and went across the street to get some food and a beer. I found a nice little place and got a ham sandwich and a French beer. The first beer tasted so good after the hectic couple of days on the trains that I had another.

I kicked back and finally realized that I was in Paris. France, the seventh country on this trip—I never thought I would be here. The city of Napoleon, de Gaulle, Louis XIV, Marie Antoinette, Picasso. Those people walked the same streets that I was about to. (Well, the royalty did not so much walk as ride or be toted about.)

Anyway, I was in Paris.

I went back into Paris Nord and asked directions to my hostel. Two different people wrote down essentially the same information in my little notebook.

So, off to find the Metro.

My first trip on the Paris Metro was unbelievably fast, efficient, and clean. I arrived at my stop in five minutes, where I consulted the handy, posted map of the general area. I was very close to my night's destination.

I headed to the one that I had called and where I reserved a bed, but it was full.

What?

No problem. He sent me to their sister hostel, which was about five hundred yards down the road.

As soon as I got there, I helped a buxom young lady with her baggage and then received my bed assignment.

It was a nice place with old brick buildings surrounding a central courtyard. I found my room on the third floor. But the only bathrooms available were on the first floor.

Uh-oh. I hoped I didn't get Petain's revenge in the middle of the night.

I was sitting on the lower bunk in a relatively clean room with three bunk beds, when a tall, thin fellow walked in. He was American and we began to talk. He seemed to be a nice a guy, and he was easy to talk to.

Josh, a physical therapist from St. Louis, had lived in Seattle for a time. He was currently traveling with his girlfriend, Lana, whom he'd met in Seattle. She was originally from Prague.

Josh invited me to tag along with them that night as they were going to dinner and then sightsee. So, I took a quick nap, and then we headed out.

Lana turned out to be a nice girl; she looked like an actress from Peyton Place.

As we walked toward the Seine, I noticed a long church on the left. It was only about a three-minute walk from the hostel.

Yep, it was Notre Dame.

Vast, magnificent, inspiring.

Sanctuary!

A mass was being conducted when we entered, so it was peaceful and solemn as well. As we explored, I noticed there were no exhibits in the church proper.

It was immense though. Its height was reminiscent of the Hoosier Dome. I got dizzy from looking up into the rafters.

Lana had lagged a bit behind, leery about entering the great church. While we were quietly traversing the floor, she said, "Smells like church—the devil," with a scrunched, disturbed look.

With my well-learned politeness, I sympathized with her taste.

We left after about twenty-five minutes and headed to the Latin Quarter to find a nice restaurant.

Walking down the cobblestone streets, we saw the innumerable restaurants, nearly all of them Greek. All with hawkers at the door, enticing people to spend in their businesses.

After about fifteen minutes, we decided on a place. The maître d' was a young Greek guy who spoke decent English—even claiming at one point to be from the U.S. He (along with many of the other hawkers) was smashing white plates onto the street—a strange custom but a sure attention-grabber.

He promised us a free drink and a chance to break some plates. Offers we couldn't refuse—in any country.

La vie en rose.

We went in and, after a glass of Sangria, we ordered. I got squid, which wasn't very good. It was rubbery and tasted like it came from a box. Do they make Squid Helper in Europe?

Dessert was feta cheese. That worked fine. It was good stuff.

While we ate, we watched the maître d' break plates on his head in perfect circles—an artist of annihilation. He placed them on customer's heads—French royalty? Grecian halos?

In the now-full restaurant and during his demolition demonstration, he danced and sang his heart out.

Before we left, we made sure that we fulfilled his promise and broke a few plates. As we took turns, he and the other customers cheered us on. We walked to the door across a floor covered in broken cheap white porcelain.

The three of us, now with full stomachs and our anger issues assuaged, found a Métro to the Eiffel Tower. On it, a tiny homeless Parisian man got a bit fresh, so we had to calm him down a bit. Too bad we didn't have any plates to huck at him.

We got to our stop and there, just out of the Métro station, was the enormous, glowing symbol of Paris, the Eiffel Tower.

We ventured to the girded tower and just stared at its majesty. I couldn't help but think of everything this structure had inspired. I thought of Delaunay's paintings and the awe that the tower must have stirred in him. I thought of all the kitsch it had elicited as well.

I also thought of the history that the tower had, well, towered over for the last 107 years. The artistic movements, World Wars I and II, ceremonies and celebrations, calamity and conquest.

We circled the tower's footprint a number of times before we began to walk away from it and cross the Seine. I caught myself continually turning back to admire it, awestruck.

We arrived at the museum opposite the Eiffel Tower and stared at it again. After about fifteen minutes we took off and headed down the Champs-Élysées to the Arc de Triomphe.

We bought some water on the way and quickly completed the mile-or-so walk. We arrived at the grand intersection and saw that there was a tunnel for pedestrians. We joined the other tourists and climbed down the stairs and through the tunnel so as not to disturb the never-ending cascade of traffic.

The Arc was huge—daunting—to stand under. On the ground and underneath the actual Arc were five plaques, commemorating the last five major French military conflicts, including the 1870s advance of Germany under Bismarck and the French conquest of Alsace-Lorraine in World War I. Another cited the men of North Africa with the Foreign Legion. The fourth was the French attempt to colonize Indochina. The last, and certainly not least, was the plate commemorating World War II. This last one included a commemoration of not just those in the military, but those in the Resistance as well. Coupled with this plaque was the transcript of a speech by Charles de Gaulle.

At the same location was the eternal flame for the French Unknown Soldier. This added even more quiet solemnity to an already somber, significant spot.

Built and conceived by Napoleon, the Arc was one of the greatest features in this stunning, amazing, beautiful city.

Time to catch up, Ketchup/Catsup.

Before heading back to the hostel, I bought another 1.5-liter bottle of water. I guess I was determined to stay hydrated.

At that point, after spending some time getting to know him, Josh started to seem a bit odd to me. He was always making comments, asides, about killing his girlfriend, Lana. He said them jokingly, but he said them enough that I had my doubts. I began to realize that his whole personality was a red flag.

That night, despite Josh sharing the room with me, I got some decent sleep—I figured he wasn't looking to sex-thrill-kill me.

I got up early, ate some French bread (what else?), and washed it down with a strong café au lait. I then found the front desk and locked my pack in their storage facility. I began the long walk to see the city and eventually find my friend Jason. I walked for an hour and a half through the overcast city of Paris, passing the Paris Opera and then finding the Boulevard Voltaire. The hotel that he was scheduled to stay was on that road.

I finally saw it, the Hotel du Prince Eugene. But just as I was about to cross the road, I saw a kid lying in the middle of the street with a blanket on him. His helmet and moped were dumped on the ground nearby—he had just been hit by a car. The police and ambulance came screeching in but I didn't stick around to rubberneck.

Once I got to the hotel, the desk clerk told me that Jason and his party had arrived but had stepped out with Clara (the photographer) to get coffee. I left the hotel and explored the neighborhood. After some time, I realized that it was early afternoon. Time for food.

I found a little pizzeria where a nice and pretty server tried to teach me French with little success.

I headed back to the hotel and finally found my friend. We went to the room he was sharing with the trip's videographer, a chunky, bearded guy named Benjamin. As soon as we got to the small room with two twin beds, Jason fell asleep as Benjamin and I talked.

Benjamin was from Griffith, Indiana. I soon got the impression that he wasn't very on top of things. I brought up some sites I had been to or planned on going to, but he wasn't familiar with any of them. He didn't know what the Louvre was, who Jim Morrison was, or what West Germany was. A bit of a dullard. Oh well.

After some casual, superficial bullshit, I decided it was time to retrieve my stored backpack. Benjamin seemed pretty tired from the travel (or conversation) as well.

I walked the entire way and back for a second time. My feet, still blistered from the previous Nike garbage shoes (despite the new pair I'd purchased in Poland), had blisters begetting blisters.

Pain.

When I got back to the hotel, Jason was awake. I made myself at home in their room as I washed my dirty clothes and took a shower in their private(!) bathroom. (I did ask them both for permission before I did it, and they laughed and said that they didn't care.)

Whoa. A room with a bathroom, shower, phone, and a color TV with remote. I was living in luxury; no more Hooterville.

Soon Clara, the photographer and leader of their party, called the room. After hearing from the boss, Jason and Benjamin sprang into action and got ready for dinner.

The three of us went down to the lobby from their second-floor room and waited nearly half an hour for the rest of the party to show up.

While we waited, I asked the girl working the front desk if it was possible to get a cot in room 105. She said that it would be no problem and assured me it would be done.

I chatted with Clara and Denise, one of the models. Clara was a French native who now lived and worked in northwest Indiana and Chicago. Denise, a pretty girl, was a whisper-thin blonde who was already homesick only eleven hours after leaving her home. She wanted to return on the next flight, she told Clara and me.

Poor kid.

Other models began to trickle down. The next was an African American model, Gretta. She was friends with Jason, and I had met her a few times but could not remember where. A Hispanic model followed closely behind her. I don't remember her name.

I scrutinized my luck to be in this model situation. Models in the media are great to look at and fantasize about. Models in the wild, not so much. They were so vapid, sallow, and shallow. If one of those ladies would have deigned to lie with a filthy traveler such as me, my commitment to my girlfriend would not have been in jeopardy. Those sullen, emaciated young women were just not my type. The modeling gene pool would be safe another day.

All seven of us began to walk the streets of Paris. Touring a big city with three female stylistas and a female photographer was not my idea of fun—we had to stop and look at everything: every store, every kiosk, every nook, every cranny.

The girls, while extremely sweet, only spoke their native tongue of fashionese, of which I was ignorant.

After quite a bit more touring, we finally decided that it was time to eat. We found a Vietnamese restaurant that the girls insisted on calling Chinese.

We were the only people inside. Great food; better service.

At the restaurant, Clara and I began to discuss many topics, including where I had been and the historical significance of many of the sites. We also talked of Van Gogh, her favorite artist.

She was mesmerized by his application of color and how perfectly he used colors to complement each other. He was such a genius, she continued, that the exactness he achieved was almost inconceivable.

Talk shifted from artistic pursuits to personal matters. I found out that Clara had photographed my cousin David's young children, Brandt and Brielle at her studio in Crown Point, Indiana, near the central courthouse square. She carried on about how adorable they were and what a pleasure it was to work with them.

The rest of the table remained quiet. Stoic. Vapid.

We finished dinner and paid the bill. Our next mission was to find a supermarket for some basic necessities.

On the way to the market, I mentioned my feet issues—blisters begetting blisters. Clara insisted that we visit a pharmacy. She translated for me as the pharmacist diagnosed my problem. Finally, he prescribed a medication as well as a set of sterile bandages.

I could not thank her enough for her help. I felt that healing was imminent.

With my medicine firmly in my hand, Jason and I split off from the group to pick up some postcards. We walked around the block, eventually meeting back with everyone at the hotel.

My bed (cot) was not in the room as the clerk had promised. Clara spoke with another hotel clerk who told her that a cot could not be brought up to the room because of its size and the fire code.

I had put my faith in the other clerk and had been drastically let down.

Well, I guess I will have to sleep on the ground, I thought.

But, before I settled on sleeping on the floor, I decided to talk to the clerk myself.

Same result.

I then began to explore the small hotel, trying to think of what to do next. On the sixth floor, while roaming the halls, I found a cot, alone and in need of a person. I grabbed it and wheeled it to Jason and Benjamin's room.

Uh-oh. About an hour later, the clerk called the room to see if we had their missing cot. Jason denied it (in French), so all seemed fine.

At eleven o'clock, I used the pay phone just outside the hotel to call my mom as I'd promised her. No answer.

As I was doing that, I got to witness a bit of police brutality. Two kids on a moped were pulled over. The first cop walked up to the driver and slapped him, knocking his helmet from his head. Five more cops showed up (including a nice-looking but loud female cop). After some verbal assaulting, the kids were sent on their way.

After the fracas, I tried to call my mom again and got through this time. We discussed the on-going process of wrapping up my dad's estate.

We then discussed some of my options regarding the planned trip to Yugoslavia. She told me that the extended Sever family and a few other close friends with relatives in Yugoslavia had agreed to wire me money to give to Jovo. Their hope was that he would be able to distribute it to a select group throughout the country. My hope was to find a way into Yugoslavia. I would need to do some investigating on that very soon.

When I got back to the hotel, ol' Jacques at the desk called for me—shit. He informed me that I could not stay in the room because of the fire code.

"I just work here, I will get in trouble," he told me.

I can't go in the street, I responded. It's too late now to find a room.

I can sell you a single room for 350 francs.

I've got no francs changed over.

We went back and forth for about fifteen minutes. He had the advantage of the rules, I had the advantage of the language—we were speaking English.

Finally, after getting pretty scared that he would kick me out, I remembered something. My ace in the hole. The girl clerk earlier had promised me that she would put a cot into room 105. I told him she said that it would be there when we returned from dinner.

With that, Jacques finally acquiesced.

Okay for tonight. But *non* tomorrow.

I shook his hand and headed to the room. There, I put in my earplugs and fell fast asleep.

September 23

I woke up at six o'clock when Jason and Benjamin were getting up to go to their first shoot. Jason handed me a crust of bread.

I went back to sleep, woke up at ten, and called another hotel—success.

I packed up my still-wet belongings, and, in the rain with no umbrella, headed to the new hotel.

It took over an hour to get there. It was located near my first hostel in Paris, across the street from the Sorbonne and a three-minute walk from Notre Dame.

I got to the Hotel Gerson about forty minutes later than expected, but I didn't think it would be an issue so early in the day. When I asked to check in, the woman at the desk told me that she had already sold the room.

Oh shit. I heard that and I dropped my coat to the floor. I was ready to blow up at this Parisian *chienne* as I had just spent a good hour and a half looking for the fucking place (in the rain), and now I was told it was all for naught!

She saw what was about to occur and, wanting to avoid a mess, told me that she would set me up at a nice place down the street. A one-minute walk, for the same price.

Okay, I cooled down and was then nice to her.

The new place, the Hotel Excelsior, really was only about one minute away; still across the street from the Sorbonne. I got the one-star hotel room, which was usually three hundred francs, for two hundred.

I stowed my bag in the relatively clean room and medicated my healing feet. Then I hit the road to be a tourist once again. This time, I went to the Louvre.

The museum was not far but I walked for quite a while because the building was under renovation and there were no clear signs for the entrance. After circling nearly the entire building for half an hour, I finally stumbled upon a ticket window and entrance.

I am more of a fan of modern art, so much of what was housed there was not in my wheelhouse. But I did enjoy seeing many of the old masters and a few specific works of the ancients and the Renaissance.

In Room 5, I stumbled (lots of stumbling going on with my blistered feet) upon the *Mona Lisa*. I sang "Mona Lisa, Mona Lisa" in my mind.

It was behind a bulletproof glass barrier, stanchions, and guards.

I then sang "Mona Lisa" aloud and received a standing ovation from the surrounding crowd.

That is a lie. I just strained and gawked like everyone else.

The work was impressive, maybe because it is so famous; maybe because it was done by Leonardo da Vinci—, for God's sake!

I took my time and examined it, noting the background most of all. It was very unique as portraits went—a curved road and a pastoral background. It was wonderful to see in person.

Next, I passed the *Winged Victory of Samothrace* and the *Raft of the Medusa* as I was making my way to the *Venus de Milo*.

I followed the signs to her, passing Roman and Greek sculptures. I did take my time appreciating those ancient pieces completed to perfection by artists lost to time.

I then saw the ol' *Venus* down a thin corridor. I walked the sixty or so yards and then stood in front of the most famous woman (in need of prosthetic arms) in the world. Fantastic to see as well.

I did not spend much more time in the Louvre; I had only wanted to see the highlights. When I began to make my way to an exit, I found a hall to the new Pei Pyramid area. The pyramid was a novel, wonderful work as it was such an aberration inside the Louvre's classical main courtyard.

September 23
(continued)

Catch-up.

I left the Louvre and walked northeast so I could pass the Georges Pompidou Center. As I was walking, I got to experience a lot of the city of Paris. I passed the tourist shops that lined the main boulevard, finally reaching a side street somewhere behind the Louvre. There I ordered a crêpe from a street vendor who spoke good English. He told me about some train wreck in the United States.

Thanks for brightening my day, *mon ami.*

As I enjoyed my crêpe, I walked past a wide array of Parisian shops—clothing boutiques, shoe stores, coin merchants, anything I wanted but didn't need.

Street entertainers became more and more plentiful as I neared the Pompidou Center. There were people dancing in a park, jugglers in colorful clothes, and a mime on a stoop. There was an old man with a soft prop bat, hitting people and ordering them where to sit. He mocked some when they retreated, all watched by an ever-increasing crowd.

I continued on and around but never entered the center (there was so much to see outside). The building was distinct from all other buildings in the city—an exoskeleton of pipes and tubes. I was glad that I'd made a special trip to see it, but how long could I stare at a building's exterior?

So I hopped on a Métro and began the long trek to the Père Lachaise Cemetery. Thankfully, the Métro stopped right in front of it, so I did not get lost in this remote area of the city.

But once I entered the cemetery I got lost immediately—it was huge. I headed back to the entrance and found a map.

First, I broke on through to Jim Morrison's grave, which was not very impressive. About five kids were sitting around it, smoking cigarettes. Five to one, they were like fools in a royal court.

Honestly, I did get a little angry at all the defacing that people had done to the graves in the area near Morrison's. With no regard for anyone, they wrote idiotic, simplistic "platitudes" extolling the forgotten virtues of a lost era.

I did not stay long at Morrison's grave as I had a few more sites in the cemetery I wanted to see.

I studied Frederic Chopin's final resting place ("A. Fred Chopin").

Then I romanticized at Eugène Delacroix's grave.

Felt witty reading the notes left for Oscar Wilde at his tomb.

I began to emote at Sarah Bernhardt's elegant monument.

Finally, I began to feel rosy at Gertrude Stein's tomb.

I then pirouetted down into the crypts looking for Isadora Duncan. It was in there that I found myself, a bit scared, standing in a huge room, alone, surrounded by hundreds, no thousands, of tiny tombs.

I walked around the vastness. I listened to the water drip as I looked at pictures on a few of the tombs.

Oh, the places the imagination will go.

I then began the long journey back up the hill where a couple of French people stopped and asked me directions to some sites in the cemetery. I was able to point them the right way—amazing myself in the process.

I found the cemetery's exit and then discovered a great small place for dinner. After that, I headed back to the hotel via the subway.

Once there, I tried to call Jason and his group, but they were not at the hotel. I decided to go to bed early. I knew I would have a long day tomorrow, Friday.

SEPTEMBER 24

On Friday morning I did not have a shower, paid twenty-five francs for the hotel breakfast, and left for the Picasso Museum at around nine thirty.

(I actually found it rather easy. I was getting to know the Métro pretty well).

At the museum ticket office, I asked for and got a student discount before heading into the twenty-gallery museum.

Working logically from Picasso's early to later years, the museum displayed countless numbers of his works. There were also pieces from his private collection, including art from Braque, Matisse, and Cézanne.

Like the Van Gogh Museum in Amsterdam, if you do not like the guy's work, you'll hate the museum. But I love Picasso, so this place was great.

The museum was designed well; it allowed one to progress through Picasso's life rationally, experiencing his development as an artist. Included in the displays were small histories regarding each portion of his life. Those were written in French, but I could, surprisingly, understand quite a bit. I grasped just enough to know what was going on in his life as Picasso produced each particular work of art.

I stayed there for a couple of hours. I really did enjoy it and would go back if I ever returned to Paris.

Next, I would be going to Versailles. I was standing in line to buy a train ticket behind two Americans in their forties when I learned that the palace would be open for only two more hours—it was to close early today, at three that afternoon. Oh well. I found the correct track and left for the uneventful thirty-minute journey.

When I got off the train, I did not know which way to walk. There were no signs, and a number of streets were closed. I soon found out that it was because a concert (Jean-Michel Jarre or some other artist I could give a shit about) was scheduled for that evening.

During my travels, I found that Europeans were very inefficient when it came to posting signs, but they were generally good at providing tourist kiosks. In Versailles, there were neither.

I, along with everyone else, began to head in all directions, looking for a ticket booth or an entrance into the palace. Gates and guards blocked the streets, and no one was around to offer any direction.

I finally got a bit of help from a near-moron cop who was nearly as feckless as his city.

After walking for nearly an hour, I found the goddamn entrance to this overly extravagant, narcissistic fool's paradise.

Once inside I understood why the French had to revolt: their kings were enjoying the most extravagant life while the people starved. I guess there is a touch of socialism in me—I could not fathom why such a huge place should be built while people suffered.

Kontrolle über das Kapital.

Vive la révolution.

Don't lose your head, Marie.

After my mental journey through Marxism and revolution, I began to be a tourist again. But I still did not have much time for Versailles. I didn't care to see the king and queen's chambers but had to walk past their vulgarity on my way to the only room I came to see.

It was, of course, the Hall of Mirrors, where the Treaty of Versailles was signed, delaying the start of World War II for a few years. It was nice to stand in such a remarkable room where such impressive incompetents hammered out the worst peace treaty of the twentieth century.

The room itself was very narrow (as were the minds of those working out the armistice) with mirrors on one side, windows on the other, and a long chandelier in the middle.

I began to work my way out with the sole intention of leaving the city of Versailles. But, as I was looking for an exit, I came across the Gallery of Battles.

This was an incredible room. Enormous. In it, the story of Gaul and France, from the fifth century to Napoleon, told through large, immense paintings (too many to count). Some of them were done by artists such as Delacroix.

Four depicted the exploits of Napoleon, one showed Joan of Arc, and one portrayed Washington at Yorktown. There were also about a crowd's worth of busts of France's greatest military leaders.

An extraordinary room for anyone who enjoys even a small taste of history. If I were a French historian, this would be the room to die for.

I left the building feeling better, having scratched my historical itch, and I made my way back to the station. On the way I asked three separate, idiotic Keystone Kops which way to go. None seemed to have a clue. With all the screwups he caused, I really hoped Jean-Michel Jarre or whoever the hell was playing there put on a great fucking show.

I boarded the train and sat next to three Parisian fellas (all about twenty years old) who smelled real bad, like cabbage or a filthy bottom. I held my nose and got off at the Invalides stop.

From there I worked my way south down the street, looking for the Rodin Museum. I found it without much of a problem.

I queued up and bought my ticket, getting an unannounced student discount. I began to my left—*The Burghers of Calais*. An amazing work commemorating the defeat of that city by the English during the Hundred Years' War. The emotional pain of the subjects, the city's leaders, screams out as they are led by their captors to their beheadings.

Next, I headed outside and walked around the huge garden. In it, there were numerous sculptures by, of course, Rodin. Lots of male nudes, which, like Michelangelo, were Rodin's preferred model form. Not as great as Michelangelo, but, in any case, he did some impressive work.

Another great piece in the garden was a massive textured door with Adam and Eve on either side. The couple from Eden, obviously just after their expulsion, were naked and ashamed, hiding their faces and bodies.

From there, I went back into the building and immediately saw *The Kiss*. I studied this as well, so it was nice to see in real life.

There was not a lot included in the small, illogically ordered museum. So, I went back outside and saw, erect and by himself, *The Thinker*, which was green from the weather in Paris. It was quite large and detailed. I noted Rodin's attention to his features as he curled the toes of the man (something that must be seen in real life) conveying that the thinker was completely strained by his thoughts—an existential dilemma to be sure. Amazing work.

After that, I slowly began my departure through the garden from the Rodin Museum. I worked my way to the Seine, intent on walking the Champs-Elysées and seeing the Arc de Triomphe not in the darkness as before, but in the bright light of day.

When I arrived at the Seine near the Pont Alexandre, I was struck by the grandeur of the surrounding area—east and west ran the Seine; to the north, the Grand and Petit Palaces; to the south, the direction I'd come from, the golden dome of Les Invalides, Napoleon's tomb.

What a sight, what a place to be. This was better than the scenery in Prague.

I worked my way to the river, between the two palaces, gaping in awe the whole time.

Then, before I was aware of it, I was standing once again on the most famous street in the world—the Champs-Élysées. As the sun was proudly shining, I looked east and clearly saw the Obelisk; I looked west and easily saw the Arc. I began to walk west. I pretended to drop my hat so I could actually touch the road itself. Trivial, I know, but I had to make contact with it.

I took in the whole—the street, the shops, the people, the smells and sounds as well.

I walked past a street named for FDR (it began as Churchill) past the Virgin Megastore, a Burger King and a McDonald's.

I arrived at the Arc de Triomphe, my feet aching. I went down into the tunnel connecting the sidewalk to the interior of the Arc as I had done a few days prior. I still thought that this was the greatest place in Paris.

I read the plaques again, noting the statues more this time. The only figure that I recognized was Napoleon—he did dominate this great city.

I must say that I really did enjoy the Arc as it represented French contemporary history with such dignity.

I left the Arc through the tunnel and boarded a Metro back to the hotel. There, I had a quick meal and then called Jason. No answer.

I wrote yesterday's journal entry and planned the agenda for my trip to Ireland, which I would be taking the next day.

I slept despite some loud Frenchman talking on his phone four stories beneath me.

September 25

Alright, so it is today.

I awoke about eight, believing that I would have an especially hectic morning as I would be catching a ferry to Ireland. I had set all of my things out the previous night and had packed everything else. I was ready for anything.

Before I hit the road, though, I needed to clean up. I left my room and walked through the rain into the courtyard (I was in room 405, fifth floor). I ventured through the tiny lobby and up to the third floor to take a shower. It was an itty-bitty tub, but I finally got clean.

When I was done, I called Jason once again. He was there. This was great news: I had to visit his hotel one last time to pick up my forgotten umbrella.

I packed up the rest of my belongings, ate, paid the clerk, and headed to Jason's. Shockingly, it only took me twenty minutes to get to the hotel.

Finding something is a lot easier when you know where it is.

I found Jason, Benjamin, and Clara all having breakfast downstairs. I got my umbrella and headed up to Jason and Benjamin's room to change, as it was quite cold in Paris, and I only had on shorts.

After I changed, I headed back to the dining room to chat a bit more with Jason. He told me that the one model who was homesick had been sent home!

But for Jason, the trip, so far, had been nothing but positive. His plan now was to lease a room for a few months from a stout old Parisian woman who worked for one of the designers. The one-week Eurail pass he'd bought (he and I had planned to briefly travel together) would be used later, if at all.

I was a bit relieved that I would not be going mad, listening to one song for six hours straight in Europe.

After a bit more small talk, it was time to leave. I said good-bye to Jason, Clara, and Benjamin. Benjamin told me that I was just like *Gulliver's Travels*. His comment confused me—I was sure the places *I'd* been to exist.

Maybe Benjamin knew something I did not.

I headed to the Metro, picked up a ticket, and took my eleventh Metro ride in Paris, this time to the St. Lazare station.

I wanted to get my itinerary to Ireland approved as I was wary of the sea crossing, so I headed to an information desk and the slowest moving line ever.

After a long wait, I finally got it okayed—I'd take 11:30 a.m. train to Cherbourg and then a 6:00 p.m. ferry to Ireland.

I found the train and boarded a second-class, non-smoking car. I was on my way.

Right now, I am in the first car, eighth seat from the front, orange seats, rain and fog outside. An obnoxious, little American girl (about eight years old) is seated next to me. Little Miss Piggy. Now, I will read and try to ignore all around me.

5

Ireland

Rosslare, Dublin, Galway

September 25
(continued)

I pretty much relaxed the rest of the train ride. I even fell asleep for the last hour or so.

The train arrived in Cherbourg on time, and I went into the terminal. As usual, I went straight to the trip information desk. There, I saw the little girl from the train with her mom. I introduced myself to Cameron and Nina, respectively.

Nina spoke French and found out where we were to catch the ferry to Ireland. I found a map and set off by myself to find the dock. After walking—in what I thought was the wrong direction—past a huge store named Continent, I stumbled upon signs that said the dock was nearby. *Whew.*

I worked my way through the town of Cherbourg (an umbrella was not necessary), past little bars and a police station. I got to the dock, which was in a vast open area. I knew that I was in the right place as I saw groups of people carrying huge amounts of beer in shopping carts to the boat.

I went inside the ferry terminal and headed straight to the Irish Ferries booth, which was easy to find in the small station. I paid the thirty-franc port tax and received my boarding pass. I had no seat assignment, so I asked the woman where I would sit.

Any place you can find, she told me.

Great, now I began to get worried. What if I couldn't find a place? Or, what if the only available area was outside, on an open deck?

Oh well, I would deal with any issues when they occurred.

I locked up my bag and started to look for lunch. Just outside the terminal, I found a food stand. I ordered a burger, chips, and a Coke from a British guy. I told him it was nice to hear English again.

Yeah, I know, he said. The French can be a little odd, he laughed.

Well, he continued, that was a terrible thing to say as they were good people.

He was a nice guy, and we talked a bit more. He told me where the nearest grocery store was as well as some other general information about the city.

I left his kiosk and found a small outside table to eat at. As I was eating, I saw Nina and her daughter Cameron. They joined me and we began to chat.

After some small talk, they headed to the terminal and I went to the grocery store, Continent, the same one I had passed earlier. It was a huge complex—a regular grocery store like in the States, but also with bars, restaurants, etc. It was essentially a big French mall.

I bought food for the trip—ham, bread, water, beer, and two packs of cheese. I then headed back to the terminal to begin my four-hour wait for departure.

At the terminal, I saw Nina and Cameron sitting in the waiting area, so I joined them. We talked and began to get to know each other.

But while we were talking, I began to worry again. I kept wondering if I would be able to find room inside on the boat. For some reason I had a terrible feeling that it was going to be an awful crossing in the cold ocean air.

I began to get my mind off my craziness by people-watching in the terminal. There was a sloshed man in his fifties who was singing "New York, New York." He was hugging everyone (especially the young ladies) and stumbling into chairs.

There were people joking, dancing, and taking photos.

Happy Irish (and French) drunks.

After some time, another young guy joined the three of us. He was a quiet, thirty-year-old Irish fisherman named Liam. He, unlike me, had a bunk reserved on the boat. He had made the crossing a number of times, so he assured us (I had succeeded in getting Nina as anxious as I), that it would not be as bad as we thought.

As time for departure neared, everyone began to line up. I panicked and headed to the line without waiting for my other three traveling companions, Nina, Liam, and Cameron.

While there, I struck up a conversation with an American, Graham. He and I were first in line for the passport and customs check.

I got through without incident, but they pulled Graham off to the side. He had darker skin and looked Greek but had a Hispanic last name. They looked through his pockets and asked if he smoked. I imagined they thought he was smuggling weed. I waited for him out of the government agent's sight, and we boarded the ship together.

It was quite a large ship, like a great big green hostel on the sea.

We stowed our bags under the carpeted stairs (along with literally hundreds of others) and looked for a place to sit.

We found a clean table near the bathrooms and duty-free shop, popped open a beer, and waited for the ship to set sail. The warm French beer was quite tasty after the long day of travel and waiting around.

Graham, my new drinking buddy, was an extremely easy going, relaxed kid. At twenty-two, he had just graduated from UC Santa Barbara with a Criminal Justice degree. He was originally from San Jose but was looking to move to San Francisco. He had been traveling with a girl, but they'd separated in France and she'd gone off to England. He planned on traveling there from Ireland on Wednesday to reunite with her.

We kept drinking for the two hours we waited for the ship to disembark. Just as we were starting to get drunk, Nina and Cameron found us—the fourth time that we had run into each other.

Nina had a beer with us while her daughter cried on and on for more candy and food. In between her daughter's screams, Nina told us about her life. She was studying agriculture in France and would be until December when she graduated. She was married and seemed like a great person.

After the boat left the harbor, we continued to drink and talk.

Cameron grumbled and griped.

Finally, Graham and I decided that more beer was in order, so we went to the duty-free shop and picked up a case of warm, cheap Irish beer.

The three of us popped open another round.

Cameron fussed and fumed.

In time, the Irish fisherman, Liam, found us. He was a nice, soft-spoken guy who masterfully rolled his own cigarettes—amazing to watch.

Our small group didn't really know how we would kill the seventeen hours of the trip, so we just hung around our small hallway table.

Cameron mumbled and moped.

We finally decided to leave our cherished table and head to the disco for the advertised ten o'clock jazz concert. But, before we went anywhere, we had to stash our precious beer. Liam offered his room as storage. We instantly agreed, since, Liam being a recovering alcoholic, would probably not pilfer it.

Liam let us in to his berth and then took off with Nina and Cameron, leaving Graham and I alone to hide the beer—which we did quietly, careful not to wake the five travelers who were already asleep there.

Graham and I left the room but had no idea where to go. We spent about fifteen minutes covering the entire boat, end to end, looking for the disco. Through the cafeteria, the pub, the restaurant, the halls, the stairwells.

We just couldn't find the club.

Finally, we stumbled onto a shadowy bar and decided enough was enough—we would just stay there. As we were looking for a place to sit, we found our three friends and they had chairs saved for us.

Yep, we had stumbled into the disco.

We all (except Cameron and Liam) got beers, kicked back, and listened to the band: a big guy playing the flute, a woman playing a trombone, a piano player, and a drummer. The first song was Louis Armstrong's "(Won't You Come Home) Bill Bailey?" The white Irish guy sang it fine.

After a few more tunes, they played "What a Wonderful World." Then came the disco favorite "I Will Survive." Graham, Nina, and I started to laugh at the cozy sound of great American disco.

I tried to make a request, surprisingly not "Dancing Queen," but some Van Morrison. I figured, what the hell, they were an Irish band.

It stoned me that they did not know any of his songs. I soon learned that this quartet did not have a large repertoire of tunes; they started to repeat their playlist after about an hour. But that was all we had. Where else could you go in a steel can floating in the Atlantic?

Eventually, Nina and Cameron left for bed, and the three males were the only ones left. Liam rolled me one of his perfect cigarettes, which I smoked (coughed), in my beer-soaked state.

We continued to talk for a while over the music, (we had already heard all the songs a few times anyway), when Liam decided that it was time to go. Graham and I followed him downstairs, gathered our beer from his room, and then stowed it with our bags.

On the way back to the disco, we ran into a group of kids. They started to tell us about some of the bad parts of Dublin. As they were telling their tales, I could not resist laying on some bullshit of my own. I told them that I was from Chicago and I was connected.

"You carry a gun?" they asked.

"Of course."

"You ever kill anyone?"

"Sure, lots of times."

It went on like that. The kid's eyes got enormous as my tales of Chicago got taller and taller.

We left the kids filled with our bullshit and found the club.

Wow! It was now a disco with a disco ball and DJ! Alright! Graham and I had a few more beers, but sadly no "Dancing Queen," so we did no dancing.

Around one fifteen in the morning, we decided it was time to find a place to sleep.

We found a deserted hallway, the main one by the information desk, and concluded that that was as good as it would get.

I put on my shorts (right in the open hall), popped out my contacts, and hopped into my hostel sheet.

September 26

The next morning, I felt a push and thought Liam was waking us up for breakfast. It was not Liam but an officer from the ship telling us that sleeping there was not a good idea. We were in the main hallway entrance, near the most trafficked area of the ferry.

I didn't care (lots of beer the night before) and went back to sleep for another hour. When I finally did awake at eight in the morning, Graham had already been up for a bit.

I got dressed (again in the hallway) and ate some of the food I had picked up in Cherbourg.

Nina and Cameron found us, and the four of us went to the cafeteria. There I, and the rest of my crew, loaded up on even more food.

Since we were extremely tired, we didn't do much talking, just kind of sat there in a daze. Liam, who was energized from sleeping in a bunk, found us after a time.

As we had three hours left until Rosslare, we decided not to loiter any more in the cafeteria. So we trudged to the ship's cinema.

We got Movie Sign! *Dennis the Menace* would be starting soon. Hooray! Something to do quietly for an hour and a half.

We paid the two pounds each and headed into the small room. There were a lot of little kids but unfortunately no smart-assed robots offering their critique. The movie started almost immediately after we took our seats.

The kids in the theater were well-behaved, good kids (even the usually crabby Cameron), but the film was not. Good, that is. No, check that—it was extremely bad, for all ages. The only redeeming aspect of that train wreck was the makeup on Christopher Lloyd. Otherwise, terrible. If I weren't on a ship, I would have walked out.

The movie ended, but we still had a bit of time until we reached Ireland. So, in our hazy, shady state, we made it back to the cafeteria and stared at each other to the sounds of silence once again.

Eventually, for a change of scenery, we left for the main hall, where Graham and I had slept the night before. In our exhaustion, and nearing the end of the trip, we just lay down on the floor to wait out the rest of the crossing.

To our dismay, after about ten minutes of peace, the hall filled with travelers getting ready to depart. We got up and joined them, making our way off the ship and then down a long tunnel and into the customs/passport check—twenty hours after boarding. We all passed the quick check and were now in Ireland.

Graham and I bid good-bye to Liam, Nina, and Cameron, as they would travel the island in Liam's car which was parked near the terminal. The two of us exchanged addresses just as Graham boarded the train to Dublin. I headed to the tourist office to find a room in Rosslare.

In the tourist office, I met an older American woman, Lilian, from River Forest, Illinois. She and I booked a room at the same bed and breakfast.

Not a room together—just at the same place.

The tourist kiosk set us up with rooms at a nearby farm B&B. Fancy Lillian's was en suite while simple mine was not.

Not an issue; I saved fourteen pounds with my simpleness.

After I booked my room, the woman working the tourist kiosk talked to me for quite some time while a line began to form behind me. She didn't seem to care as she handed me countless maps and told me some sites to see in Dublin and Galway (my desired destination in Ireland).

I was about to set off, when I decided to get dinner at the station. The talkative kiosk lady had told me there weren't any restaurants near the farm I was going to.

After a bad sandwich but good fries (chips), I went outside and saw Lilian. Together, we waited for our ride to the B&B in the misty Irish air.

Lilian, originally from Minnesota, was about my mother's age and had done a lot of solo travel since her kids had grown. While she was traveling through Europe this time, she was putting together a family genealogy.

Finally, and about an hour late, the owner of the B&B arrived. She was a short, fat, gray-haired bitch. Before even introducing herself, she laid into Lillian and I as we had apparently been waiting in the wrong place, blah fucking blah.

The two of us got into her car, and she immediately started in. "I won't take you back here in the morning. You have to take a cab. The tourist girl had no right to tell you I would. I run a business."

What the fuck. Nice to meet you too, asshole.

She then complained about how the "book" was wrong— "I won't do this and that!" The "book" was a popular (not Frommer's) travel guide that had her place listed as a recommended accommodation.

Miserable, contemptible old bat. If I hadn't been so fucking tired, I would have walked on her. But I desperately needed some post-hangover sleep.

On the ride to her place, she kept complaining. She was a wretched person. Ireland will be a shinier emerald the day of her reckoning.

The three-mile ride took an eternity.

We got to her place, and I got my room.

"Make sure you shut the lights when you leave," the miser was sure to tell me.

Lilian and I met in the living room for tea and talked with a couple of other people staying at the B&B. After some small talk, Lilian went for a walk, and I returned to my room. It really was a great place, despite the owner. Rolling grass hills overlooked the ocean; I could see a lighthouse about four miles down the coast.

It was especially picturesque, but at that point I didn't really care. All I wanted was to avoid the owner and get some sleep. It was beyond my comprehension how such a lovely spot and such an evil woman got paired together.

I took a nap until eight that evening, and then I hesitantly exited my room, looking to plan my cab for the next morning as my train to Dublin left rather early, 7:30 a.m.

I walked into the living room and found three older women and a man sitting around drinking tea. It was straight out of a movie, like *The Earth Dies Screaming*, or something like that.

I nodded "cheerio" and moved on.

I found the owner's daughter, who told me that my new friend Lilian, who had intended to leave when I did tomorrow morning, had fallen in love with the beauty of the coast and would stay a few more days.

The daughter then informed me that her mom, the mean old broad, had decided that a cab would be too expensive for me to handle alone. So, for a fee (of course), she would take me to the station in the morning (which is what the tourist girl at the station told me would happen anyway).

Bless her evil heart.

I hung out with the older folks, had a spot of tea, and then went back to bed. Pathetic; the geriatrics had more energy than me.

September 27

My alarm woke me at 6:30 a.m., and I took a much-needed shower. After that, I headed to the kitchen where, I must say, Monday morning breakfast was quite good—tea, OJ, sausage, ham, eggs, and bread. I ate it all.

The charming owner and I got into her car, and she took me to the station for £2.50, complaining all the way. I bid my farewell and then made a wish that later editions of that travel book didn't include her place.

I boarded the train to Dublin without any issues. I sat next to a mother and her son, a twelve-year-old redhead who looked like an old high school friend of mine. Very nice people. The young man was well-behaved and respectful—he was like a classy, miniature adult.

Through most of the trip, I gazed out the window at the rolling countryside and the ocean. Beautiful. Ancient.

Along the way I noticed a lot of Monty Pythonesque stone fences, but sadly saw no peasants digging in mud while arguing political science with coconut-laden kings.

Around eleven in the morning, we finally got to Dublin. I oriented myself (the streets had markings warning tourists to look right when crossing) and walked a short way down the road to the bus station.

I was planning on going to Galway immediately, but during the ten-minute walk to the terminal I decided that I would stay in Dublin a few days—it seemed like an interesting place.

I found a computer kiosk where I picked up some information on local accommodations. There, I called to price some bed and breakfasts—all were around twenty pounds. I finally found one I thought was nearby for eighteen pounds. But I was very wrong as the woman on the phone told me it was about an hour's walk. As it was too far, I lied and said I'd take it, gave her a bullshit name (Jim), and hung up.

What a jerk I am.

I gave up at the kiosk and went to the bank around the corner and changed $190 into £122.

Then I looked at one of the Dublin maps the Rosslare tourist woman had given me. There was a hostel listed that was about thirty feet from where I stood—the Isaacs Hostel.

I went inside and got a bed for six and a quarter pounds, but I could not enter the dorms until five o'clock. So I stored my pack at the front desk and headed off to explore another big city.

My main goal was the Guinness Brewery. I followed the map, which took me down the river road for about a forty-five-minute walk. Thankfully, my feet had not bothered me once since arriving in Dublin. Thank you, Clara and French medicine!

I walked down main drags and side streets—passing run-down neighborhoods and garbage dumps that surrounded the celebrated brewery.

After I made a few wrong turns, I found my way to the old hop storage building that housed the brewery museum.

I went inside and learned that a tour would begin in fifteen minutes. Until that time, the tour group of ten were free to look around at the exhibits. Those mainly explained how beer was made. There were a few other displays, such as an old wooden pipe and old brewery tanks. But the most prominent feature of the room was the smell. The odor of spoiled hops, like dirty feet, pervaded the air even though they had not been stored there for forty years.

The doors to the theater opened, and the ten of us went inside. The film was unintentionally funny. It was just a twenty-minute-long commercial for Guinness, with not a whiff of historical fact.

According to the film and in all earnestness, Guinness could save people's lives, give artists inspiration, give athletes strength, heal lepers, turn water into wine, walk on water, etc.

It was bad, but in a good way.

After the film, the doors opened into another room with more exhibits, such as an old delivery apparatus and a video presentation about the barrel making process. I stayed there for about ten minutes and then headed for the bar.

Once there, I was about to grab my one allotted "sample" of Guinness and then head back onto the streets of Dublin to find some lunch.

At the bar, watching the Guinness settle, I felt a tap on my shoulder. It was Graham, from the boat!

I grabbed a pint and joined him and his new crew that he met on the train into Dublin—two New Zealanders, Casey and Rachel, and a girl from Vancouver.

The five of us sat and drank a few "samples" for about an hour, making fun of the tour we'd just been on. They also told me about some drunk guys in the Rosslare train station who were telling a young couple how they'd survived, for a few weeks, on Guinness alone. Also, how it would heal the sick.

Damn, was this a beer or a religion?

We left the brewery through the gift shop. Once outside, in the fresh air, Rachel decided to go back to the hostel where they were all staying.

As it was lunchtime, the remaining four went in search of a restaurant.

We started by going to a few pubs, but they only served cold sandwiches. We all agreed that we wanted something hot on this rather cold day. But unable to control his hunger, Casey bought a disgusting cold beef kidney pie. He took a couple of bites but chucked it into the nearest trash can.

We continued our quest, now walking back toward the city center. Finally, we came upon a take-out fish and chips place. It was a unanimous choice; we all had to eat. Inside the tidy little shop, we all placed sizeable orders. I got, well, fish and chips, as well as a Coke.

From there, we started to walk to a nearby park to eat. Neither I nor anyone else could wait, so we dug in while we were walking. Once at the park, we found some benches and finished up our meal.

So hot.

So greasy.

I was thankful that I didn't have high blood pressure.

Next, we went through the park to the pedestrian-only shopping district of Dublin. There was a myriad of clothing stores and numerous bars and restaurants (including a Subway).

So, we started visiting the stores. I ventured into a few but had no intention of buying any of the clothes. Finally, we reached a famous sweater shop, a place Graham had discovered on a pamphlet in his hostel. It was a nice little shop filled with—no way(!)—sweaters.

As Graham was headed home in a week, and still had a bit of money left over and room in his bag, he was a serious buyer. After twenty minutes and the two New Zealanders and I getting quite antsy, he bought one.

Next, we made our way through the university district (Trinity University) on our way to the River Liffey. We made plans to meet at the Half Penny Bridge at eight that evening before splitting up to our respective hostels.

Back at my hostel, the downstairs was very crowded. I looked around a bit and then headed upstairs to find my room and bed assignment (109E, Bed 3). I ended up lying on a bed in room 108, thinking it was my room and my bed. I'd been there for a while before I somehow realized that I was in the wrong room. I left and quickly found my assigned room and bed. I must say, all the rooms looked the same: ten bunk beds each and all pretty grimy. I lay down again but didn't sleep.

At seven o'clock in the evening, I peeled myself off the bed and went downstairs to get my backpack. It was in the damp, dingy, musty storage area. The bag itself was stinky and a bit wet, but nothing inside seemed damaged.

I brought it upstairs and locked it away in one of the ten lockers in my room for fifty pence.

I left the hostel at 7:35 p.m. and headed to the rendezvous at the bridge. It was closer than I remembered, and I got there with fifteen minutes to spare.

As I waited on the bridge, I really got to see and appreciate Dublin. "The Dead" from James Joyce's *Dubliners* flashed into my mind. I visualized the city at the turn of the twentieth century. I envisioned the party at the beginning of the story and how it developed; "The Lass of Aughrim." I pictured how it took place in one of the buildings of the town that I was now in. I imagined Gabriel and Gretta's ride in the carriage, making their way home through the snowy Dublin streets. I thought about the story's last, nearly perfect paragraph of sorrow and loss.

It was very haunting to have such pictures in your mind, standing all alone on a quiet (pedestrian-only) bridge surrounded by the story itself. Joyce painted such a vivid picture of the city that I almost felt I was there at the turn of the century, during a Christmas blizzard.

As I pondered, my "soul swooned slowly."
Grief is love with nowhere to go.
Joyce sure understood that.
What a story. What a writer. No words.

I was driven back to reality by the sight of a man waterskiing behind a motorboat through the city. Waterskiing in forty-degree weather through a major world capital! He passed under the bridge three times before I saw my party—Graham, Rachel, Casey, and the other girl (I am pissed that I didn't remember her name).

We walked down the street that paralleled the River Liffey. On the way, we passed an archeological dig of an old tower, a portion of the city walls, built in the eleventh century AD. But we didn't stay there long. Rachel, in the lead, was hustling everyone to get to a pub—she hadn't eaten all day.

We got to the Brazen Head, Ireland's oldest pub, established in 1198 AD, about a hundred years after the old tower we had just passed.

It was way too crowded. It had no seats but a hell of an atmosphere—customers were singing Irish folk tunes.

Despite the songs, we left, still in search of food. We looked around and finally found an Italian/Irish restaurant. When we entered there was a homeless guy aggravating the hostess by refusing to leave.

We bypassed that matter and took a seat. We ate rather quickly, paid the bill, and then took off as we really wanted to find a pub.

We got directions to The Globe from a passerby. It was a nice place, but not really what we were looking for; it was just like any other upwardly mobile yuppie bar. We sat, had a beer, and then headed out.

I needed to find a bathroom, so we quickly found a quiet neighborhood bar. This one suited us, so we each ordered a Guinness and relaxed.

The place began to get crowded as our conversation moved from baseball and basketball to movies—a violent film festival was being held there in the pub. *Scarface*, *Midnight Express*, *Jaws*, and *Once Upon a Time in America* were all showing at different times throughout the evening.

Rachel, who looked like Yeardley Smith, told us disturbing stories of her solo travels. She had been groped and grabbed everywhere on her body. Shockingly, she had taken it all in stride.

I decided that I didn't want to spend a lot of money there since it was already eleven and the pubs closed at eleven-thirty. Also, I had to wake up early, so it would have been a wasted drunk. I decided to leave. I said good-bye to everyone and promised to get their addresses from Graham. All of them were very nice people whom I was glad I got to know.

September 28

This morning, I got up with help from my alarm. I made a lot of noise as I struggled with my bag in the dark. I was sure I woke everyone in my room. Oh well, I wouldn't see any one of them ever again, so who cared? Fuck 'em.

I didn't shower—yuck. I headed right downstairs for a £2.50 Irish breakfast of ham, sausage, eggs, toast, tea, and baked beans.

Then I was out the door and on my way to Connolly Station to catch a bus to Heuston Station (where I would catch my train to Galway). The bus I was on was due at Heuston at 10:25, and my train was due to depart at 11:00. That should have been enough time, but, when I was in a bit of a time crunch I noticed how slowly people got off and on buses.

I did make my train, but with only ten minutes to spare. I took a seat and began writing in this journal. I also did some math to figure out my money situation. I figured that the money that I had already exchanged would be enough to live on for four more days.

I wrote nearly the whole trip to Galway, which is on Ireland's southwest coast. When I arrived, it was raining rather hard.

I went to the tourist office (or what I thought was the tourist office). It was instead just a room with one a phone and a listing of local accommodations.

There, I ran into a pushy American from Connecticut who insisted that I stay in a hostel that he knew. The guy would not leave me alone, telling me how he couldn't believe I wouldn't stay in this shitty hostel as it was so cheap. I tried to explain to this dickhead that I was fine with a B&B.

"I spent ten pounds on a hostel last night and got breakfast too," he continued.

"Great, the bed and breakfasts here are twelve pounds," I retorted.

What a fucking idiot—it was two extra pounds for a private room away from the body stench.

Eventually, he did show me the way to the real tourist office, as I needed to get a map. Unfortunately, he tagged along. Just as we got to the office, we ran into an old guy who said he would take us to a clean B&B, two minutes away, that offered a huge buffet breakfast, all for £12.50.

Perfect. That was my call. But the fuckwad still wanted a hostel. At that point, I decided that I would ignore idiot boy and work with the old man. I grabbed a map from the tourist office and began to chat with the old guy. Hostel Boy finally got the hint and departed to find his holy hostel.

I followed the old fellow to a nearby building, the unfortunately named Hollywood Bed and Breakfast, then up a few flights of stairs to room twelve. It was a very comfortable room with a bathroom and shower next door.

I took it and paid him twenty-five pounds for two nights.

Later, I found out that the old man was a B&B hawker for the woman who owned it. She was very sweet, adorning the place with pictures of her family.

Laundry was next on my agenda. I washed a shirt and a pair of socks in the sink, set them to dry, and headed out to see the charming seaside town.

It was quaint, like a town in Michigan—shops, restaurants, art galleries, and pubs—everywhere pubs.

I decided to have a splurge dinner and even got dessert.

I walked some more, finally reaching the ocean. It was raining, but it was still terrific to see Ireland's west coast. Strangely, it was stormy and serene at the same time.

September 29

I awoke early, around seven, and went downstairs at eight to eat. I sat at a table with an Asian guy and two Britons. Another great Irish breakfast.

From there, I walked around the town again. I stopped at a travel agent and confirmed my Friday night ferry crossing. I figured that, if I saved money today and tomorrow, I would be able to afford both a bunk and the movie during the ferry crossing back to France on Friday. That would sure make it more enjoyable than sleeping in a hallway.

I did do some unplanned spending: my camera had not been working right, so I took a twenty-four-count roll of film to be developed. It was pricey, but I needed to know if I was wasting my time, taking pictures of nothing. I would know the results in two hours.

After dropping off the film, I got some lunch. While I sat there, I had a couple of ideas for a short story. Not much yet, but I sketched out some themes. By the way, I had been using another notebook to record any ideas as I didn't want to include those in these journals.

Next, I went to the pub next door to my B&B. There, I had two pints of Guinness but remained mortal.

It was the quintessential Irish pub—comfy booths, horse racing on TV, people playing cards and throwing darts. The bartender did change the TV to *Charlie's Angels* but, eh, can't win 'em all.

When it was time to pick up my pictures, I paid my bill and went back to the film shop. Whew, they came out fine. But I realized that I should have taken more in a few places.

I didn't worry long, though; I would be returning to where I wanted to take more photos soon. I would be sure to take more in Dublin tomorrow. Friday, more pictures on the ferry. The next day I would take a few more in Paris.

After that, I decided to call it an early day. I had spent too much money, as the pictures were a bit expensive. It was also raining. But all in all, Galway had been a nice rest.

September 30

I got up early, 6:30 a.m., because my train would be departing at 8:00 a.m. I didn't shower since I'd had such a horrible one yesterday that I must have blanked and forgot to recount it.

So, here goes: I had lathered up in the second-floor shower because the one closest to my room was running only cold water. When I was completely covered in soap, the fucking water shut off. I tried everything to get it working, even knocking off the shower rod in my spastic gyrations, but to no avail. Finally, I decided to use the sink if it worked. As it was a dual faucet sink, I turned on both. The left faucet's water was so hot that it was almost boiling, while the right faucet's water was nearly freezing. I grabbed a full-length towel, got it soaked and wet from both and rinsed off all the soap. After that worked so well, I figured, what the hell? I washed my hair the same way.

The room was a mess. I was clean.

Back to today. I ate with the pleasant owner, who was not a certified plumber. Then I went through the front gate and walked about a hundred yards in the rain to the train station.

No problems. Easy ride. I mostly read.

In Dublin, I hopped on one of the many city buses and sat next to a nun. The bus was crowded with junior high age kids who seemed to be on a field trip. It was not a fun ride, since I kept my backpack on. It was a short one though.

I got off at Connolly Station and saw a train that was leaving for Belfast. What the hell, I figured. I'll get on it.

As it was Northern Ireland, another country (a hated other country), I had to go through a metal detector to get to the proper track. No problems there. But the only car that had a vacant seat was in first-class. My Eurail pass did not cover that, and I certainly didn't want to pay the extra fees.

So, I jumped off just as the train was about to roll. Back to the nearby Isaacs Hostel to find a bed.

I had no problems there, and I lingered a while, eating my last bit of cheese and finishing off a Coke.

Then, it was off to the streets of Dublin once again.

My first stop was the ferry company where I hoped to secure a bunk for the crossing back to France tomorrow. No issues, quick line, paid the five-pound fee.

I was a happy fella. I would sleep in a bed and could do so whenever I wanted. Whew. Relief.

The clerk working the ticket counter sent me to my next stop with some decent directions. I was headed to the United States Embassy. I was going to see what the restrictions were on a possible trip to Yugoslavia.

I walked nearly an hour in intermittent and sometimes heavy rainfall, constantly holding my trusted umbrella. The neighborhoods I walked through were definitely not on the tourist track. They were residential districts lined with red brick buildings, straight out of a film—boys' school this, girls' school that. Trees and white fences. The Irish upper middle class.

Eventually, I ran into another commercial area which looked like any other big city—not a lot of character. As I had been walking down the same street for quite some time, I asked a businessman if the embassy was still on this same road. After confirmation, I continued on my way.

Finally, I reached the ugly, circular embassy.

Once I went in, I learned I was in the wrong place. I needed the Hume House for all travel information.

Thankfully, it was across the street.

Just as I entered the correct bureaucratic building, the rain began to fall with a vengeance. The Irish gods were pissed at America. I figured that potatoes probably played some part.

I went up to the third floor, through a metal detector (which went off because of all the coins I was carrying), and then to the desk. There, I let my fellow countryperson know why I was there, took a seat, and waited.

It only took about ten minutes for me to be directed to window one. There, an Irish woman told me it was not advisable to go to Yugoslavia.

She handed me three documents that seemed outdated (signed by former Secretary of State, James Baker, not Warren Christopher, the current one). But she assured me they were still accurate. One of the documents contained the Yugoslavian embassy's phone number in Washington, D.C. Another listed the entrance requirements for every country on Earth. The last was a bleak five-page U.S. State Department report on travel to the Balkans.

There was no mention of a special visa to enter Yugoslavia. All the documents stated that only a passport was required. However, I did learn that no trains were crossing the Yugoslavian frontier, so that took train passage to Sombor off the table.

I began to have second thoughts. Maybe I shouldn't go to Yugoslavia? But I quickly shelved them. I had made this commitment, and I wanted to see it through.

I left the room and went back downstairs. I waited a bit for the rain to let up, which, thankfully, it did. I had heard earlier that the National Gallery of Ireland offered free admission, so that was where I headed next.

It was a beautiful place but quite small. Well-ordered, though. Some Rembrandts, one Picasso, one Gris a lot by Jack Yeats. I think the latter was the brother of W.B. Yeats. Well, it was the Irish fucking National Gallery—it should have some Irish art!

I must say that one piece did catch my eye. It was a still life by Heda. Amazing. Done in the late sixteenth century—it looked like a snapshot. Even up close, I could not see the brush strokes. I'm sure he took a lot of flak from the church for creating such realistic images—torture the witch!

His work genuinely illustrated why the artists of the late nineteenth and early twentieth century moved away from realistic portraiture and into Cubism. Photography had just been invented, rendering the need for such realism obsolete. If artists such as Heda were able to create works like that three-hundred years prior, there frankly was nothing to improve upon. A different, more analytical path needed to be blazed, and Cezanne, Picasso, and Braque did just that.

I stayed at the gallery for about an hour and a half. Then, off to another free admission gallery—the National Museum.

Here was a logical display of the Irish isles through the millennia. Vikings, human skulls, examples of homes. Golden trinkets and jewelry. The "Tara" brooch was a highlight.

After an hour, something happened there that I still have trouble believing. I heard a little kid say something. She sounded like she was talking to me. I ignored it—who did I know in Ireland? But I heard it again. I looked down to see who was talking and saw a stout little girl.

Remember Cameron? Well, it was her and her mother Nina, one of my drinking buddies from the Irish crossing.

After six separations we ran into each other again. Like Graham at the Guinness brewery, it was a small world after all, blah fucking blah.

I must admit, I was amazed and will forever be amazed at the coincidence. They weren't even supposed to be in Dublin. They had gone to Galway. They were there in that small town at the same time as me, but we never ran into each other. It had to be in the big city.

We left the galleries and went to the museum café, where Nina told me that she'd hung out with Liam and had a great time in Galway. I told her I'd had a great time there as well, making sure not to mention the plumbing issues.

We decided to leave together and find some food. Not ten feet out of the museum and Cameron's whining began. *Ugh.* We walked about ten minutes with the kid screaming the whole time.

I couldn't handle it, so (knowing Cameron couldn't go in) I said to Nina, "You know, this pub looks fine. I'll just eat here." I had no clue about the place, but if it meant some peace from the screaming, it would do just fine.

As I entered, I told her I'd see her in Rosslare tomorrow, as they were bound for the ferry back to France as well. Bye.

I did end up eating there. Good, cheap, and a lot of food. Hooray. Just what I needed.

After I left, I got lost for a bit but quickly reoriented myself. I was nearly in front of Trinity College when I saw Nina and Cameron again—jeez, I had left them over an hour ago, for God's sake.

It was getting weird. It was like a *Twilight Zone* episode: every move I made, every corner I turned, they'd be there. If I went to Las Vegas, boom. Together, they'd be my blackjack dealers. If I went to the Arctic, bam. The two of them would be just finishing a snowman. I couldn't shake 'em.

So I walked with them for a bit. But after five minutes, once again, the little piggy began to squeal.

Oh no. I lied and said I forgot my newspaper (which I never had) at the pub. I told them that I had to go back and get it as there was a great article I was reading. I said good-bye again knowing full well that I would see them again soon.

I finally got back to the hostel, where I picked up my bag from storage. I went up to my horrible dorm, stowed the bag in a room locker, and then took off my sweaty and wet shirt and socks. From there, I carefully walked across the cold linoleum floor and climbed into my nasty hostel bed, one of eight in the room. I matched the bunk as I was filthy as well. My feet also stunk but I didn't care. I put in my earplugs to block the sound of trains clattering directly outside of my window. With those in my ears, I expected a good night's sleep.

October 1

I did not have a good night's sleep—I shouldn't have jinxed it by writing that.

Anyway, I got up around eight thirty and took a shower around nine. Went downstairs and had an Irish breakfast in the hostel dining hall. Great food. I really did love those Irish breakfasts—meats and fats, yum.

After that, I just kind of loitered in the dining hall through three dreadful rushes of stinky hostelers. I sat there for two hours reading my Hemingway book. When I saw the kitchen helpers begin to bring the lunch food out, I decided to split.

I walked out and gave two German girls directions to the hostel. They in turn pointed me to the train station. The circle of life. Kumbaya and all that shit.

At the station, I grabbed a seat and read more of my book. I ended up sitting next to a chick who was puffing a cigarette and blowing smoke in my face. But I didn't spend much time near her, as my train boarded soon.

I hopped on and took a seat. I ended up finishing the book, *For Whom the Bell Tolls*, before the train left the station.

It was a great novel. I had no preconceived notions when I began the book. In fact, once I started it, I did not think the entire story would concern the mission to destroy the Segovia bridge and end with the hero's death. In addition, just like Hemingway's *A Farewell to Arms*, the plot was not like any other war novel I had read. I was blindsided by it.

This "war" story was not concerned with battles, but with people, their development, and the loss of their ideals. When the bell tolled, it tolled for everyone; all people were together as one—the camaraderie of the human experience.

Fascism was a known, worldwide evil by the time Hemingway published this book in 1940. The novel explored the pre-World War II days of this vile political theory using the Spanish Civil War as a backdrop. Hemingway reminded us that we cannot ignore what goes on in other parts of the world—anything may affect us.

I hope that synopsis sounded alright, as I was quite distracted when I wrote it. I will explain what was going on in a few lines.

On the crowded train, I was sitting in a car with an older woman, her middle-aged daughter and her little, itty-bitty daughter Kayleigh. We eventually began to talk, mostly about comparisons between Ireland and the United States. But it was the little girl, Kayleigh, who rightly got the most attention.

She was an adorable, incredibly well-behaved little two- or three-year-old. I couldn't understand much of what she said, but she did sing "choo-choo, toot-toot" to mimic the (silent electric) train we were on. Terrific little kid!

The family got off one stop before mine and Kayleigh said "bye-bye" to me. Steal my heart.

I relaxed for the final leg of the journey.

I disembarked and, like before, headed right to the Irish Ferries desk. I paid the port tax, got my bunk assignment, and met up with Nina and Cameron once again. (They had been on the same train).

We decided that Nina would get some food for us while I watched Cameron. I gave her two pounds, and Cameron and I headed upstairs to keep an eye on the bags.

Once there, Cameron told me some disturbing, sexual-like stuff that she said went on at her afterschool day care. I really did not want to hear it and then have to deal with it.

But deal with it I did.

As soon as Nina came back, I took her to the side and told her what her charming daughter had just related to me.

"Cameron fibs a lot," she told me.

From what Nina said, she did that often.

I remembered some of Cameron's other stories—for example, angrily insisting that "cavemen" had matches—so I tended to believe her mom. I really, truly hoped my intuition was correct. Otherwise, fuck. What a mess.

After that hilarity, we sat quietly chatting at the restaurant for quite a while. As time dragged on, I realized that it had been over two hours since we ordered any food. I was afraid that we were going to get booted, so I convinced Nina that it was time to move on. She agreed, so we headed to the boat's waiting area. That is where I wrote this.

Once at the waiting area, Cameron began to run on the seats of the chairs. The minute Nina told her to stop it— "there's no doctor here, Cameron,"—Cameron took a dive headfirst into the seats.

Down goes Frazier.

She then began to scream and yell at the top of her husky lungs.

That's what was going on while I wrote about *For Whom the Bell Tolls*. I was completely distracted with the kid yelping bloody murder. Who knows if I made sense.

Anyway, Cameron the tuba, still blowing her horn, had a scuffed chin and fat lip to match her body.

I'm distracted. Time to stop writing.

Good times.

October 1

(CONTINUED)

After I quit writing another girl, Hannah (quite attractive), who Nina had met at her hostel, joined us. The four of us waited together. Finally, it was time to set sail.

I boarded the ferry but got lost on my way to my cabin (Promenade Deck, thank you Purser Gopher and Cruise Director Julie).

The cabin was cramped, six beds, no storage. But good news: only four of the beds were booked—by a French kid, an Irish kid, an older Irish man named Abel, and me.

I got situated and picked the furthest bunk from the door (and a lower one as well) and then headed out. As I was going up the stairs, I ran into Abel, who had left the room about five minutes before I did.

He asked if I was going up for a pint.

Indeed I was.

So we headed up together. We found the mellow pub (not the disco). (We were on the same ferry, the Killian II, that I took across a week prior).

Abel and I ordered two Guinnesses (what else?) and found a table.

As we sat at the dock waiting to depart, I noticed how desolate the ship was compared to the previous crossing. I guess no one wanted to go to France—wah, wah.

Abel and I chatted and ordered more and more beer. Finally, Nina and Cameron (who now reminded me of Veruca from Willy Wonka— the spoiled, "bad egg"), found us.

They joined us, and Abel bought Nina a beer. Just when Nina took a sip, Cameron began to scream, "I'm tired," and started to freak out, eventually hitting her mother in the face. We had yet to leave the dock and this little shit was already going bananas.

Nina reprimanded her, but the kid started again just as her mother resumed talking to Abel and me. I'm not a fan of spoiled kids.

Well, needless to say, Nina and Cameron left soon after. Abel and I were left at the table, so we ordered a few more beers and talked.

Abel told me about the Irish attitude toward world events—the Irish hate the British.

The situation in Northern Ireland—the Irish hate the British.

We talked of Churchill and the role of England in WWII—the Irish hate the British.

We talked of Normandy (where I will be visiting next)—the Irish hate the British.

After this Irish-Anglo lovefest, Abel told me his plans for travel in France. He explained that he was simply taking a vacation (um, holiday), a break from Ireland (where they hate the British, I've been told), and just decided to go to France.

He called his wife and let her know. He was only supposed to be gone for a few days, but after this ferry trip, he'll have been traveling for over two weeks (a fortnight, sorry). Interesting story—he was probably not going back to his wife, who, I was sure, hated the British.

After chatting a bit more, we decided to head down to the empty disco. No groovy jazz band this time. Only bad music was in the air tonight. We stayed just for a bit and headed back up to the pub. We each had one more pint before the bar closed.

October 2

Then back to the bunk, where I had an amazingly good sleep—probably due to the waves which rocked me like a baby.

Damn! Slept until eleven! I went back up to the mellow bar and found Abel, having his morning beer. I ordered a half pint of Budweiser and joined him. (Are you nuts! Guinness, baby.)

After I finished my mini beer, I went to the cafeteria, leaving Abel in the bar with his beloved Guinness. Nina and Cameron were there. I didn't eat; nothing looked very good. I didn't stay and hang out—I decided to go back to my cabin for my first shave in twelve days.

As I was getting ready for my shave, I saw that all my shaving cream had leaked out. No problem. I lathered up with lots of soap, took my time, and gave myself a pretty damn good shave (only one nick).

I went upstairs to the nicer restaurant, where I finally felt comfortable burning some of the money I had been so careful with for the last week. I paid the £6.90 and gorged on the all-you-can-eat (and drink) buffet.

I sat for a bit on deck and then headed to the cinema to catch the ferry's only flick, *Sleepless in Seattle*. A decent film that leaned on emotional themes but ignored rational ones. Because of that, I thought it would have made a better silent film. Strangely, I believe that I would have related to it more if it were not a "talkie." I began to think that early in the movie, and that idea just kind of stuck in my head. It would have been more enjoyable to see Lillian Gish or Mae Marsh in the female lead using their finely tuned face and body movements to better express the emotions. But, even with the handicap of sound, it was fine.

I hope that little aside didn't make me sound like one of those curmudgeons (Leslie Halliwell) who always wished for the "good old days" of film. I am a true believer that, in most instances, artistic expression must strive to advance. But, in a few cases, like here, the older methods and styles would have benefited the script much more.

Okay, with the film over, I headed back down to my bunk where I intended to take just a quick nap. I slept until France. When I awoke, I found that everyone had packed up their property and had headed to the ferry lobby to disembark.

I quickly packed up and headed upstairs. There, I saw Hannah for the first time on the boat. She told me she had slept for the last three hours of the trip as well. She said she woke up at one point and thought it was midnight. Nope, it was noon the next day.

Nina and the kid found us as I was hastily filling out a departure card just before we disembarked.

I have to say, this trip was a thousand times more bearable than the last. The cabin and bunk kept my anxiety at bay.

6

France (part II)

Bayeux, Normandy Beaches

A s I was in Cherbourg again, I made sure that I had my umbrella. Since Nina and the kid would be staying in a hotel in town, we bid our adieus for the last time. I did not plan on running into them again. Hannah and I then walked to the train station.

On the way, we ran into my Irish drinking buddy, Abel. He would also be staying in Cherbourg.

Hannah and I made it to the station in about twenty minutes and went directly to the information booth. Just in time—we were the next-to-last people they let in as the doors closed and locked behind us.

We learned the time the train departed to Bayeux and then I found out some information about my pending trip to Madrid.

We headed to the platform of the tiny train station, found a bench, and then polished off the last five beers that Graham and I had picked up on the first crossing.

As we were sitting there enjoying our beers, a little French girl bit it, falling to the floor and spilling all of her fries (I mean chips).

Sad.

The train arrived.

It was a pretty uneventful one-hour trip. Hannah and I just chatted. She would be settling in Galway to write fiction after her one month of continental European travel was completed.

In Bayeux, we got off the train and onto the outside platform. It was dark, quiet, and desolate. We didn't really know where to go, so we just walked into the miniature station.

There, we started to organize ourselves. As we were doing this, an Australian, Sharon, found us and asked if she could join us in finding a room.

Sure, why not, Hannah and I agreed.

We went outside and saw a hotel very close, the Hotel de la Gare, with rooms for one hundred and fifty francs.

There was a mustachioed English-speaking French fellow working the desk. After signing in, he brought us up to the top floor of the hotel to show us the room. Two beds, two separate rooms—yes! I would have a private room for only fifty francs.

We paid the man and then headed out into the small Norman village. The girls wanted to eat, but I really didn't care what we did. I was just happy to have a room and a cheap bed.

Wait.

Shhh.

The town was very quiet.

We walked the short distance to the city center and saw the majestic cathedral. The cathedral in Cologne blew it away, but this was a small town, so it dominated the townscape.

We found a restaurant. They ordered food, but I didn't, as that buffet splurge from earlier held me just fine. We all shared a bottle of wine and chatted. That's it. They finished their meals and we headed back to the hotel, making sure to match the hush of the town.

October 3

Hannah took off at eight (early train), leaving me with Sharon, whom I did not particularly care for.

I took a shower and put on cleanish clothes for the first time in twelve(!) days.

Sharon then informed me that she would not be able to share the room with me tonight, as I snored too loud. The desk clerk had told us last night that he would only rent the room to two or more people.

With that, the inexpensive room was lost.

That meant I would have to find another place, and, most likely, pay a lot more for a bed.

Damn, strike one.

The next strike was that the Normandy beach tours (the D-day invasion) did not run on Sundays, and, of course, it was Sunday. On top of that, the ones for tomorrow were already booked.

Well, I still intended to stay in Bayeux to see the tapestry. So I walked the short distance to the train station and paid eighteen francs to make my reservation for the Paris to Madrid TGV, via Irun, in two days.

Strike three of that fine morning came when I discovered that I could not change money today or Monday at French banks, and I only had 112 F left. I did have my Visa, but I did not want to use it and create a lot of debt.

Shit. I really wanted to go to the D-day invasion beaches. I decided I would use my Visa to rent a car to drive there myself. I would use the cash for room and board only.

But no car rentals on Sunday—strike four?!

Failure after failure.

Pretty good day so far, huh?

Forget it, I decided. I would change my plans and get a room at the most expensive hotel in town. I called them, but they didn't take credit cards.

Strike fuck-it.

Enough. I ditched Sharon the Aussie, who I blamed those troubles on, illogically reasoning that she'd set this all in motion by screwing up my perfect accommodations.

In the city, I walked for about half an hour looking for any type of lodging. Finally, I found the one-star Notre Dame Hotel. It was 220 F, but it included breakfast and dinner. If I stayed at any other place in town, I would have been charged the same or more just for the room.

I went in and got a room. The desk clerk, a beautiful older woman, was very helpful. She knew where I could exchange money tomorrow—from the travel information office one block away.

I told her about my desire to see the beaches. She said she would call in a favor from a friend to book me on tomorrow's tour. She was confident it would be no problem.

Then she gave me maps and more information about her town.

She was my French savior.

My naughty Norman.

My Bayeux beauty.

I fell in love.

I went to my room and stayed classy, washing three sets of underwear and two pairs of socks in the sink. As I was doing this, I put together my clothes strategy for the rest of my travel. I figured that I would only have to wash one pair of shorts and two pairs of long pants for the remainder of the trip.

Wow, I am gross.

At two in the afternoon, I bid *adieu* to *mon amour* at the front desk and headed to the Tapestry Museum. There, I would see the nearly one-thousand-year-old Bayeux Tapestry. I'd studied the Norman Invasion in an undergraduate English history course my sophomore year, so I was familiar with this subsequent work.

At the ticket office, I paid the eleven francs (that's with a student discount—otherwise it would have been twenty-eight) and went right in.

The first section of the museum was a history of Normandy and England just preceding the creation of the Tapestry. This was written out in the modern era on a tapestry itself, which I think fooled some people as they believed it to be the thousand-year-old Bayeux Tapestry.

I read this for a while and then headed to the cinema. They were showing the English version of the Tapestry documentary when I walked in.

Great info but a bit boring.

I got a quick refresher on the subject and then headed to see the work.

I paid the five francs for a headset and entered the climate-controlled room that housed the seventy-meter cloth. There was a crowd of people fighting for the best view. Of course, I decided to join them and weaseled my way to the front. I had a great view as the narrator on my headset explained the cloth and its near thousand-year history.

It was difficult to imagine that those who commissioned this amazing object envisioned it to simply hang in the open in the Cathedral—it was just too precious an artifact.

Again, incredible to see something that I studied. I never imagined that I would see this beautiful work of art in person.

After taking in the entirety of the museum, I exited onto the ancient, narrow streets and headed to the Normandy War Museum.

I walked the short distance and found it rather easy.

More great history—Eisenhower, Montgomery, Bradley, Rommel—all the major players from the great invasion were represented.

Weapons and uniforms adorned the walls.

Maps and reconnaissance photos; posters and personal letters filled the rooms.

In addition, there were all sorts of newspapers and magazine clippings behind glass or posted on the walls.

The only thing that was missing were songs in the air from Vera Lynn and the Andrews Sisters.

The museum was what history should be about—a still-living present so the future may learn from the past.

I took my time and looked at literally thousands of artifacts on display. I also watched the half-hour film of the conquest of Normandy.

Finally, I walked through the Eisenhower room—named for the former President and Supreme Allied Commander. This room was filled to the rafters with tanks, cars, jeeps, motorcycles, and flags from every imaginable command.

Walking through this beautiful museum gave me a strange sense of hope. I, of course, knew precisely how and when the Nazi horror would end, but seeing those wonderful displays brought a peculiar air of relief.

October 4

I slept very well and awoke around 8:30. I went downstairs to the dining room where I ate the usual French breakfast—four pieces of bread with butter, jam, and strong coffee.

I found out that my French protector, the magnificent desk clerk, was able to get me on the afternoon tour of the Normandy beaches.

My love for her now knew no bounds. To her, I will dedicate songs and sonnets, symphonies and sonatas, poems and prose.

But, as it was still the morning, it was too early to be creative.

So I went to the tourist office and exchanged some more money, as it was the only place in town where I could.

I then hit the town. Well, village. I took some pictures of the river and then the working old mill. I snapped some more pictures of a street filled with flags that looked just like an André Derain fauvist painting.

Bayeux was a great town. I really loved this almost-rural France, away from Paris. I also loved the people of France despite expecting the contrary. I had believed all the French-haters; I had let my prejudice overwhelm me. I now understood that I must experience something, anything, anyone, before I realized its true nature.

After my short walk, I headed to a journal store and bought a *USA Today*, three postcards, and an envelope. I took a seat by the old cathedral and read the paper. The Chicago White Sox were in the American League Championship Series.

After a brief rest, I made my way back to the hotel and my room, where I began to write the postcards.

I also wrote a letter to my mom, as she'd requested, giving her power of attorney regarding the sale of my father's business. She was hoping that it would speed up the sale. So was I.

I left to mail my postcards and letter and pick up some food for the next day. I bought three small salamis, some cheese, and a three-foot-long loaf of French bread. That would do for tomorrow's travels. I then headed back to the hotel and waited half an hour for one o'clock.

I saw the tour van, and out came our guide. It was the same fellow from two nights ago who was working the front desk at the hotel I'd stayed at near the station. I'd kind of screwed him over yesterday by taking off without telling him (in my fit of rage—strike three and all). But, today, he didn't seem to mind.

I got in the small van with two couples, one in their fifties and one in their sixties. There were two Dutch guys in their sixties already sitting in the back, and I joined them. The last person to board was a man in his seventies who, like me, was by himself. Except for the two Dutch men, we were all American. It was an older group, but I did not care. I was ready to see the beaches.

It was a beautiful day—sunny, no wind, a bit cool. A perfect day for an American (and Dutch?) invasion.

On the way, the guide told us tidbits of information, but the two Dutch jerks keep talking. After I shot them some dirty looks (and, I do confess, a few well-placed elbows into their fat guts), they quieted down.

Our first stop was the American Cemetery overlooking Omaha Beach. A small sign simply read "Silence and Respect." To me, that sign was preaching to the converted.

Before I entered the solemn field, I walked past a time capsule that is to be opened in 2044 (one hundred years after the invasion). It was created by the press corps that covered the attack. There were a few other plaques as well, which we read before we entered.

It was a sizable place. The sight of over nine thousand headstones with their Stars of David and Latin crosses was overwhelming.

All Americans.

My small group headed to the semicircular stone memorial commemorating the Allied advance into Europe. The monument included inscriptions noting the other war theaters and other battles both on land and sea.

In the center were the poignant words of General Eisenhower:

"To these we owe the high resolve that the cause for which they died shall live."

We then moved to the cliffs overlooking the Atlantic, and I saw the beaches for the first time. I did not get a fantastically good look there, but our guide assured us that we would be getting closer soon.

We walked around the reflecting pond, to the sculptures and finally through the seemingly endless rows of white stone markers. On my way I read a few of the inscriptions. I found (and photographed) the grave of one of the 233 unknown soldiers in the American Cemetery who gave their precious lives to defeat totalitarian fascism.

I then came upon a soldier's grave who died at the end of April 1945—so close to V-E Day.

Sadness.

Finally, we walked to the chapel and past two large American flags. "Silence and Respect."

Outside was an engraved a tribute to the "Grateful Memory" of those who gave their lives in the Normandy invasion.

This was a moving place—I have no words. It was an experience unparalleled.

The group headed back to the van, and we drove from the high cliffs to the beaches themselves.

At ground level, beneath those tremendous cliffs once held by the Germans, we got our first glimpse of the great obstacles the invasion force overcame.

We arrived at the beach at high tide, so the beach itself appeared extremely small and narrow. It seemed impossible to land any invasion force, let alone the most significant amphibious assault in history. However, the primary invasion came between the tides, so there was much more room to operate. As the day progressed, we were able to see the beach at low tide, which made the seemingly impossible a bit more probable.

Omaha Beach was buffeted by high cliffs, with pillbox machine-gun nests built into the rock and beach itself. The nests were not pointed out to sea but aimed at the beach. It was a great tactical placement as that enabled the Germans to catch the Americans in a horrendous crossfire.

To add to the American's woes, two German divisions just happened to be on maneuvers nearby, which added to the complexity of completing the American objective.

So, the Germans had the high ground with crossfire from the pillboxes aiding their cause. They also had a strong secondary force nearby if needed. It was a fucking miracle of sheer willpower that the U.S. troops survived, let alone established a beachhead at Omaha. The mission succeeded, but only after four-thousand American men died in the two days it took to firmly establish the foothold. Truly one of the great successes in the annals of warfare.

We then headed to Pointe du Hoc to learn of one of the most incredible military missions of the war. The promontory was between Omaha and Utah beach, a strategically important high point that had to be taken to halt the constant assault the Germans were raining down on the two American positions at Omaha and Utah.

The Germans knew of its value when they built numerous machine-gun and cannon nests on top of the hundred-foot cliff.

The allies recognized its significance as well. For months prior to the manned invasion, the Allies continually bombed the area. Today, that was well-evidenced. There were still innumerable bomb craters littering the area. Some were quite deep, scarring the area for millennia to come. Adding to the carnage were several pillboxes in ruins due to the constant Allied bombing.

The Army Second Ranger Battalion was the group chosen to make the assault on Pointe du Hoc during the initial phase of the invasion. Using medieval castle-storming techniques, the Rangers catapulted rope ladders up the hundred-foot cliffs. Under unimaginably heavy fire, they eventually reached the top. Once there, they had to struggle inch by inch through showers of bullets (and "friendly" Allied bombs) to clear the area. Finally, across the huge craters, the Rangers finally secured the high ground.

For the American invading force, this was one of the most important operations because it allowed the two U.S. forces the opportunity to unite.

The immensity of the task the Rangers accomplished was nearly unfathomable. This handful of men achieved their objective and secured the area from their most despicable foe. An inspiration to experience.

As I explored, I saw that there was still barbed wire strewn across the cliff's edge. The Rangers had been forced to navigate through it to reach the top. For obvious reasons, this area was considered too hazardous to allow tourists to get too close.

Also deemed too dangerous for us were the bomb craters. They were roped off, allowing no one near as the chances of unexploded ordnances, nearly fifty years after the invasion, were still quite high.

However, the German pillboxes, small and claustrophobic, were opened to explore. The Army Rangers took their time and methodically cleared each one of those. They are forever scarred with machine gun and grenade holes.

We left Pointe du Hoc and headed down the coast. On the way, we stopped and investigated more German pillboxes. Those, once positioned for Allied ships, still had their huge six-inch cannons aimed out to sea.

We continued, making our way to Gold Beach, part of the British sector. It was there, in Arromanches, that the main thrust of the supply lines had entered.

Today, the D-Day Museum overlooks what remains of the vast, man-made harbor. During the invasion, the port was assembled and made operational in three(!) days.

About a mile out to sea were some of the remains of the port—huge concrete breakwaters called mulberries. The water there was filled with rotting steel and iron left from the days this quiet beach was the main crux of the Allied invasion into Europe. I snapped a few pictures and then headed into the museum.

The museum was reminiscent of the one yesterday. Although this one had a film which told the story of the construction of the artificial port—an engineering marvel.

I went back outside and looked out over the land, sky, and sea. Here, as opposed to the American sector, the terrain was very flat, with none of the towering cliffs the Americans had to contend with.

As the day was coming to an end, I realized that throughout this tour of Normandy, I had made friends with everyone but the butthole Dutch guys. The seventy-something solo gentleman was a WWII veteran who was stationed in the Pacific during the war. He was well-schooled in military history, so he was great to chat with.

The fifty-something couple had just been to a White Sox game, so that was kind of cool.

The husband of the couple in their sixties was an officer during the Korean War. There, he was stationed under General Paul Tibbits (the pilot of the Enola Gay, dropper of the atomic bomb Tibbits). Both he and his wife told me that Tibbits was extremely weird—he would turn to face the wall in a crowded officers' club rather than look at anyone.

These two also told me to go to the National Museum of the Pacific War in Texas and the Churchill War Rooms in London. The former had an atomic bomb shell, and the latter was sealed just after V-E Day, leaving everything as it was the moment victory was achieved.

I also spoke with the tour guide. We discussed how my earlier plans had fallen through. But, as he observed, the weather was much nicer today.

Just as we reached the van after the five-hour tour, it began to rain—perfect timing.

On the way back, I was quiet but happy that I spent the extra day in Bayeux to see the beaches.

I also felt reassured as I reflected.

My European crusade was nearly half over. But after the past two days, I already felt a sense of closure on two fronts. The first was minor, and it concerned the Bayeux Tapestry. The Normans invaded Britain to take it for themselves, and then the British (and the Allies) took Normandy to give it back to the French nearly a thousand years later. A fantastic, ironic twist that could never be dreamt of in any work of fiction.

The other sense of closure had to do with this journey and what I had seen and experienced. When I started, I allotted myself two months to achieve the trip's ultimate design of remembering my father by helping our relatives. However, in this first month, the trip had taken me to other meaningful sites that had greatly affected me. Many of those pertained to World War II.

I began in Amsterdam with the Anne Frank House. Next, to Oświęcim and Auschwitz-Birkenau. Finally, Bayeux and these beaches.

This beautiful Norman coast and her tranquil villages would see the start of the death knell for the aggressors of World War II. It would mark the beginning of the end for those that murdered Anne Frank and so many others with their military aggression and their death camps.

Those Allied troops proved that despite hardship, pain, and death, when man is pushed to the limit, he really is good at heart.

That when some people have a purpose, nothing can stop them.

I hope that I can complete my task as well.

As soon as I got back to the hotel, I began to write about the day.

I eventually went down to dinner, where I spent one and a half hours on a four-course meal. I lingered as long as I could because my new love, *la magnifique* older French beauty, served me.

After all that food and wine, I was more than ready for bed. Also, I had to get up early in the morning to start a three-train, twenty-hour odyssey to Madrid.

Although it started with five strikes, Bayeux was a home run.

October 5

Today I got up late, as my damned alarm clock did not go off. The only job that fucking thing had to do, and it could not do it right. Fuck. I nearly threw it out the window.

So, I quickly ate, showered (my sixteenth shower—I counted), and said farewell to my love.

We'll always have Bayeux.

I rushed through the town, hoping not to miss my train.

I made it out of Bayeux and got to Paris in three hours.

In Paris, I bought a newspaper and read about the Russian and Yugoslavian wars. After three hours of reading and waiting, the TGV arrived. I mistakenly boarded a smoking car that was filled with four adults and one asshole kid.

As I wrote this, I sat on that TGV, from Paris to Irun, listening to the jerky kid make grating noises, disturbing everyone in the car. Incomprehensible sounds flowed from this idiot's mouth, keeping everyone in the car awake.

Anyway, enough of the Grinch. (Goddamn, this kid is getting on my nerves—I hope there are no kids in Spain.)

There are two hours left, so I put in my earplugs and will try to sleep.

I just remembered that I didn't buy a sleeping car bed for the next and final leg which will be a ten-hour trip from Irun at the border to Madrid.

(Slow trains in Spain travel mainly in the rain.)

I still may buy a bed though.

Update: Relief, as I was not the only one annoyed. The woman in front of me just turned around and glared at the foul kid. I caught her eye, and she just kind of smiled with disgust. Maybe someone will come by and conk the kid on the head. Maybe that someone will be me.

7

Spain

Madrid, Barcelona

October 6

It is nighttime in Madrid, and it seems like quite a while since I have written in this journal.

Anyway, I did not assault the child.

Not a lot happened on the TGV after I stopped writing. The kid and his mother got off and a loud Spaniard got on. He was cracking jokes (I guess) and kept the people in the back laughing.

I got off the train in Irun. I was in Spain, just over the border, so I had to go through a passport check inside the train station.

After that, I found the train to Madrid and met an American couple. I talked with them as I boarded and claimed my cabin on the empty train.

Time passed, and I faked being asleep whenever we made a stop. By doing this I was able to keep the cabin to myself for the first part of the trip.

The conductor came by to check tickets and I handed him my pass without thinking twice. He didn't speak English, but I soon realized there was a problem. He told me that I owed four hundred pesetas (less than four dollars). I tried to argue with him that it was paid for with the pass. I even showed him "Spain" written on the flap of the pass in the list of countries the pass was good in.

"No. Four hundred pesetas."

I then panicked as I did not have any Spanish money on me.

"No money?" he asked.

"American money," I replied.

"OK."

I handed him a five, and he gave me back one hundred pesetas in change.

I don't think he played me, since he would have taken me for more than four dollars. It was probably some extra fee tacked on to nickel and dime Eurail travelers.

I lay back down and tried to get back to sleep on the narrow row of four seats.

Shit, the door opened again and in walked another Spanish man.

"Four hundred pesetas!"

Just kidding!

He was another passenger like me—a small, older guy, looking a bit disheveled.

He asked if he could come into my car.

I was an old pro at this train thing, so I asked, *"¿Solo tu?"* rather sternly.

"Sí."

I let him in. Frankly, he did not need my permission.

He took a seat and began to talk at me despite my firm and fierce body language displaying my complete opposition to this.

"¿Estados Unidos?"

"Yeah."

"¿California?"

"No."

I had just met José from Pamplona. Pamplona Joe, I called him in my mind. (I guess the rampaging bulls missed this one.)

Pamplona Joe was one friendly guy. While we were talking, he got up, patted my back and thanked me for giving him a place to sit.

Didn't he buy a ticket? Why the fuck was he thanking me? Thank the fucking Spanish Railway, not me.

He bothered me a few more times about the open window but then settled down. He was certainly no little kid from the last leg. In fact, after a while, he became quite tolerable.

I must say that he did earn some high marks for what he did

next. At the subsequent stop, a man came into the car and José said something that sent the man scurrying.

José jostled me, and I thanked him for not letting more people in to crowd the car.

With José keeping the car cleared, I thought I could finally relax and get some sleep. But, at the next stop, my bodyguard, my concierge, José, departed. Not a tearful good-bye, but his Spanish speaking coupled with his intolerance would be missed.

In the now cleared car, I fell asleep. Around one in the morning, I awoke and saw that I had been joined by two more travelers—a *chico* and his *novia* were seated on the opposite side of me.

No problem, I decided. They didn't wake me up when they came in, so I didn't expect to be bothered by them now.

I fell back asleep. I woke up four separate times, but, all in all, did get some quality sleep.

At seven fifteen I awoke for the day. I cleaned up in the train WC, ate some of my packed food, and then went back to my car to watch the scenery until the train pulled into the station.

At exactly quarter to eight, we arrived in brilliant Madrid.

Early morning sunshine tell me all I need to know.

In the station I made reservations for a hostel, changed some money, and then looked for the Metro. It took some time to find. Subways always seemed to be hidden in the main train stations.

But it was a decent subway system. I got to my stop with no issues. I also found my hostel with no problems.

The Concha Hostela was on the second floor of a row house that contained a few other government-regulated hostels. I rang the appropriate bell and headed upstairs to get my room and bed assignment. On the way, I also located the shower, which I did plan to use.

It was unbelievably cheap, small, low-end accommodations. But that didn't matter at the moment, as I was in desperate need of a nap. I needed some regular sleep as opposed to the inefficient train sleep from the night before.

I awoke after a couple of hours of REM sleep a shinier, happier person, and headed out.

My first stop was a cheap counter café where I grabbed a sandwich and fries.

I then went south, in search of the Prado. After getting turned around and asking for directions, I finally found the massive museum. I went to the desk and paid the 450-peseta entrance fee.

I spent nearly three hours in this enormous warehouse filled with thirteenth- to eighteenth-century treasures of primarily Spanish and Italian artists.

As I have noted earlier, this is not my favorite artistic era. But I did begin to appreciate a few of the artists.

I really enjoyed Hieronymus Bosch's bizarre, sin-inspired works, such as *The Garden of Earthly Delights*. I also appreciated Goya's *Black Paintings*, which cleverly depicted fear and insanity.

As I toured the museum, my feet began to ache, so I took several seat-breaks, feigning to admire large pieces but only sitting to rest.

However, every time I took a seat, I was able to smell my fabulously stinky feet. I could not stay at one place very long, as their stench would permeate the area and make me woozy. My feet would have been right at home in Bosch's sinful garden or in Goya's giant oils.

But fuck it. I decided that I would not do the right thing and tend to my odor and filth. Instead, I would ignore them and search for Picasso's *Guernica*—funky feet be damned.

I asked a guard where it was, and he told me it had recently been moved to another museum. (Of course, the shitty Frommer book said it was there—worthless).

I left the Prado and followed the guard's directions the best I could. I traveled down a host of small side streets, getting a taste of Madrid. I passed a school letting out and saw a group of kids heading home. I gazed into small neighborhood shops (as opposed to the tourist shops on the main thoroughfares). I wandered past families walking and pets milling about. It was a genuine experience—slow life in a world metropolis.

I eventually found a main artery and headed to a pharmacy. I eagerly went in and, for 130 pesetas, bought a bottle of talcum powder to rid my feet of their now (nearly) unbearable stench.

I left the store and began again to look for the elusive museum that housed the Picasso masterpiece. After about forty-five minutes of walking, I was approached by two security officers, both holding bags of money. They saw me fumbling with my map and offered to help me out—not with a bag of cash, as I had hoped, but with directions. Those guys knew their stuff; I finally received some decent directions. They were even cool enough to recommend a couple of places to get some decent food.

Following their advice, I found San Mateo Street and then a great place to eat. I ordered a tortilla and a Coke. I sat down and shoveled it in.

At the little bar, I decided to hang around and watch some TV—a bullfight. I really had intended to stick around to see one live when I was in Spain. But once I saw just a bit of one on TV, I decided against it. I am not a PETA freak, but the whole spectacle became grotesque. Twenty guys in the ring, tormenting and taunting a bull. Three fighters then went in and, with extreme, cartoonish arrogance, shoved six knives into its back.

The defenseless, wounded animal, innocent, was left staggering about. Then, "Mr. Cool," the top fighter, came in and taunted the beast some more. As he did this, his cocky face exemplified the proud power he felt over this now helpless creature.

The crowd wildly cheered.

I nearly retched.

With all my heart I was rooting, in vain, for *el toro*.

I could only hope the next bull he tormented left him in the same condition as Jake Barnes.

After about twenty minutes of this, I decided to split—yuck.

Back to the hostel—to rest and powder my nose, I mean feet.

October 7

I am halfway through this journey.

I have to catch up from yesterday to today.

I slept pretty well—long into Thursday morning.

I showered and then left the Concha Hostela. I grabbed some food at a café (a different place from yesterday, but similar). I ordered something that looked great on the posted picture behind the counter, which unexpectedly turned out to be an anchovy sandwich. It was quite good. Decent price as well.

Today, before continuing my search for the elusive *Guernica*, I intended to go to the naval museum, because shitty Frommer's said it contained the first map that included the Americas. But, like nearly everything else in Frommer's, this was a false lead. The museum had closed in December.

Well, I then continued south to the Alcala Station. I was looking for the Reina Sofía Museum, the modern art museum that now housed the *Guernica* (Fuck Frommer's).

I then had a flash—I could find the tourist information booth at the station and get exact directions.

I entered the station and realized that it was, frankly, the greatest train station I had ever been in. It was like an ecological habitat—huge ceilings, rooms filled with palm trees and exotic vegetation, steam, flowing water—it was amazing. It was a tourist destination all in itself.

I explored for a while, and then found the tourist kiosk.

My destination was directly across the street.

Gracias.

I paid the 450 Pts and headed to the twenty rooms of the permanent collection of the Reina Sofía.

In my opinion, the greatest era of art—Picasso, Miró, Dalí, etc.

I hold the cubists and their immediate predecessors in the highest esteem. Cézanne's work, which was greatly expanded upon through the analytical cubism of Picasso and Braque, astounds me. It amazes me that they had the genius to depict every possible angle and all temporal perspectives of a subject as well as its entire nature using only a single-plane canvas.

As I was enjoying the entirety of this incredible collection, I stumbled upon room seven. In room seven, I found *Guernica*. Even after reading about it and studying it, I was not prepared. I thought the black and white masterpiece was large but still of a regular size. But it was the largest modern art painting I had ever seen.

It was mounted in a separate room, behind glass. In the anteroom of gallery seven, before reaching the masterpiece, there were sketches Picasso made during the four months he spent preparing for the project. He wanted the anti-war, anti-fascist piece to be perfect.

He achieved that as this is the greatest anti-war piece I, or anyone else, has ever seen.

After taking my time in room seven (there was not a lot of traffic coming through), I continued into the other rooms of the permanent collection, including entire rooms of Dalí and Miró.

I thoroughly enjoyed the entire experience of the permanent collection for an hour and a half.

From there, I went upstairs to *Expo 57*. This exhibit included a group of painters from the late 1950s who experimented with shapes and colors. It was very interesting. The sketches that led up to the finished pieces were included, and the development of those final works, simple shapes and colors, is evinced. Despite looking to the contrary, the exhibit showed that a lot of thought and preparation went into each of those one hundred works.

The other display in the upper floor was the *1900 Exhibit*, which had opened only the day before.

This show concerned the Austrian empire just prior to World War I. There was a great deal of variety on display: architecture, clothing, music, scholarship (an original letter from Freud), and, of course, art.

The art included Klimt and his *Judith I* portrait, a work I had studied. That piece, as opposed to Picasso's early cubist work in the museum, was much smaller than I had thought. But not any less impressive.

Also in the exhibit were two other artists that I had studied and enjoyed—Schiele and Kokoschka. I was happy to see one of my favorite

Germanic expressionist works, Kokoschka's *The Lunatic Girl,* hanging in a prominent place.

It was also nice to see photos of those artists—some quite misunderstood, but geniuses nonetheless.

After three hours, I left the Reina Sofía, which I now viewed as one of the greatest art museums in the world.

My next stop was not a stop—I was going to explore the city of Madrid, walking.

Today, I ventured down main drags. After about forty-five minutes I came upon the Palace. It was large, but it paled in comparison to Versailles. You know, it was pretty ugly. The best feature of this Spanish palace was where it was located—on a hill with valleys on both sides.

I continued past the Plaza Mayor and into the new section of Madrid.

I began to head back to the Concha (Ka-chonk, Ka-chonk) Hostela. As I was walking, I saw a stand selling the *USA Today*. I had no intention of buying one until I read the headline. Yep. "Michael Jordan Quits the NBA."

I immediately bought one and read it right there, standing on the street. I then kind of wandered around in a circle, in a daze. I felt like I was in a movie with tunnel vision—I was on a crowded street but could not see nor hear anything clearly. It was weird.

It actually is a good story though: "Where were you when you heard Jordan retired?"

"Oh, on the Gran Vía in Madrid at a newspaper kiosk in between a KFC and a sex shop."

October 8

The next day, I got up early but could not clean up as someone beat me to the shower. So, I got dressed, paid the woman at the desk, and headed to the train station to make the ten o'clock to Barcelona.

I made it in time but quickly found out that there *was* no ten o'clock train. Oh no. Before I panicked and changed all of my plans, I saw that there was an eleven o'clock. Panic-attack averted.

I bought some travel food and sat and waited on a hard metal train station bench.

I boarded the train and readied myself for the seven-hour trip. Nothing of interest happened except that I was able to read two hundred pages of my next book, *War and Peace*.

The best thing about the trip was the scenery. Mountains, hills, rocks—like California. I guess that was why the sixteenth-century Spaniards liked the American Southwest so much. It looked just like their home country.

Eventually, the train got to the coast where I saw the Mediterranean for the first time.

Bright sky and blue water.

Shining sun and sandy beaches,

Colorful parasols and palm trees.

I was glad it was such a beautiful day.

At around six fifteen, as the sun was setting, the train arrived in Barcelona.

As was now my custom in new cities, I headed straight for the information desk. But here the clerk only gave me a hostel list and a map. Not as helpful as some of the desks, but they did provide me with a phone where I was able to find a hostel with an open bed.

Just before I left the booking office, it was interesting to see two middle-aged American women not think twice about booking an 8,500 Pts room.

Well, fuck them. I've got a lopsided bed for one thousand pesetas at a filthy hostel.

(Oh God, please don't make it that filthy).

I hopped on the Metro and arrived at my stop at La Rambla, the "cruising" street of Barcelona. This must be where the term *to ramble* comes from; it was a huge street with four lanes of traffic in both directions. In between, there was a vast middle sidewalk filled with pedestrians.

Out of the Metro station, I, of course, walked the wrong way. But, after a quick consultation for directions with an old man and woman, I found my hostel destination.

It was in the Plaça del Rei, the Plaza Mayor of Barcelona.

I entered and paid.

As I went up the stairs, I finally started to be honest with myself. I began to come to terms with my hatred of hostels.

I stowed my pack in the too-small locker in a room with over twenty beds. There was a Rastafarian and another fellow already asleep.

I went downstairs and paid for a terrible dinner.

Next, I left the hostel and walked a short distance. I then realized that my accommodations were near the Mediterranean. It was so beautiful that I hung out at the waterfront looking over the darkened sea for about half an hour.

It was getting late, so I went back to the hostel, where I wrote this. I sat in the cafeteria with foosball and pool tables nearby. There were about thirty fellow travelers milling about. It was just after ten at night.

Like I wrote earlier, I have begun to be honest with myself and admit that I hate these places. There is no privacy, and I am extremely private and introverted. These places are dirty, stinky, public, loud, bright. They are not worth the little savings they promise. At this point I seriously doubt that I will stay in another on this trip. This was my sixth one, and, except for Gimmelwald in Switzerland, will be my last. I will sacrifice large meals and such just so I don't have to stay in these shitholes anymore.

Next, I went to the front desk and called my mom. I told her my thoughts on hostels. She told me of the ongoing difficulties in selling the company to Uncle Nick. We were equal in our exasperation.

Then I mentioned that I was getting nervous about the plan to bring currency into Yugoslavia. I didn't even know how much I would be bringing, as we had not settled on a final amount. Added to that, I had yet to formalize a scheme on how I would get into the country.

At that point, I, only half joking, told her I didn't want to get caught smuggling in so much money that it created an international incident.

She tried to allay my fears by telling me that I didn't have to do this; I could back out at any time. I kept my mouth shut, knowing that I had to see this through—it was a pact with myself, and I had to fulfill it.

We ended with her telling me that she was about to go on a lady's day with my cousin, Jane; my sister, Nadene; and my girlfriend, Carly. They would go shopping and then have a nice dinner while I slept in this nasty hostel.

I did not look forward to that night.

O<small>CTOBER</small> 9

Well, it wasn't that bad—as my late father used to say, "everything came out in the wash." Not literally though, as I hadn't done laundry for a while—I was out of clean pants.

I slept until a quarter after eight. Then I went to the nearest shower room, but it was fully *ocupado*. I walked down the hall and found another washroom. As I was heading in, a girl in a towel walked out and told me that it was the ladies' shower—the other one was the men's.

No shit.

But I soon found out that both of us were mistaken.

I walked back and went into the first shower room I had stumbled across.

There were four private stalls but only one was occupied. I entered a stall and lathered up. As I was doing that, I saw that the other person had left their stall and was now bending down, drying off. The person then looked up and we caught each other's eyes. We both stared, trying to focus through the water. I just couldn't tell what this person looked like.

"Oh, is this co-ed?" the girl toweling off calmly asked me.

I said, "No, I don't think so. But it is now."

"Shit," she said, and then asked me to give her a couple of minutes.

I grabbed my towel and left the shower room.

In no time at all, the tall redheaded girl apologized and left.

Alright.

I finished my shower, a bit discombobulated, went back to my noxious, all-male room, and dressed in the dark.

I left the hostel and returned to the train station via the Metro. I would be off to Nice this evening.

As I had some time to kill, I found a locker to stow my pack in and headed out for one last bit of sightseeing in Barcelona.

I walked an hour or so to Gaudí's Cathedral. Throughout the entire walk, I had to use the bathroom—take a seat, that is—and I did not want to use the dirty squat and aim ones at the train station.

Against the wishes of my intestines, I made it to the Cathedral.

Very large, very gaudy(!), very ugly. It will probably never be completed.

I walked around the structure (and the twentieth-century construction equipment), found a bench, and took a seat.

There was not a lot to do there—I was just looking at something with no other purpose than seeing it. I bobbed my head a couple of times, like Chevy Chase looking at the Grand Canyon, and then decided to take off.

Also, by this time, my *servicio* calling was getting to be almost an *emergencia*.

I headed into a small café to do my work.

After I completed my business there, I remembered that I'd forgotten my hostel card at my last accommodations. Not a great surprise—that was the first hostel in Europe that even asked for the damn thing.

I boarded a Metro, found my stop, and then got lost again on La Rambla, walking the wrong way a second time. Finally, I found the place—still stinky—and got my card. I didn't think I would need it much more on the trip, as I didn't plan on staying at many more hostels, but you never know.

I left and walked the correct direction on La Rambla, north to the station. I journeyed down the whole impressive avenue, past the university, past Joan Miró Park. There were a lot of people there—crowds just enjoying the day.

After I had rambled on, I arrived back at the station, gathered my pack, and bought a newspaper and a bottle of water.

I then boarded a train which would take me my on first step toward Nice, a French border town named Cerbère.

It was a completely uneventful ride. I read the paper in an empty four-seat car the entire three-hour ride.

Once I got into the town of Cerbère, I realized I was back in France, so I had to go through customs once again. After a fully forgettable border crossing, I headed to the travel kiosk where a pleasant and competent clerk was working the counter. There, I made a reservation on the train to Nice. But I also found out that it was not leaving until midnight (it was five in the evening) and that it was an eight-hour trip.

Yikes.

I decided to opt for a couchette. I left the travel desk and found a small bank, where I exchanged seventy dollars. Back at the kiosk, there was no line, so I returned to the same clerk and told him what I wanted.

The clerk looked at me with blank eyes and no clue to what I was requesting. He said something back to me and received the same response in turn. Neither of us knew what the hell the other was saying. So, without anything else left to do, we began to laugh.

Finally, we got on each other's wavelength and figured it out. I paid him the equivalent of seventeen dollars for a couchette and what I hoped would be a good night's sleep. Not a bad price. I chose the top bunk in the hopes of not being disturbed.

Prior to leaving Spain, I had forgotten to change or spend, all of my pesetas, so I returned to the bank just before it closed and exchanged the small amount. I stored my pack and began the walk to town.

I followed a sign that said the beach and town center were the same way. But it was not a very inviting walk—that path led me through a long, dark underpass. It was like walking through a large sewer tunnel—and it smelled like it too.

So, for protection, I took out my small Swiss Army knife. I was sure that if I had to use it, I would get confused and wrongly pull out one of its many non-knife components. I would then be forced to pluck the nose hairs from any potential thieves.

Thankfully, I didn't need to use it for any purposes, protection or grooming, as I made it to the beach safely.

There were some shops still open, so I picked up some film and then found a seat.

It was a beautiful cove with a hill on the right and old houses surrounding it on all sides. Palm trees, boats, and small cafés. If Jimmy Buffet saw this place, he would write a song about it.

I wrote this while sitting on rock steps about ten feet from the beach. The sun was setting. There was a cool breeze, and it seemed that I had all the time in the world. It was so great to get out of the cities and take a breather. If I had not bought a couchette ticket, I might have stayed the night there.

Well, maybe not, I reconsidered. I was on a tight self-imposed schedule to see and do everything I planned. I still had Switzerland, Italy, Austria, Hungary, and Yugoslavia (hopefully).

I left the beach and decided to walk to the town. I was about fifty feet from the town center and walking up a narrow uphill street when a tremendous wind forced me to turn around and find another way. Crazy.

I finally trudged my way into the village and found a bar in the tiny town square, which is where I wrote this.

There were several people inside when I arrived, but after some time, the number dwindled to about ten customers (and four dogs). All were in good spirits, and nearly everyone had a beer or glass of wine in front of them. Sadly, the dogs did not.

I had been there about two hours and had that many beers—one an hour. During my leisurely drinking, I had some time to chat with the bartender in this harbor town who was a young, pretty woman. She seemed like a fine girl although her name was Aimée, not Brandy as I had suspected.

I didn't do much else—a bit of travel planning (the Alps), but that was about it. After one last beer, I plan on making my way back to the station, popping out my contacts, and reading.

8

France (part III), Monaco

Nice, Monaco-Ville

October 10

H ey, I did do that, just as I planned!
In addition, I tried to call Carly, but could only leave her a message.

Next, I met two Americans. Actually, it was the two women who bought the 8,500 Pts room in Barcelona! Small fucking world again. They were from Chicago and worked for some type of medical facility (I wasn't paying the closest of attention). They told me that they would be traveling for three weeks through southwestern Europe and they were off to Nice as well.

Well, howzabout that?

I was thankful that I was in the station, as the train boarded very early—about an hour before it was scheduled to depart. No lights were on in the train, which was filled with a group of older Americans on a trip from Seattle(!).

There was a lot of commotion as we boarded, owing to the near-complete interior darkness coupled with the unfamiliar surroundings. But I made it to my car with minimal issues.

I shared my four-bed couchette with a German couple and another guy who was asleep on the train before we boarded into this clusterfuck.

I climbed to my top bunk easily but had a tough time getting situated. I struggled with the sheet and then with the blanket. Then I had to contend with my property falling to the floor numerous times.

Finally, I got it right.

I took off my shoes but—uh-oh—my feet smelled like good cheese or bad meat. My stench, mixed with the terrible aroma of the actual camembert cheese I had in my bag, made me gag. No one else seemed to mind though. Or they played it off well.

After that, I put in my earplugs and closed my eyes. I knew the conductor had to be coming by soon, so I knew I couldn't fall asleep quite yet.

So, I immediately fell asleep.

When the conductor did come, forty-five minutes later, I grudgingly showed him my pass. I really didn't think he looked at it. Back to sleep.

After a short but decent sleep, I awoke with my alarm. I knew I had to hustle to get off the train in Nice. If I did not, I would end up in Rome, the train's final destination.

I hopped off and into the rather small station. Immediately a man ran up to me and handed me a hostel card—another hostel hustler.

I told him no thanks and I hit the road into the early morning air of the rainy French Riviera town.

I walked south, looking for cheap accommodations, but didn't see any places that appealed to me. Finally, after an hour of walking in the rain, I found a decent-looking pension. I took a chance that it would be inexpensive as well and knocked on the door.

A sweet woman (who I woke-up) answered my knock. She quoted me a price of only one hundred francs.

"I'll take it," I tried to communicate with her, but she spoke little to no English. After some gesturing and rudimentary English and French, we figured it out.

Eventually, I learned that her husband, who was not there, spoke English quite well. I also found out that her son loved America. Relief! I had not stumbled upon American-hating Frenchies.

So, in Nice, I would be staying at the Selecty Home Pension.

She took me upstairs and across the hall into my room. Huge— kitchen, couch, table.

But, unfortunately, it was not the cleanest. I noticed crumbs on the counter the moment I looked at it.

Are the French as unclean as it is said? Perhaps.

Oh well, who cares? It was cheap. I'd wear my damn sandals while I was there and I'd shower a lot (that would be a change on this trip). I was on the French fucking Riviera for 100 francs a night at the Selecty Home Pension.

The next thing I did was an absolute necessity—laundry. I did it all in the kitchen sink. A lot.

After that, I put on a pair of shorts (both of my long pants were now drying) and napped for an hour or so.

I woke up and decided it was time to eat and exchange some more money. I headed to the train station, but once I got about a quarter of the way there, I remembered that I didn't have a map. Nor did I have the Selecty Home Pension's address.

I'd been lost quite a bit on this trip, but this time seemed different. I was hopelessly disoriented. I figured I would remember my way back if I kept walking, looking for landmarks I'd passed earlier in the day. I tried to remember street names.

Nothing.

I got to the station and changed some money. I was able to help a guy with directions for what he was looking for, a laundromat, as I had just passed one. But he had no such advice for me.

I was not yet panicking.

I decided to relax and eat to clear my mind. I found a nice little place with good food. I had some lamb and a quarter carafe of wine.

It did not work. Clearing my mind, that is. Now, I was a bit tipsy and woefully lost. I had no clue whatsoever where I was.

One positive was that I did remember the name of the Selecty Home Pension for some crazy fucking reason. Otherwise, seriously, I'd still be looking.

So, I asked countless people on the street, "Where is the Selecty Home Pension?"

Nothing.

Where the fuck was the Selecty Home Pension?! (See, how the hell did I remember that stupid name and nothing else?).

I journeyed into bars, stores—nobody knew this place, the Selecty Home fucking Pension.

Finally, I found a small market with a nice cashier and a phone book. There was no listing for the Selecty Home Pension. Suddenly, I remembered the name of a hotel near it, the Hotel de la Fleur. Nope, that goddamn place wasn't listed either.

I was stuck.

Lost forever in France.

I would buy a beret and a loaf of long bread. I would wear black clothes and smoke clove cigarettes. Existentialism would become my mistress. The Selecty Home Pension would fade from my memory.

But what was this?

One last chance. I saw a police station.

Fuck, thank God I remembered the name of the place, the Selecty Home Pension. (Remember?)

A really nice officer understood my dilemma and handed me a folder with a list of all the registered accommodations in the city.

Holy mother of fuck, there it was—the Selecty Home Pension. It was there—its elusive address and its worthless phone number.

I shook the officer's hand, genuinely thanking him, as he handed me a stack of maps (I get it; much appreciated, guy) and went on my way.

I carefully followed the maps and realized that I was only a few blocks from the goddamn place.

I got back to the Selecty Home Pension and went upstairs to my room. It was already six in the evening.

I wanted to use the phone, which was located just outside my door. I couldn't get it to work, so I found the family and asked the husband for help.

He spoke great English and broke the ice by telling me, like his wife had, that his son loved America. Whew, relief, as I would not have to defend my country's honor in that home.

His wife soon joined us as we tried to figure out how to call the United States. I gave it one more attempt and, amazingly, I was able to get through.

I got through to Carly, who had lost her voice and couldn't really talk. So much for that.

I then called Uncle Nick to discuss my possible trip to Yugoslavia. Teta Jean got on the phone immediately and told me her elderly sister (who my family had stayed with in Yugoslavia in 1985) was killed in the war yesterday.

Terrible.

I then spoke with Uncle Nick a bit more. He'd been able to contact Jovo in Sombor and tell him that I intended to travel there within the month. Through Uncle Nick, Jovo had advised me to bring American dollars and Deutsche Marks, as those were the most widely accepted currencies in Yugoslavia.

Even though Jovo now knew my plan and expected me to bring in money, fear overtook me, and I began to have second thoughts. After the news of the death of someone I knew, the idea of war really hit me. I tried to think of alternative plans.

Maybe I could call Jovo and have him and his family just meet me in Budapest and not go into Serbia? I could pass on the money there without jeopardizing my life.

All those thoughts were careening through my head as I ended the call and lay down to get my thoughts in order. As I weighed the pros and cons of entry into Yugoslavia, I concluded that I would finish what I had planned.

I had made this deal with myself, and I would do everything I could do to get into that country.

I then fell soundly asleep, now sure of my goal.

October 11

In the morning, I ate the bread I had bought at the end of yesterday's adventure and took off, this time with a map and the pension's address.

I was off to catch a train for a day trip to another country, Monaco. But first, I would stop by the ticket agent and buy a couchette for the trip to Geneva tomorrow.

I waited in line for quite a while, not sure of what was going on. I had only about ten minutes left before my train to Monaco was set to leave by the time it was finally my turn.

I asked the woman at the desk, who thankfully spoke English, about a couchette from Nice to Geneva, via Interlaken. That would not be possible, she said, as there was a planned strike by the SNCF scheduled for all day tomorrow.

Uh-oh—that meant an extra day in Nice. Damn, I had spent so much time last night planning the rest of the trip, and now that would all go to waste.

But I started to reconsider. It wouldn't be much of a problem. Nice is nice (hooray for my word play). I would cut out the day I'd planned on the Italian Riviera (the Cinque Terre), as I was on the French one already. One Riviera would work out fine.

So, I bought my couchette for a day later than expected and then hopped on the already moving train to Monaco.

My new normal was to head straight to the tourist office, but it was closed. Instead, I found a store and bought a huge map of the tiny country. Although, with or without a map, I was doomed to get lost, which I did almost immediately while looking for the Oceanographic Museum. A friend had told me that this was a place I just could not miss, as it was founded by Jacques Cousteau.

Really, how lost could I be, though? Monaco is one of the smallest countries (political anomalies) on earth.

So, as I was lost, I kept my cool and decided to get lunch.

I found a quiet restaurant and ordered the plate of the day and a Coke. The Coke was twenty-five francs, which made the whole meal seventy-three francs. I needed to learn to order wine in France (shitty little Monaco I mean), as it was ten francs for a glass of red. I was not happy; I had already spent too much in this weird little place.

After a few wrong turns, I used my map and found my way (through this shitty little "country") to the museum. It was up a tremendous hill and past the royal palace.

Thankfully, Jimmy Stewart was not looking through any rear windows.

(By the way, I hate royalty).

I found the entrance and paid the sixty(!) francs. Great. Now I had two francs left for two days if I didn't change any more money.

I guess I planned on starving.

First, I headed to the aquarium, which was not bad. I hadn't been to one in a long time, but it seemed to be what I remembered—fish behind glass. It was peaceful, though, with some pretty bizarre species. Relaxing.

After that I went up to the museum. Big disappointment. Extremely boring—mussels, shells, and fish corpses. Hell, I could have ordered the variety platter at Red Lobster and seen the same shit.

I realized that my taste in attractions was the polar opposite of the friend who'd advised me to go to this fish necropolis. Unless he'd pulled a fast one on me, this place sucked. I would much rather see art than nature.

But I did make it through the museum in its entirety—I'd better—I'd spent 60 francs. Hell, I even stayed and watched the incomprehensible French language film about Cousteau to make sure I got my money's worth.

I beat it out of there and went to the casino. That was more my style anyway.

On my way, I had to make my way around the port. I had seen the port a million times in pictures, including in the *Guinness Book of World Records* when I was a kid (Aristotle Onassis's yacht was parked there when it was the largest in the world).

It was beautiful though. Monaco, despite being such an aberration, was inspiring. It looked as if the city (country, I mean) rose from the Mediterranean and climbed the side of a mountain.

I found my way to the casino. The same one where Charles Wells "broke the bank."

It was not much different than American casinos.

I exchanged the last of my budgeted money, put five francs into a slot machine, and lost.

"I have now gambled in Monaco," I told myself.

I was a high roller. *Une grosse affaire.*

Champagne and caviar for *déjeuner.*

Toute la nuit, I would dance with *les belles femmes.*

On second thought, it was time to leave the casino. I was out of francs.

I had failed in my quest to break the bank, so I decided it was time to bid *adieu* to Monaco as well. I found the train station with surprisingly little problem.

Other than its beauty, Monaco was a bit of a disappointment. But I was still happy I'd made the day-trip excursion to see this odd little place.

Back in Nice, I found my pension with no problem. Damn, I was getting good at not getting lost.

Sure.

I then went to a grocery store and bought sixteen francs worth of food. As I had a kitchen in my place, I believed this would be a wise move.

When I got back, I told the owners that I would be there another night and paid them one hundred more francs. As they were telling me they hoped the weather would get better, I watched their American-loving son steal a smoke from his mother's purse.

Anyway, the people in Nice are nice (happy to write that again).

I then retired to my room.

My clothes were still not dry. But the extra day would only help remedy that.

I replanned the trip and got everything back in order.

October 12

Nice. Shit, I'm still only in Nice.

Thankfully, there were no Valkyries outside my window.

Yesterday, Tuesday, I slept in and then wandered to the beach, which was about five blocks away. The beach was not sand but large, sometimes sharp, rocks. I did get a nice view of Nice (last one).

The city was built around a cove, right into the outlying hills. It was not as impressive as Monaco, but still something to see.

I strolled for about an hour and then headed to the grocery store to pick up a snack. As I was looking for a place to sit and eat, I ran into the owner of the pension, the English-speaking husband. I told him I was going to one of the small towns in the Alps next. He told me that was great, but the large Swiss cities, like Bern, were wonderful to see as well. We chatted for a bit, and then I headed off to eat.

After my snack I made my way to the Fine Arts Museum of Nice. It was a decent little institution for not being in a huge metropolis.

There, I discovered that I really enjoyed Jules Chéret's poster art. Early twentieth century; gauzy women in bright colors. Through his works I was brought to circa 1908 France, one of my favorite periods and places, as the entire concept of visual art was being redefined.

But, again, Frommer misled me, the dickhead. The book said that the fauvist works of Dufy would be there. But they'd been moved. I was pretty disappointed; I really liked Dufy. About par for Frommer's, though.

I headed back to the pension earlier than expected and read *War and Peace.* As I sat there reading, the bar next door and one floor below kept playing not "Dancing Queen" but Whitney Houston's "I Will Always Love You." It was a fine song (not as good as ABBA's hit), but not ten times in a row. Were they trying to get customers to leave? Was she down there having a cheap beer? Were the local French drunkards involved in some strange love cult?

How will I know the answers to those questions? I wouldn't, as I did not investigate. I just finished reading, put in my glorious earplugs, and went to sleep.

October 13

In the morning, I packed up my now-dry clothes and readied myself for my last day in the south of France—I would be taking a night train to Switzerland and the Alps.

Like yesterday, I slept in and decided that, if I was going to limit my writing to two journals, I would need to write smaller.

As I had all day to kill, I took my time, read, updated my log, and putzed around. I then went across the hall to give my key to the wife. She asked me if everything was alright.

Of course it was. I smiled.

She then led me to my side of the hall and pointed to a bulletin board of postcards. She asked me to send her one when I got back to the States. I planned on doing that—this was a great, if a little dirty, pension. I just hoped my mail could find its way to the Selecty Home Pension without getting lost.

I got to the Nice train station and stowed my bag in a locker. I had some time to kill before my train, so I decided to take one last long walk through the city.

I rambled to but didn't stop at the Marc Chagall National Museum, as it was much too expensive. I then found the long and winding road, Avenue de Cimiez, and worked my way to the *Musée Matisse*. After getting lost for a time in a park (lost in a *park* was a new one), I finally stumbled upon the museum.

It was housed in a brand-new building which was constructed half above and half below ground. The museum had a fine representation of Matisse's later works, but I wanted to see more of his oil paintings, works from his early days when he was experimenting, like a wild animal, with color.

Instead, it was mainly sketches. He probably threw those out a dime a dozen—using them to pay for some meals and a few prostitutes along the way.

There were also a lot of his sculptures and paper cut-outs. The latter were colorful but not from his fauve period—I was bummed.

When I ventured outside to stroll the gardens, I discovered something that made this museum quite memorable and worth the walk—the final resting place of the artist. His grave was marked by a large stone slab near the museum.

Next, I headed to the Roman ruins of Cimiez, which were in the same park as the *Musée Matisse*. There was an Archaeological Museum next to the dig, and I paid the small entrance fee. However, I could not understand much, as most of the inscriptions were in Latin. Where there were translations, they were only in French and no other language. I did my best but only understood a small fragment of what was there. I should have listened more in high school French class—I would have really liked to have learned what the ancients had known.

Near the museum's exit, I had the option of viewing the ancient city through a window or walking through it. As it was fifty francs to stroll through the town, I saved my money and peeped through the glass.

It was an impressive museum despite the financial and linguistic obstructions.

Time to get back to the station.

Once there, I primarily read *War and Peace*.

But, after some time, I began to write in this journal, which is what I am doing right now.

I just noticed that there is a pizzeria across the street. I've got some time to kill, so I am going to get a pizza and spend about an hour enjoying it. Once I pay for it, I figure I will have one franc left over. That will work out perfectly—no francs to exchange, and I will stay near my budget.

9

Switzerland

Gimmelwald, Mürren

OCTOBER 14

I took my time eating the pizza, and then I went back into the station and waited the last few minutes for the train to arrive.

I got on the train and found my couchette. At first there was only an old man sharing the six-bed car. He was kind of a dick, bitching about this and that, but I was able to sleep a bit despite his dickishness and the interior heat (well over ninety degrees).

After some travel, more people boarded, including a screaming kid (not Cameron). This little shit cried so loud, he woke everyone up. But, after some time, he did settle down.

All in all, I got a terrible night's sleep. The full car, with the body heat, made the temperature and aroma nearly unbearable.

Finally, the lights came on as the trip neared its end. I immediately perked up, knowing that I would soon be out of the crowded, boiling tin can.

I detrained and saw two girls that I had briefly spoken with in Nice. They were from Augustana College in Illinois. They planned to study for a time in Europe before they went traveling with full force. We talked for a bit.

I then left to catch my train to Bern. Once on it, I convinced myself that it was not the correct train.

I am nuts.

To be fair to myself, the ticket-counter clerk in Nice gave me the wrong time this train was to arrive in Bern. So each minute that crept past the stated arrival time, my worry increased exponentially. I startled two people on the train making sure we were on the way to Bern. They assured me we were, but I still had my crazy doubts.

The train was the correct one, and we arrived in Bern about twenty minutes after the time I was quoted.

At the station, I changed money and waited thirty or so minutes for the train to Interlaken. Goddamn, I was catching a lot of trains.

Once I arrived at Interlaken, I noticed that I was in the West Station but needed to be in the East Station.

I exited and headed through the very touristy Swiss town. There was one cool thing among all the tourist shops—an open field, in the middle of town, filled with grazing cows.

They seemed so benign, eating the grass and chewing their cud. But as I walked past, I must admit, the cows were intimidating. Fucking enormous animals that could really do some damage if motivated. Thankfully, man had bred out any trace of will; those beasts were simply submissive, mindless milk and meat machines.

Once past the field, I was relieved to be safe from the city cows.

I arrived at the East Station and just missed the train that would have taken me to my day's next destination, Stechelberg.

I had some time, so I bought my ticket at the station (instead of on the train as I'd planned) and went across the small Swiss street to buy some groceries. I shopped quickly, knowing my time was short.

Ten minutes later, the train to Stechelberg arrived. Those trains ran like subways!

Uneventful.

From Stechelberg I took a bus to the next stop of this crazy day, Trümmelbach, which is in a deep valley.

Once there, I got to experience the amazing Trümmelbach Falls. Everything was colorful—beautiful and breathtaking.

The little town, dominated by the falls, was filled with a rainbow array of wildflowers. The tiny Swiss houses were quaint and straight out of a 1960's technicolor film.

But, of course, a mini disaster struck: I noticed I had left my umbrella on the bus. I went to the counter at the bus station, and they told me not to worry. The bus was on a tight circuit and returned every twenty minutes.

Whew, disaster averted. It was early fall in Switzerland—rain season.

As I was killing the twenty minutes, I chatted with two American girls who were debating whether to go up into the mountains any further. As I was trying to convince them to do it, the bus returned.

Farewell, indecisive ladies, I've got an umbrella to fetch and a funicular to board.

After retrieving my precious umbrella, I headed straight for the funicular, or gondola.

It seemed quite unstable, swaying precariously on what looked, to me at least, like dental floss.

I boarded for the five-minute ride. There were four others on board with me.

Oh man. I was in the Alps. On the Alps?. Holy fuck. *Beautiful* cannot describe it. Again, no words for this scenery.

I got off at the first of four stops on that gondola route, Gimmelwald, the village that travel guru Rick Steves popularized.

I was the only one who got off at that stop.

Quiet.

Cowbells.

There was a tiny, pedestrian-only road. Empty.

I followed it to the hostel where I got a bed assignment.

I went up to the bunk room and began to introduce myself to a few people. Eventually, I chatted a lot with an Australian accountant named Ron. Rocket Ron, as he was known.

Soon, five of us decided we needed a beer. We took the hiking trail up the mountain to the town of Mürren (which was the next stop on the gondola). It took about forty minutes of intense walking.

The hike took us over mountain streams and past goats, cows, horses, caged rabbits—and lots of dung.

What's brown and sounds like a bell?

By the time we arrived in Mürren, I was beat. We had essentially climbed up a Swiss Alp, for God's sake.

Mürren was a much larger village than Gimmelwald. It had actual streets and money exchanges.

My little group bought some beer and then headed back down. As we trudged down the same path, my left knee began to hurt. I even contemplated stopping. But I toughed it out and made it back to the hostel, where beer awaited me.

Nearly everyone staying there was now back in the common room. We played cards and drank. I taught the group a drinking game, "Drug Dealer," which we played for quite a while.

As we played, more hostelers showed up, including a guy who came in with some wild mushrooms he had found (not the psychedelic kind).

Beer continued to flow as we listened to some of my tapes, including the "Polish Beer Drinking Songs" cassette and some Pink Floyd, "The Final Cut." We did not listen to the latter for six hours straight, though.

We were pretty loaded by the time nine o'clock came around. That was when we decided it was time to go to Walter's, a hotel with a bar, just up the mountain.

Five of us made the initial trek, with three following soon after. We drank more beer. I made friends with another accountant, Jim, from California. Lots of drinking and fun.

At midnight it was time to hit the downslope and return to the hostel. Once there, a few of us chatted in the dining room. Finally, I decided enough was enough and went to bed.

Of course, I slept in until after eleven that morning. I went downstairs to clean up but could not take a shower as all the hot water had already been used.

I got myself situated and headed into the dining hall. As I wrote this, it was just about noon. I was the only one here. It was very peaceful. I caught up on my writing, so I am going to hike the Swiss Alps and see what I can see.

October 15

After I quit writing on Friday, I took a nice, leisurely walk up to Mürren. On the way up the mountain, I stopped a few times and read.

Once I arrived in Mürren, I found a quiet restaurant and bought myself a great Swiss lunch—ham and Swiss cheese, hot, on a bed of hash browns. I planned to recreate it at home.

After lunch, I strolled through the town. Eventually I found another quiet place and continued to read.

Peaceful and calm.

I left Mürren and went back down the mountain to tiny Gimmelwald. I saw a couple of cars and wondered how they got them up the side of a mountain. There must be a crazy, steep road filled with cutbacks to access the town.

I even saw one small truck. I discovered later that that truck and driver had the fabulous job of delivering the liquid fertilizer (liquid shit) up and down the mountain. Yum.

I hiked the path through the little village and found another seat. Read more *War and Peace*. I must admit that, in the cold alpine air, I dozed off a few times while taking a break from the book.

After an hour or so, with the majestic Alps spread out in front of me, I decided to go back to the hostel. There were about twenty more people there, so I grabbed a seat and joined them. But the peaceful camaraderie of yesterday was gone. There were too many people looking to be the boss.

I did talk to a beefy American girl who had been traveling through Europe off and on since 1988. This year, since May, she had only spent $418, including airfare. She told me that she was sick of museums and culture. She just liked to sit back and do nothing all day.

After listening to her, I thought of some of the other people I had come across on this trip. They had come to view traveling in the same light.

What the fuck kind of life was that? Traveling should not revert to idleness. If it does, stop, reexamine your existence, and find another direction in which to evolve, as you have obviously reached the end of one journey.

Perhaps that was the reason I did not like hostels. When I started this trip, I truly had no idea what they were about. But now, after experiencing hostels, especially the same, unchanging type of person in them, I realized it was the people that inhabited them that turned me off more than anything else.

I then began to reexamine myself, trying to be as honest as possible—I was taking a journey, a brief diversion to accomplish a goal. I was not trying to escape into a life of lethargy. My father died and I moved to Seattle. I simply had a desire to do something in his memory.

I was, more than anything, overwhelmed.

After talking with the American girl for a short time more, Rocket Ron let me know that a few people were headed outside. I joined them, took a seat with about eight others, and popped open another beer.

As we were talking and relaxing in the mountain air, I met another Aussie guy who had completed about half of his six weeks of traveling. Nice guy.

Nearly everyone outside in the tiny Alpine village seemed to get along well—the air? The beer?

I gave Rocket Ron my address in Seattle; he might come to the States after he was done with Europe.

I finished my beer and went to bed.

During the night a girl (the dorm was co-ed) woke me up and asked, very politely, I must say, if I could roll off my back, as my snoring was keeping her awake.

Hostels.

The next morning, I woke up early, or so I thought. It was only seven-thirty, but I missed the first gondola down the mountain and, thus, the first train to Florence.

At eight I got on the gondola, but it was going up. I had to ride it all the way to the top before I could get off at the bottom. Are you kidding me!? It wasn't too bad; I got to see all of the villages at all of the stops. Also, I was in the fucking Swiss Alps, so the scenery wasn't awful.

At the bottom of the mountain—relief.

I got on the circuit bus, the same one I took before, and then onto the privately owned train. At Interlaken I was able to buy some food while I waited for the next train.

I caught that one, to Spiez. From there I hopped on another one to Brig. After about an hour of waiting, I got on the next one to Milan.

What, was that like my sixth fucking transfer today? I didn't remember, nor did I care.

But I was on my way, from the country that gave the world the cuckoo clock, to the country that gave the world the Renaissance.

Thank you, Harry Lime.

10

Italy (part I)

Florence, Pisa, Orvieto, Bagnoregio

OCTOBER 16

The train to Milan was completely full, so I had to stand for half of the two-hour trip. That train, maybe because it was so full, was slow. It was so slow that, once it arrived in Milan, I nearly missed my next transfer.

But those bad times only got worse.

I made the transfer onto the train to Naples, via Florence (my intended destination) but wished I had not. I was so late in boarding that I did not have a seat. But unlike the last segment, where it was for only half the trip, I did not have a seat for the entire three hours of bouncing and battering travel.

Italian trains are too full. Stop overselling them, damn Italians.

At a quarter till six in the evening, after eight transfers, I finally made it to Florence, Italy. The Renaissance. I hoped for a rebirth for my beaten body as well.

After consulting the warnings from the Frommer book (I know, why; it had been extremely unreliable), I expected the Florence train station to be overwhelmed with gypsies, tramps and thieves ready to rob me blind.

Of course, there were none.

I changed some money at the rate of about fifteen hundred lire to one American dollar.

I then turned down a solicitor that offered me a sixty-thousand-lire pension and went to the tourist office. I booked a room, picked up a map (see, I was learning), and headed out into the moped-filled streets of Florence.

All the mopeds reminded me of an old joke.

What do sleeping with a big girl and driving a moped have in common? They're both great to ride until your friends see you.

Those Italians did not seem to mind how dorky they look though.

I soon discovered that, unlike many other European cities, Florence was very compact. In fact, I found my hotel's street with absolutely no problem. I finally did not get lost.

I checked in to the hotel, paid a couple of extra lire for use of the shower, and then went up to my room. Three beds. Will I have to share this with others? I was genuinely worried, so I headed back down to the front desk to ask the manager. I also needed to ask him how to lock the door to the damn room.

My man assured me it was my own room, no sharing. I then thought, maybe I should push all the mattresses together for a jumbo bed.

Although tempting, I did not do that.

After my reverie, he told me the key did not lock the door from the inside, a latch did—no extra charge.

Relieved, I headed out into the early dusk of my first Italian city. I had not eaten since breakfast in Gimmelwald, so that was first on my to-do list. I was glad I liked Italian food—I planned on eating a lot.

But there didn't seem to be a lot of restaurants there. After I walked around for some time, I found one. A pizzeria.

Hooray!

Great food and a lot, just as I had planned.

After that, I was very tired but very sated.

As the bill was a bit higher than I expected, I decided to pay with a credit card. When the server was returning it to me, he saw my name, Michael.

"Michael Corleone!" he exclaimed.

Great, my first night in Italy, and the mob is going to have a contract on me.

To my dismay, the server continued. "The mob is just a business here," he explained as I squirmed.

I now became paranoid and scurried out the door, hoping that Luca Brasi or Sollozzo weren't at a nearby table, ready to follow me and whack me in a back alley.

After this minor excitement, I went back to the hotel, extremely tired but safe from la Cosa Nostra. I fell asleep early with my earplugs in as the street below was a major thoroughfare and very loud.

October 17

Today, I woke up and decided to take a shower (I did pay a bit extra, might as well use it)—my first one in four days. But the door to the shower room was locked with no one inside.

I headed down to the manager again (I am quite sure he was happy to see me again with more issues). I could use another floor's bathroom and shower, he told me.

Surprisingly, he did not seem to be that annoyed with me. I'm sure the poor guy had built up a thick facade dealing with complaining Americans (and Germans) on a regular basis.

I used the other floor's facilities as he suggested. I even shaved for the first time in a week. Now fresh and clean, I went back downstairs to my room and got dressed.

As I was putting on my shoes, it dawned on me why the restroom was locked and had no entrance key that morning. Last night, as I was using the bathroom around midnight, one of the two German girls sharing a room on my floor knocked on the door. I told her it was occupied, and she said something back to me in a huff. After I had returned to my room, she probably went back to the bathroom, grabbed the key, and then stowed it in her room so that only she and her roomie would have access to the facilities. They must have decided that they did not want to share the bathroom and shower.

As I was about to unlock my door to leave, I heard them trudging up the stairs. My suspicions were confirmed when they went directly to the bathroom.

I also heard the key.

Scoundrels!

I quickly devised a plan.

I waited in my room until they were out of the bathroom and back in their room.

Just as I suspected. They left the key in the bathroom door. They didn't care who used it during the day. They would claim it again tonight.

Devious. I could appreciate it.

But I could be devious too.

I stealthily exited my room, went to the bathroom door, and gently locked it.

Locked it? Why?

I locked it so they would have to use the downstairs bathroom as I'd had to.

Oh, yes. I hid the key in my room.

Bring a flashlight when you climb the stairs tonight, ladies.

The ugly American was unleashed in *Firenze*.

After my spy mission, I left the hotel and headed to the Academia. It was about a two-minute walk from where I was staying, so I only got lost for an hour. Just kidding. I found it without any problem, using one of the multitude of maps I picked up earlier.

I expected a huge crowd, but there was none. At first, I thought it was closed. But it was open—it was just that no one was there that early in the day. I walked right in.

Very early, very exceptional Italo-Byzantine and Renaissance art.

As I wandered through the galleries, I turned a corner and, down a long hall, saw Michelangelo's *David*. From that distance he looked both pissed off and worried.

I've been there, Dave.

But before I got to the mammoth masterpiece, I walked past eight unfinished Michelangelo sculptures. Most of those were meant as decorations for some long-forgotten Pope's tomb (I forgot the fellow's name at least). Fuck him. I wondered what they used to decorate his tomb, since those were never completed. Probably something stolen.

Those unfinished works were incredible. They looked like they were in the process of a dynamic metamorphosis; but a transformation that was halted. Time had stopped for those creations, and they would remain in this half sculpture, half rock form for eternity. The viewer sadly understood that the process of creation would never restart.

David. He was next. Huge, incomparable to anything else. The veins in his stone arms looked supple, as if they were pumping blood.

From there, to his meaningful gaze. He looked scared, but also determined.

He would not fail in his mission to kill the giant Goliath.

Perfection.

I walked around the bulletproof glass shield for over twenty minutes, taking in the divine piece. Photographs truly did not do it justice.

After my time in front of *David*, I worked through the rest of the Academia. Early Renaissance art, altarpieces and objects filled the galleries. It reminded me of the old Serbian Orthodox church in Gary, Indiana.

This period of art had never meant much to me. However, as I made my way through the Academia, I felt my appreciation for this era begin to grow. It was breathtaking. These pieces were hundreds of years old. There were hundreds of years of innovation, both artistic and technical, separating the present day from these works. But they achieved their artistic goal, even today, of inspiring the souls of humanity.

The Academia was much more than one—albeit incredible—sculpture.

I exited this transformative building and began to walk to the Basilica of Santa Croce. I was still inspired, so I found the church with no problem. I even stopped for a gelato on the way.

I entered the Catholic church with shorts on, as there was no dress code sign requiring long pants. I did feel a bit odd, though.

The first tomb I came to was that of Michelangelo.

Next was Dante.

A few popes.

Then Machiavelli.

The composer Rossini.

Finally, Galileo.

Are you fucking kidding me? I had never heard of this church before this trip, so I never knew that all of these luminaries (popes, not so much) were entombed there. A humbling experience, to say the least.

As a mass was being conducted, I felt a bit underdressed and decided to leave out of respect. I planned on coming back there with long pants and a camera (which I forgot when I hurriedly exited my room this morning).

I then strolled around the town—Florence! The Medicis!

I decided to scope out some places I would visit tomorrow and Wednesday. It was such a small town that I could do that and still have time to be leisurely.

But, before I started my *passeggiare,* it was time for more pizza. Hot damn, do I love traditional Italian pizza. Who knew it was better than Domino's? Just kidding. Fuck Domino's and their thirty minutes.

My next stop shocked me: I decided to follow Frommer's advice one last time, and I actually found the Tivoli gelateria that the book highly recommended. That was the first time I ate at a place recommended in that book.

Second surprise—it was exceptional. I still say forget Frommer's. One good take did not negate all of the bad.

I finished my gelato and walked some more, the perfect tourist. I arrived at the Baptistry and its venerated doors. Michelangelo himself dubbed them the "Gates of Paradise" because of their splendor. There was a bit of a crowd around them, so I decided to get a better look at them later this week when I had my camera.

Back to the hotel at two thirty in the afternoon. Everything would be closed for a couple of hours for the daily Italian-style siesta. So, I decided to do the same.

I went upstairs to my floor, and, oops, the hotel manager was there letting a middle-aged woman into the shower room. I'd thought it was only myself and the two girls on my floor, but I was wrong. I shouldn't have taken the key. I really screwed with this innocent lady by fucking with those girls.

So I waited for her to finish and then headed to the bathroom. I washed a pair of really stinky shorts. (How did they get that bad?) I kept the key but left the door unlocked.

Relaxing now. After this day filled with Catholic churches and sepulchers, I will rest in peace myself tonight.

October 18

Today I got up early and took a shower. I paid the small extra stipend, so you're damn right I was going to use it. The door was locked, of course, but I had the key. As the shower was a charged commodity here, the management must have to be really vigilant about who used it. Sucked for them.

After all of this shower drama, I decided I'd had enough of these surreptitious, miserly shenanigans. Time for a hotel switch. I saw a tourist office down the street and made that my first stop. But they didn't make reservations.

On the way there I passed the American Express office so, just for the heck of it, I checked Frommer's. Nope, it had its location across town. Frommer's.

I did remember that the train station had a tourist office that made reservations, so I went there. I quickly booked a room that was five thousand lire cheaper (I know, like four dollars, but still).

I then went back to the American Express office (I was on my way back to the old hotel, where I was headed to pick up my pack) and changed some AmEx traveler's checks. The rate and the fees were generous, so I changed enough money for a week.

I then ventured to look for my newly booked hotel. Amazingly, I found it quickly. I say amazingly as, one, I get lost a lot, and, two, it was on a side street, out of the way. I was relieved at that—it was much quieter than the last hotel.

I paid the nice old lady, headed to a nearby grocery, and picked up enough food to last me a few days.

I stored all of it in my new room and then headed to the nearby train station to catch a train to Pisa for a day trip. But before I got on the train (they departed every hour for Pisa), I met two American women.

As we chatted and waited for the train, they quickly became friendly traveling companions. The taller one, Shirley, was very talkative. The short, stocky one, Judy, didn't say much. Abbott and Costello in reverse. They both worked for the U.S. Defense Department as auditors, or so they said—I was sure they were spies. Just kidding.

Shirley had been traveling since early September. Before heading off with Judy, she spent twenty-two days on a Rick Steves' tour.

The three of us talked for the one-hour trip through central Italy. Once we got to Pisa, we all left the train together, with Shirley in the lead. She had been to Pisa before and knew the quickest bus routes to get to the tourist sites.

We bought our bus tickets and boarded the number one for a ten-minute ride. At the last stop, we disembarked. All I could see was a large, domed *duomo*. We walked toward it, and there it was, my first glimpse of the Leaning Tower of Pisa. A very strange sight.

Again, as I keep saying, I never thought I would have any reason for coming here and seeing this magnificent, yet odd, building.

The three of us took our time walking, taking in all of the tacky souvenir stands that lined the streets. As we were screwing around, I kept glancing at the strange sight. The tower sat at such a precarious angle. The damn thing looked like it could topple at any moment, taking a few tourists (and a bar across the street) along with it.

I had a feeling the city fathers must have felt the same way. There were literally tons of weights stacked on the rising side. Those were certainly just delaying its inevitable collapse.

When you looked at it closely, you could see that it was constructed differently; its upper section was different from its lower. It seemed that during its construction, it had already started to lean, so the builders tried to correct it by making the top section perpendicular to the ground rather than following the building's already fierce angle. The correction failed.

We stuck around, tower-watching as well as people-watching. We saw numerous people do the ubiquitous holding the tower pose, not caring how stupid they looked.

After some laughs, we bought ice cream and then walked the streets of Pisa. On our walk, we saw a little kid nearly get nailed by a car, along with some "Yankee Go Home" graffiti and a few Soviet-era hammer and sickle posters. Also, a lot of dirt and depression.

Besides the heavily touristed area, Pisa was a filthy, depressing little town. I had debated whether to stay overnight there. I am glad I decided against it. Maybe Italy should start shoveling some of their tourist tax dollars into helping this city's outlying areas.

Just a thought—European Socialism ain't perfect, I guess.

After our dismal trek through town, my traveling trio found the number one bus to the train station and then hightailed it out of the city.

On the ride back, I read about my upcoming trip to Rome while the girls played with an adorable three-year-old boy.

When we arrived back in Florence, the three of us made plans to meet at seven to go out for dinner. I had a few hours to kill, so I went back to my new hotel and began working out some sentences in Serbian I could say to Jovo regarding my attempted trip to Yugoslavia. I studied the phrase book and wrote down some rudimentary phrases that I hoped he would understand.

My plan will be to meet him at Keleti train station, track one, in Budapest at eleven in the morning on October 31. From there, we will drive to Sombor, crossing the border on the way, somewhere I hoped there would be no problems.

So, before meeting the girls for dinner, I needed to find a place where I could make a long-distance call. Reluctantly, I conferred with Frommer's, which said the main post office was the place. I walked twenty minutes there, but Frommer's was wrong again.

Fuck Frommer's.

I decided that would be the last time I consulted that trash publication. (It was not. I continued to go back to it like an insane person).

At the post office, they did steer me to the train station, where I would be able to make a long-distance call.

Once I arrived at the appropriate desk at the train station, I saw that the post office was correct. I got a phone booth and made my call.

Holy shit, it worked—I reached my cousin Jovo.

But my joy was short-lived. Hardly anything was understood by either of us during the six-thousand-lire call except "Nikola y Jagoda," (my Uncle Nick and Teta Jean). As I understood him, he wanted me to contact them in the States and have them relay back to him what I wanted to tell him. Not a bad idea, Jovo.

I followed his suggestion and called my aunt and uncle. Teta Jean answered and I was able to tell her the whole plan while she took notes. I then asked her to call Jovo and relay the message. I told her I would call her back in twenty minutes for his reply.

I stayed in the booth, pretending to use the phone. In reality I was killing time and taking in the atmosphere of the Florence train station. It smelled like dill pickles—usually yum, but odd for a train station. Also, garbage was everywhere. I guess I was in too much of a hurry earlier to really grasp how nasty this place was. And, my, it was nasty.

I called my aunt back after the requisite time. She told me it would work; it was a doable plan and Jovo had agreed to everything I had laid out.

I then asked her about the money. She said they had collected quite a bit, nearly ten thousand dollars so far. They would be wiring it to me in about a week. It would be in two separate American Express accounts, both under my name.

Now I had to rearrange my schedule a bit. But, more importantly, I needed to collect the cash I would be bringing (smuggling) across a war zone border.

Why was I doing this again?

Kicks, baby!

No. I reminded myself that, despite the possible danger, I was doing this to honor my late father. It was his side of the family that was suffering through this stupid conflict.

Shit, I then realized it was close to seven and I had a date with two, count 'em, two ladies.

Ménage à trois, and this wasn't even Amsterdam!

Absolutely not.

I walked to the church where Judy, Shirley, and I planned to meet. They were right on time; their hotel was next door to the church.

They recommended a famous restaurant, Da Pinocchio, that I had never heard of. This landmark restaurant was on a busy, main thoroughfare and filled with tourists. Included in the horde was a large group of Americans, all in their seventies. Loud, obnoxious, unsatisfied, ethno-centric fun. They truly put the *glee* in *ugly American*.

The three of us took a seat away from that group and ordered off the menu *tourista* to save some money. Small portions, but not bad.

After dinner we strolled *la dolce vita* and then called it an early night. The three of us got along very well. So well, in fact, that we made plans to meet for dinner again the next day. Same time, same church.

I guess I just can't keep the ladies away...

October 19

Today, I woke up early.

I could not figure out how to get the hot water to work in the shower, so I just cleaned up, via Irish shower, in the sink. Why are the bathrooms so difficult to decrypt in Italy?

Oh well, today would be a big tourist day. Since I would be heading into Catholic churches, I made sure to wear long pants, even if they were a bit, well, ripe. I would have to reassess their condition after a very hot, Italian day of perspiration. I hoped they wouldn't be so foul by tonight that I'd have to discard them.

My first goal was to repeat one of my visits from the other day. So, I bought some film and headed to Santa Croce. I photographed the resting sites of Michelangelo, Dante, Machiavelli, and Galileo. I skipped the popes.

My next stop would be the Uffizi, "The Palace of Offices," Florence's most famous art museum.

After waiting in a short line, I headed in. My first destination: a Michelangelo oil. Apparently, I didn't get enough of him at the Academia two days ago.

I did not note the name of the piece, but it was colorful, almost fauvist. Cartoony in a strange way.

From there I ventured through the galleries, past Roman sculptures of emperors and gods (the former believing they were the latter in most cases).

I arrived at a room filled with sketches. Sketches by some of the greatest artists in history—Michelangelo, Botticelli, Raphael, and Leonardo da Vinci.

One of the da Vincis was simply amazing. Created with a pencil, it was of a black cloth on a black background—all done with shading. It looked like a photograph. In fact, it was about the size of a thirty-five-millimeter photo. After getting in as close as possible, I saw that the detail was incredible. It still looked like a film-captured image.

"He's the devil! Burn him!" I thought with a grin.

From there, the Byzantine era. OK, all right. Religious art, icons, and altarpieces. Flat, until the arrival of Giotto and his contemporaries.

This proto-Renaissance art began the move to a more dimensional perspective portrayal of the subject. Shadows, diminishing lines, and faint backgrounds all added to the three-dimensional illusion. Painted, vaulted arched churches began to have volume. Even facial features became more realistic, no longer simply flat profiles on a two-dimensional canvas.

Next, the inevitable. Drum roll... The star of the show—the reason why folks have been flocking to this obscure little town on the Arno for five hundred years—the Renaissance itself!

The Botticelli Room.

My heart skipped a beat as I entered the massive room with his most famous works.

I saw the *Birth of Venus* first. I believe that if I saw the real birth of the goddess, it would have had less effect on me.

It was much larger than I had imagined.

It brings the viewer into a dynamic state; the movement of the water, the wind, and the peripheral characters—all coalesced into the foaming birth of the goddess herself.

I turned my head and there was *La Primavera* (the *Allegory of Spring*) in the same fucking room!

A celebration of fertility. A blue figure on the right, winter, is desperately trying to hold back a spring cherub. But to no avail. Spring, fertility, will win the day, always.

As I've said countless times during this trip, I never thought I would have a reason to be there to see these immaculate creations.

I continued through the Renaissance. I realized that I was taken by Filippo Lippi's work of the late fifteenth century. I made a note to research him more when I was able.

I passed two more "minor" Leonardo Da Vinci oils, and I was spent.

The Uffizi was marvelous. Da Vinci, Michelangelo, Botticelli, Raphael, Rome. Not a bad collection of office art.

I dragged my body outside as I was determined to be the *übermensch* tourist in this over-the-top city.

Beware! Here comes Tourist Boy, heading for the Pitti Palace via the Ponte Vecchio Bridge, the only medieval bridge to survive WWII. Today, the bridge is filled with tourists like me, now at war with the street hawkers.

I arrived at the Palace but didn't feel like paying, as I was a bit burned out—so much for the *übermensch*.

I instead picked up a *USA Today*. The White Sox lost in the playoffs. Oh well, Chicago baseball sucks anyway. *Go Cubs.*

I read that the United States was sending troops into Haiti now. More military action, as we'd just pulled out of Somalia. I was sure that most of the American people would fully embrace this new front—the sunshine patriots. With the war in Yugoslavia heating up, I figured that would be the next place for American ground troops. I just hoped to get there to help Jovo and the rest of my extended family fulfill their basic needs before that happened.

I journeyed back to my hotel to rest, read, and write (what I am doing at this moment). It was still early, as I planned on going back out after a brief *riposo*.

Back out on the street. To the Medici-Riccardi Palace. There was no entry fee (man, the Medicis would be pissed), so I went in. There was not a lot there. An oil painting by Lippi, who I now quite enjoyed, was great to see. There was a beautiful, domed room, which I snapped a picture of.

I stayed there for only twenty minutes or so. Then I walked past another repeat site, the Baptistry and the *Gates of Paradise*. I snapped a shot there as well. Next, I was off to the Duomo and another picture.

I then journeyed to the fourteenth century Orsanmichele but only popped my head in as a mass was being conducted. I do not want to burst into Catholic flames.

I then returned to the Baptistry. The crowd had thinned, so I was able to get in. I took a picture of the huge domed room that was filled with art. However, I did not stay long, as I did not require a baptism, nor did I have a towel.

At that point, I concluded that my sightseeing in Florence was over. I was saturated, mind, body, and soul. I was relieved that I would be taking it a bit easier tomorrow before I hit the road to Rome.

I decided to go to the train station to confirm my trip for tomorrow. The first clerk I asked said no, there was no train from Florence to Orvieto tomorrow. I didn't panic. I was learning that traveling in

Europe was like getting a diagnosis from a doctor: never trust the first opinion.

I went to another clerk and asked the very same question. Of course there was a train to Orvieto tomorrow, he said. It was only a two-hour trip; it was very close.

Ah, Europe.

Ah, Italy.

At this moment I am back in my hotel room, airing out the socks, shoes, pants, and shirt that I wore today. I will soon be putting them back on as I have a dinner date (remember my two Pisa companions) again tonight at seven. I should be freshly aired out and at minimal odor by then. Still, all in all, feeling pretty well.

October 20

After I finished writing yesterday, I went to meet the girls, Trudi (not Judy, oops) and Shirley. We met at the church and then went back to their room so they could pick up their laundry. (They had someone else do their laundry? What a novel concept!).

From there, we set off to another restaurant of their choosing. Another highly touristed restaurant that is.

There, we got to experience what I understand is a worldwide phenomenon—an asshole server.

As soon as we entered the restaurant, the server, our new star, told us he wanted to sit down but couldn't because of "you customers."

He continued, "Thank God, tomorrow off."

Why was he speaking in English?

He was a prick, that's why, and he wanted us to know it.

And he was just getting started. Shirley began a conversation with an American couple at the table next to ours. Server Guy made some smartass comments that I did not hear. But Shirley sure did, and she got pissed. I think she wanted to kick his ass right there. We calmed her down and just waited for him to do something else.

He did not disappoint.

He was taking the order of another English-speaking customer when he said, "No, I'm a-sorry. I won't bring you that."

For us, it just got worse. Fuck-o brought us no bread as well as no dessert—which we'd paid for.

As time passed, we saw the jackass start an argument with his manager and the restaurant's cashier.

During their fracas, the cashier sent me a glance that could only be interpreted as, "I know. He's a cock."

After some time, the manager, reading the room, sent us a round of drinks and some cookies. He knew he had an asshole working for him.

Then, obviously sent by the manager, the dickhead came by and, very insincerely, apologized. I was sure his manager said do it or you're out of a job.

But Assface was not done! He still intended to fuck with us. He brought us the bill, and it was way too high. Yes, we checked it. we'd had a suspicion he would try to cheat us.

Not today, fuckhead. We called Cock-face over, and he brought us another bill, apologizing. We checked it again, and again, he'd tried to overcharge us. Wow!

Finally, he got it correct. We paid and left him with nothing but a "fuck-you" and finger flip out the door.

After this unfortunate dinner, we went back to the girls' hotel and chatted for about a half an hour.

Shirley confessed that she would be spending about eight thousand dollars on this trip. Damn, I'd be spending much less than half of that. Now I didn't feel so bad about my few splurges.

I said good-bye to the girls, headed back to my humble one-star hotel, and crashed.

Today, I woke up and desperately needed a shower. I found the hotel manager and got the shower key from her. There was no drama as I casually took what was my third shower in nine days. Whew. I felt a lot better.

I left the hotel a bit earlier than I needed and headed to the waiting room at the train station. There, I met a middle-aged man from Portland, Oregon. We began to chat about basketball, languages, trips, etc. He told me that his mother and grandmother used to run a boarding house in Crawfordsville, Indiana. He believed they used to house students who attended Indiana University.

Small world, I guess.

He told me his son lived in Alaska. He then gave me his son's name and the name of the Podunk town he lived in.

I would not be going there.

After some time, I boarded my train and took an uneventful trip south, down the Italian peninsula. I read and watched the wind pass the window.

Once in Orvieto, I located a small, cheapie hotel, booked a room, stored my pack, and hit the streets.

My first stop was the bus station. I planned to take a bus to the small village of Civita di Bagnoregio, one of the hidden "backdoor" gems discussed in Rick Steves' book.

Once I got the bus ticket, I could not figure out where to catch the damn bus—there were no signs pointing the way. But I asked a nice little redheaded Italian girl, and she gingerly pointed me the way.

On the bus I quickly realized I'd boarded a local. It was going all over the place, making numerous stops. Oh, I then realized it was not just a city/regional transport, but a school bus filled with children as well. Wonderful.

I finally made it up the Umbrian hill to Bagnoregio, which was more like a small city than a town. But my goal was not there, but the little village of Civita. However, there were no signs marking the way. After asking a few locals, I was able to find my way to this "backdoor" site without getting lost.

The tiny little village was about a half-hour walk away from the center of Bagnoregio. Before one entered the town proper of Civita di Bagnoregio, though, one had to traverse a quarter-mile, winding bridge. The village sat atop a small mesa amidst the Umbrian hills.

It looked like one of those old Christian cartoons where people were lined up to enter a walled city.

I arrived at the mesa and then at a tunnel leading to an archway entrance. Once inside (I was careful not to step on one of the countless feral cats), I was immediately in the main square. This square had truly been lost to history. I half expected a man to be ringing a cowbell and yelling for people to bring out their dead.

The small square was surrounded by medieval rock buildings. It felt like time had stopped in the thirteenth century. It looked like nothing had changed for hundreds of years. The main street (the only path I would refer to as such) was just a small—albeit wider than the others—lane. There were ancient homes of rock and mud, storage areas that resembled prison cells, and just a scattering of scurrying inhabitants.

I walked through the strange little anachronism and reached the end of the path in about five minutes. There stood an elderly woman with a bent arm and hand. With her good hand she waved me on. She wanted me to come into her garden and see the "panorama," as she kept repeating.

I judged my environment and figured this would be a safe stop.

I doubted that she was the bait for an international kidnapping syndicate.

It was a beautiful view from the "panorama" of her garden.

How lovely for this kind woman to offer this to wide-eyed tourists.

I got ready to leave, and she tried to sell me an old book of scraped parchment for ten thousand lire.

No thanks.

But then the hustler came out. I owed her one thousand lire for the use of her garden for "panorama."

I started to laugh. I'd just got beat by her. I paid her the equivalent of sixty cents.

Swindled in Civita di Bagnoregio.

I left the player to work another sucker and started down another, smaller path to exit the city. To my surprise, there was a rudimentary souvenir stand built into one of the homes. Thankfully, it was not open today, or I probably would have been worked over by another one of the village grifters.

I left the mesa and arrived back in Bagnoregio and the twentieth century. I started to hurry, as I knew the bus I needed to catch left the top of this hill at 2:25 P.M.

Oh shit, it was two thirty. Did I miss it?

I did. But I figured there would be another running soon. I found the bus schedule and saw that the next one was due to leave down the mountain at 5:25—in three hours.

"Whoa," I said out loud, as two people turned to look at me. Well, I was really going to experience the town of Bagnoregio.

After cursing some under my breath, I weighed my options. What the hell, I figured. I'd try to hitchhike a ride down to Orvieto.

I walked about ten minutes to the outskirts of town and then onto the main road. There, I tried my best with my thumb. I would have tried another way, but I did not have the legs of Claudette Colbert.

I kept trying for an hour or so, but nearly everyone pointed to the left, down the road. I finally realized that there were several other small towns in that direction and the cars were going to those towns, not all the way down to Orvieto.

So, sullen and defeated, I walked back into Bagnoregio and found a store. There I picked up a liter of water and sat with a couple of locals to watch a soccer match in absolute silence.

I took my leave of those sports fanatics and explored more of this Umbrian town. It was beautiful. High in the green and sunny hills of central Italy. It was the former land of the Etruscans, just bordering Tuscany.

As it neared five, I started to make my way back to the center of town so I would not miss the next bus. I grabbed a seat on a park bench as two Americans passed by. They took a seat, and we began to talk. They were from Chicago, very nice, and pleasant to talk to on that warm day.

The couple, Jim and Karen, told me that they were taken by the Civita hustler as well, paying her the equivalent of about a dollar.

With that kind of take, how did she sleep at night?

Finally, the bus came. On time. Thank you, Mussolini?

I did not take the bus all the way down to my hotel, as I wanted to see the upper part of Orvieto. There was a gondola that would take me down to my hotel after I had explored a bit there. The gondolas left every half an hour until eight-thirty, so I decided I would kill about an hour poking around.

I looked for and found the restaurant in upper Orvieto that both my friend back home and Jim and Karen recommended.

But I shocked myself and decided that I was not quite ready for dinner.

I popped in to a few shops and had some rudimentary conversations with the small city shopkeepers. I'm sure I disappointed all of them, as I bought absolutely nothing.

On time, I returned to the gondola, bought a ticket, and got in the swaying car.

As I sat waiting for the descent, trying not to throw up, a younger fellow got on. We were the only two passengers, so we chatted. I found out that he was a private in the Italian Army, stationed in Orvieto. When he was younger, he'd lived in New York City, in the Bronx. His father still did.

Wow, imagine that. An Italian in New York City? Now I've heard everything.

Nice kid. We talked the whole way down and shook hands when we reached the base of the hill.

I headed back to my little hotel and figured it was time to eat. I asked the desk clerk where I could get a pizza.

As I was getting this local man's valued recommendation, a pesky, nervous American woman began yelling at me about the place where she ate earlier that day.

She approached us, and I saw that she was so amped up that she was trembling. I knew this wasn't Amsterdam, but I suspected there was another junkie in my midst.

As the clerk began to laugh at her, I got a bit freaked out. I decided it would be best to go back to my room and wait for her to leave.

Nope. As I headed up the stairs, she followed me. I went into my room, shut my door, and then made doubly sure it was locked.

Yep, she was nuts. She stayed just outside of my door, talking to me as if I were still in front of her.

Then, the lights went out in the whole building.

What the fuck?!

I gathered myself, unlocked the door, and stepped out—I had to see what was going on. Also, I figured that if it came down to it, fuck-it, she was a little chick. I'd smack her upside the head if I had to defend myself.

As I stepped out of my room, I saw that the crazy lady was as mystified as me. Just as I was about to speak, the hotel clerk came flying up the stairs. He went directly to the shower/bathroom and knocked on the door. A half-naked Frenchman peeked his head out, and the clerk told him to turn the switch off and on.

That restarted the whole system, and the lights came back on.

Apparently, the electrical system in the hotel was so fucked up that some switches can overload and shut the entire system. There are other switches, like the one in the bathroom, that seemed to be master reset controls.

What the hell, Italy? Time to revamp the construction racket and get some decent laws passed.

But one good thing: Nervous Nancy, the creepy pest, was freaked out as well. She returned to her room, finally leaving me alone.

I felt rejuvenated for some reason. Sure, I might die in an electrical fire tonight, but now it was time for pizza!

Yay, me!

The clerk sent me to a pizzeria near the gondola. I went inside and saw my old soldier buddy finishing off his dinner. We briefly talked, but he had to catch a train, so we said farewell one last time.

I ordered some food, took a seat, and people-watched. The little place had a lot of atmosphere but never got too crowded—just a steady stream of local characters and tourists in and out. Some got a bite to eat, some a drink. Some just came to watch and cheer on the ubiquitous soccer on the televisions.

The pizza was cheap. It was tasty. I was happy.

I returned to the electrical trap of a hotel and went back up to my room. Thankfully, no problems with Henrietta Heroin this time.

As I write this, I am sitting on my comfy twin bed. I have prepared for the morning with a newly washed pair of socks and a newly washed pair of boxers resting on the back of the desk chair. They are patiently waiting for me to put them on fresh in the morning. My stinky towel is airing out on the window ledge, and my Polish shoes are unlaced and wide open, airing out on the ledge as well. The fine life of travel.

11

Italy (part II), Vatican City State

Rome, Vatican City, Naples, Pompeii, Venice

October 21

I got up late and showered. I was hesitant to touch the light switch, but I braved it out. Nothing disastrous happened. I then went to the lobby to check out. It was raining like I had never seen it rain before. As I waited in the lobby for it to let up, I checked peripherally for Nervous Nancy, but she never showed.

The rain never eased, so I decided it was time to run the two hundred or so yards to the train station; my train would be leaving soon.

As I sat in the station, writing about yesterday, the American couple I'd met in Bagnoregio, Jim and Karen, arrived. We talked, killing time until the train arrived. Once it did, we had to hop on quickly; Orvieto was just a stopover on the way to Rome. Unfortunately, they had first-class tickets and I was in steerage.

Please, don't sink in this rain like the Titanic.

It was an uneventful ride, and we arrived in Rome in about an hour.

Yes, I was in Rome, the Eternal City, the city of kings and emperors; popes and peasants; Mussolini and Fellini; Sophia Loren and Isabela Rossellini.

Being a jaded traveler, I knew to go directly to the tourist office to book a cheapskate room. I was in line for over twenty minutes before I got the bad news. At the window, I found out that there were no vacant, affordable places in the highly touristed areas. But there were a lot of cheap rooms in the shitty parts of town.

I had to quickly assess my options. I hesitantly decided to accept a pension that the girl behind the desk told me was not in a great part of town. I took the slip but did not put down any money to reserve the room.

Next, I found the Metro stop in the station. The Metro was only two lines, so it was a snap to master. The subway arrived at my stop, and I exited the tunnel into a magnificent rainstorm. I had absolutely no clue where I was or which way to walk. I began to wander in the deluge, a rider in the storm.

It was terrible—I was carrying a cold, wet, heavy pack, and there were no hotels in sight. I decided to forget the pension that was booked and wander to another, better neighborhood to find a place on my own.

After some time, I found a four-star hotel. I was not too proud to tell them they were much too expensive and request that they point me to a three star. They happily obliged. I figured they didn't want some water-drenched punk besmirching their lovely little palace anyway.

The four-star did do me right, though. They gave me fantastic directions to a very suitable three-star hotel. I asked the desk person their terms. Ninety-five dollars a night, which included an en suite room and an all-you-can-eat breakfast buffet.

I inquired about what kind of food they would serve at this "Grand Buffet." I had seen twelve-course buffets in which one course consisted of a pat of butter, the next a thimble of jelly, and so on. He assured me it was legit, and I somewhat believed him.

So, now I had to rationalize this expenditure. So far, I had spent way less than I'd budgeted. On top of that, I would spend no money for a week if I could make it to Jovo's in Yugoslavia. I hadn't accumulated any substantial credit card debt. I didn't want to stay in the cheap places in Rome—they were way too seedy. And, after all, I was in Rome, one of the most historic places on Earth.

I eventually decided that I would take the room just to get out of the storm. I told myself I would find another place tomorrow.

I rode the open, art deco elevator to my "luxury" room, still not completely satisfied with my decision.

Maybe I am just a cheapskate?

I got to my room, which was small but clean. And: it had a bathroom inside the room.

Not down the hall. *Inside* the room!

But it was a strange bathroom set-up, as that room was quite tiny. When the shower was on, water ran over the whole room, toilet, sink and all. There was no separate area to shower. The one saving grace was a steel cover over the toilet paper dispenser protecting it from the water flow of the shower.

After that odd discovery, I set my alarm for later that night, intending to call my mom for her opinion regarding my decision.

I put my bag down and then headed out into the streets of Rome. The rain had let up, so I could take my time and stroll a bit more easily. As I made my way to the Tiber River, I checked a map to see the location of my hotel. I found its position by luck; I truly had no idea where I was. I was happy to see that I was in a surprisingly good locale, about a ten-minute walk from St. Peter's Basilica in Vatican City.

I crossed the Tiber and arrived at Augustus's tomb and the Ara Pacis. The hall that housed the Ara Pacis was closed, but the building was made of glass, so I could see inside. The altar, dedicated to the goddess of peace, and which actually ushered in about two hundred years of Roman "peaceful" dominance, was clearly visible. I briefly studied this structure as an undergrad, so it was very gratifying to see.

But I began to fear that I was becoming a bit oversaturated with tourism. Maybe the day had simply gotten off to a rough start, but I was feeling lethargic, jaded at what I suspected the rest of the trip would hold for me—especially if I failed in my quest to reach Yugoslavia.

I honestly hoped that this feeling passed; I really wanted to appreciate Rome. I was determined that the splendor and grandeur of this incredible city that gave birth to a magnificent empire would not be lost on me.

I took a deep breath and tried to find my center, my soul, and carried on.

I continued my trek, careful to follow the map. I arrived at the Pantheon, which I'd studied in the same class as the Ara Pacis. Frankly, it was amazing to see how large it was. If I remember correctly, it was the largest domed structure in the world until the Houston Astrodome was completed in 1968. This place was completed in 125 AD!

It was strange to see that it was located in a neighborhood, surrounded by other buildings. I entered the ancient marvel and stood inside, looking up and gawking at its glory.

It was astounding that this could have been built two thousand years ago, I thought, as I took a few pictures.

Then I noticed that the Catholics had appropriated this pantheon meant for all gods and turned it into a church for only their jealous God. Yes, the Pantheon was now a Catholic church.

The damned monolithic Catholic church take and take, never fully sated in their lust for wealth and power. The greed of this "Universal" organization will never stop impressing (and depressing) me.

I was still jaded, I guess. Time to move on.

I found a pizzeria in one of the many neighborhood storefronts overlooking the Pantheon. Like an alcoholic with a drink, I needed a pizza to settle down and relax my spirit. So, I got a pizza with everything, which, here in Rome, I guess included canned corn.

Better than moonshine.

After my corny pizza I walked to the Trevi Fountain. It was much larger than I'd anticipated. Majestic carvings and a horde of tourists. I did not stay long, and I did not throw a coin in the fountain. I guess I will not be returning to Rome.

The Roman Forum was next.

At this point, I am going to stop writing. I am just not feeling it. I want to be able to express what I felt properly, but right now I just can't seem to find that groove. Maybe it's the length of travel, maybe the room, maybe the fear of failing at my task, but something is keeping me from feeling it. I will be back to finish soon.

October 21
(continued)

Alright, I am feeling a bit better, so I am ready to finish yesterday.

I walked to the Forum, the center of the ancient Roman world, which I also studied in a Roman culture class my sophomore year. I honestly did not remember much about the Forum from that class (except that Romans "dry cleaned" their togas with varying solutions of urine), so I had to consult a pamphlet which explained all the sections.

Ruins is the perfect word to describe the Forum today. It was difficult to grasp its former scope and splendor. But I spent quite some time there in the dreary rain, trying to imagine what it looked like with thousands of Romans milling about, shopping, worshipping, eating, and just generally fucking around.

From the Forum I walked down along the crazy busy Roman streets to the Colosseum. Again, tremendous—the Romans did not do anything small. I must say, it was more impressive than the Eiffel Tower and nearly ten times as old. And, unlike the Forum, it looked exactly as I had pictured it in my mind.

I snapped a photo and walked in. I noticed that the floor had been removed, and the various tunnels that were used for the events were visible. Animals and people were once shuttled around in those depths, getting in position to rise to the surface to satisfy the Roman crowds. Usually satisfying their blood lust, but satisfying them, nonetheless.

I remembered from the Roman culture course that the empire hired several builders to construct this mammoth monument. One's bid was considerably less than all the others. The area where that builder worked is the only area that has collapsed. His shitty workmanship was still on display after two millennia. I guess the axiom has always been true: you get what you pay for.

I took a few more pictures and then found a seat in the mammoth arena. I spent a lot of time there, imagining what it was like to be in the teeming masses, in a full crowd of toga-wearing Romans. I conjured up screaming crowds eating the ancient Roman equivalent of hot dogs and Cracker Jack. Thumbs up or down? Praise the gods with sacrifice!

The rain started to pick up again, so I decided to make my way back to the hotel. It was only a drizzle, so I figured I would walk the hour or so back. I wanted to experience the entirety of Rome. I made a few stops early in my walk, picking up another map and another small book detailing more of the sites. Those would be helpful in getting a better understanding of what I would be looking at.

As I thought that, walking in the light sprinkle, the deluge began. I mean it began raining hard and it showed no signs of letting up. Buckets of water from Neptune's seas and bolts of lightning from Jupiter's wrath kind of weather.

But ha! Fuck you, pagan gods. I had my defense against you, a good old twentieth century umbrella. So, with my sturdy vinyl armor, I decided, screw-it, I'm still going to check out some sites.

I crossed the Tiber and saw the enormous Castel Sant'Angelo, built by the Emperor Hadrian. I even stopped in the torrent to take a quick picture of this cylindrical landmark that was built as a mausoleum but has been used as a circus, a fortress, a hideout for popes, and now a museum.

I continued on my walk, stepping it up as it was getting dark. I had a lot of trouble with getting lost in the daylight, so God only knew what would happen if I got lost at night. I'd probably end up in Carthage.

I finally arrived at my three-star hotel and realized I was soaked—literally soaked through all of my clothing, underwear and all.

I guessed I didn't have to do laundry now?

I called my girlfriend, Carly, and we chatted for some time. Then I wrote in this old journal. That was when I had to stop writing and regroup yesterday. Remembering what I had just gone through, I see why I had lost my "groove."

Next, I set my alarm for eleven at night so I could call my mother at a decent hour in her time zone. Then I went to bed earlier than normal which was fine as it would end this rather dismal day.

The alarm did not go off—one fucking job, and it failed. But for some reason I awoke at two in the morning and called my mom. She allayed some of my monetary concerns.

The trip was almost complete, she reassured me. I'd spent much less than expected; charge the rest. Don't worry, get the experience and see my goals to the end.

All good advice, repeating what I knew to be true. I only needed to hear it from another, trusted person.

She also told me there was some legal paperwork waiting for me to sign regarding the sale of the business.

Finally, she told me that all was set for the money to be wired to me. They would send it tomorrow, as planned. There would be two separate accounts, each with five thousand dollars for me to exchange for hard currency.

I called Carly again. She told me some bad news. The Chicago radio duo that I grew up listening to, Steve Dahl and Garry Meier, had split up, called it quits. That made me sad. I had listened to their radio foolishness every day after school. Seven years ago, I would have thought the world was coming to an end. But now? Oh well, as I was learning, easy come, easy go; nothing lasts forever.

Not even Rome.

October 22

I woke up surprisingly early and got dressed. As today would be church day, I would be sporting long pants.

I headed down to the dining room for the "Grand Buffet" I was promised. My hesitancy was misplaced, as it was truly a grand buffet. Damn, those Italians could cook! I ate a lot—probably my best meal in three weeks. Also, I was aware that I had already paid for this meal, so I loaded up. So much so that I planned on not buying lunch.

It was time for the Vatican. It was nearby, so I was confident I wouldn't get lost.

I got lost immediately.

I had to ask two people for directions before I got situated and finally found the entrance to this (like Monaco) political anomaly, this strange little country in a city. This one was not run by kings and former actress/princesses but by Popes. I was not expecting a progressive experience.

The first thing I saw in this country was St. Peter's Basilica. I took a picture.

I would be returning there, but my first stop would be the Vatican Museum.

On my way, I saw that this country, Vatican City, was surrounded by a huge wall, three times the size of the Berlin Wall. Why did the church do this? Invaders, perhaps? But why was it still there? I thought religion was intended to comfort people, to give them a place, to extend hope. But I saw that the Catholic church, in its universal wisdom, had decided that power and glory for the clerical elite was the only goal. They had placed great barriers and hoarded precious treasures from countless cultures, all to satisfy their lust for power and purse.

I truly did not understand how visitors could see those grand buildings, that stolen art, and those daunting walls and feel anything but contempt. But they did not. I believe a lot of people rationalized those riches. A lot of people saw this accumulation as a sign that God had shone his light down on this, his universal faith.

That's a lot of bullshit, and so is the Roman Catholic Church. Christianity, in the early days, was intended for the meek, the poor, that whole camel through the eye of a needle thing. It was beyond any doubt that now, logically or emotionally, the church of power-hungry elites had lost sight of that initial ethos.

The church leaders, from the time of Constantine to the present, have not had their hearts aimed at the poor nor the afterlife—never mind the worship of God or Christ. They worship only weight and wealth. Earthly weight and earthly wealth.

Separate the church leaders from the common horde and sell everlasting life. What a racket—give us your money or spend eternity in hell. The church exploits the most basic human emotions, especially guilt, to satisfy their ends.

The church is worse than the Mafia. The Mafia will just kill you, not damn your soul to everlasting torment. Perhaps that is why the Mafia started in Italy; it used the church as an example.

After that aside, I certainly won't be suffering from any stigmata. But I had to write that. It had been swelling up in me since I entered that place.

Anyway.

The museum had an expensive entry fee, but it was filled with classic, world-famous art and artifacts, so I paid at the kiosk. Although I was a bit tired of museums, I did look forward to this one. I was especially drawn to the slew of signs that announced what awaited me at the end of the tour, the Sistine Chapel.

But those Sistine Chapel signs seemed to lead the visitor in all sorts of random directions. Maybe that was a way to disperse people and thin out the crowds that inexorably were headed to only see the Chapel? Who knows, as I was there to see the place in its entirety. I would get to the Sistine Chapel when I got to the Sistine Chapel.

There were some truly legendary works there: da Vinci's *Saint Jerome in the Wilderness*, Raphael's *Transfiguration*, the ancient *Laocoön and His Sons*, and countless others by artists from Caravaggio to Titian.

There was even art from the modern era. I was quite surprised to see an oil from the German expressionist Emil Nolde.

I reached the end of the museum proper and arrived at the Sistine Chapel.

The Sistine Chapel.

Despite my earlier thoughts regarding this iniquitous setting, this chapel was beyond my expectations. Describing it as *incredible* or *beautiful* does not give do the justice it deserves.

Michelangelo, forced by the church to complete it at an advanced age, did some pretty fucking amazing work. It was by far the largest, maybe even the greatest work of art that I had ever seen.

Paid for and hoarded by the Catholic Church.

I strained my head for a good bit of time. I also referred to my pamphlet guide so I could better understand each individual part.

I left dazed and confused from the art and the loss of blood to my cricked neck.

As soon as I left, I got lost.

Yes, I got lost in the smallest country on earth.

I asked a misguided bride of God the earthly way to St. Peter's Basilica, and she pointed me the way out of force of habit.

A nun and a pun.

When I got inside the basilica, I realized that it was a massive space.

Disgust washed over me again, but I still checked my palms for bleeding. Padre Pio will have no competition from this sinner.

I strolled through the church. I saw Bernini's massive altar and people giving confession.

I watched them and thought, "I don't know if, as Marx wrote, religion is the opiate of the masses. But I am sure that the Catholic church is the sword that both keeps them at bay and then shovels in their wealth."

Time to leave this odd little country before I burst into flames.

I continued back to my hotel to catch an hour's nap and say one hundred rosaries (just kidding).

I awoke and continued on with church day. There were three more churches on my agenda, all with some type of Christian artifact housed in them.

My first stop in the second round was the Basilica Papale di Santa Maria Maggiore. There, I had come to see what sat in an urn underneath the main altar. The relics were pieces of the crib, the manger, of Jesus Christ. I snapped a picture.

Unbeknownst to me, there was another piece there that I was interested in: Michelangelo's *Pietà*. The famous sculpture of the Virgin Mary holding her son, who had just been crucified. Although the artist created the work when he was quite young, it was still remarkable. The Christ figure was so small, dominated by the figure of the Virgin. It was stunning to see in real life and not just as a picture in a book.

My next stop was the Basilica di San Pietro in Vincoli. There were two sights there that I was interested in. But on my way, I passed by a nasty park. The smell of excrement filled the Roman air. *La dolce vita* it was not.

After clearing my nose, I arrived at the basilica. The first site I saw was the Michelangelo (damn, that guy was everywhere) sculpture of Moses. This was the piece that depicted Moses with horns, as he was described, erroneously, in a very early translation of Exodus.

After I studied the sculpture, I walked forward to where, as at the previous church, the relic resided, underneath the high altar. Clearly visible and protected inside a glass case were the chains that held St. Peter. With those shackling his body, St. Peter was crucified, upside down, on Vatican Hill. I took a picture there as well.

From there I trudged the long distance to the Scala Santa. Inside were five separate flights of twenty-eight stairs. However, the middle flight was the one I had come to see. According to Christian tradition, those were the marble steps (now protected with a covering of oak) that led to the praetorium of Pontius Pilate in Jerusalem. Christ was to have walked down those after his death sentence and on the way to his crucifixion.

There were numerous faithful walking—crawling really—on their knees up the stairs. They stopped on each step and recited a prayer.

I hesitantly touched a step and then took a picture.

As a person who loves history and was raised as an Eastern Orthodox Christian, those three religious pilgrimage sites were a wonder to see. All were free, and the relics were truly powerful to experience. I was in awe that I had the chance to see them. Before this trip I had never even known such relics existed. But now I had stood before some of the most powerful symbols of the religion that I was raised to believe in.

After the Scala Santa, I intended to find a bus to get me near my hotel. As I was looking, I saw the ancient walls of Rome. They were quite large (smaller than the Vatican walls, though). But they weren't large enough to keep out the fifth- and sixth-century horde of Huns and other invaders. I took a picture (it would last longer).

I ended up finding a bus and returned to my hotel without much problem. I got back to my room and remembered that, incredibly, I had a television in my room. A tiny one, but a television, where I was able to watch some European women's basketball.

After a little TV time, I began to write in this journal, which I am doing right now. I am at my desk (yes, there is a fucking desk in this room too—I'm living the life!), with my foot powder, contact solution, and comb to my left; my hat, glasses, and newly purchased guide to Rome in front of me; and an empty water bottle, the room phone, and coins to my right. Church day is complete, and I am a tired boy.

I hope I can rest if and when I get to Yugoslavia.

October 23

I got up early today with the intention of seeing absolutely everything in Rome. That's ridiculous, so I settled on walking through the city on my way to the ancient catacombs.

I showered quickly and then headed down to the buffet to gorge on breakfast.

I was remarkably successful at eating.

Next, I rolled myself to the front desk to tell the desk clerk that I had changed my mind and would be staying one to two more days.

An extra day was fine, he said. But, not so the second day, as he had my room already booked. He offered me another room, not en suite, for that added day. It would be about fifty percent cheaper.

Wait.

What?

Well then let's just cancel the room I'm in and get that cheap sucker for tonight and tomorrow. I didn't need a tiny little shower/toilet room. That was a bit creepy anyway.

That change would also save me time tomorrow; I could leave earlier for Naples as I would not have to do a room change in the morning.

I was out the door when I realized that I forgot my map and city guide in my new room. I went back to get it, and in my food coma state, lay down for what I thought would be a brief time on my new bed.

Three hours later(!), I woke up. It was half past noon. Time to leave.

I got on one of the two lines of the tiny Roman subway system and arrived at the Pyramid stop. This pyramid, located in the middle of this urban jungle, was built before the empire in the days of the Republic. I took a couple of pictures before heading down the street.

I wound my way over to the large open field that was once the Circus Maximus, the chariot racetrack. The outline of the oval (the circus) was almost fully intact. It was a massive site, a huge stadium that could house over two hundred thousand spectators.

I imagined being there, as a spectator in ancient Rome, watching those insane races straight out of *Ben Hur*.

Go, Chuck Heston, go!

"Take your stinking paws off me, you damn dirty ape."

Oops—right guy, wrong film.

I continued through the city, past the gates and onto the Palatine Hill. It was massive; the first and original of the seven hills of Rome (Palatine, Capitoline, Quirinal, Viminal, Esquiline, Caelian, and Aventine). At the top, I took some pictures of some very early Roman ruins.

I pushed on and passed the Colosseum once more. I then walked parallel to the Walls of Rome, finally reaching the Porta San Sebastiano, the gates that mark the beginning of the ancient Appian Way. I then started an ill-advised journey. I was determined to walk that archaic road, like a Roman, to the catacombs, despite it looking to be quite a distance. Distance be damned, I was going to do it.

It was a busy, narrow old road. There was a wall to my left, so I could not move far from the cars racing past me.

It was also a long, grueling walk; I even jogged some of the way. I continued on this inane path for a couple of hours, cars speeding two to three feet from me the whole way. I feared that I might be the next one entombed in the catacombs.

Finally, I got to a food stand and bought a bus ticket to take me the rest of the way and then later return me to the city.

At the Catacombs of San Sebastiano, I paid the nominal fee and joined an English-language tour that was starting just as I arrived. Lucky me.

This was one creepy place. An arm bone here, a leg bone there, intact skulls, children's caskets. It was dark and smelly. (It out-stank me and the clothes I had been wearing the whole week.)

The catacombs were built upon three levels, patrician pagans on one level, Christians the next, and then the church. The patricians had been stored outside, but their internment area was eventually buried.

As my group went deeper into the caverns, we entered the rooms where the earliest Christians celebrated their outlawed, illegal mass in secret. A fish figure (ichthys) was etched into the walls throughout the catacombs. This symbol was used as an anagram for a statement regarding Christ. The sight of the ichthys let the early Christians know that this was a safe place to worship their new religion.

A room on the second level was filled with ancient graffiti asking saints Peter and Paul to pray for specific early Christians. One theory is that this room was the actual first resting spot for both saints—their bodies may have once been entombed there. Early Christians would come there to feast and pay homage to both saints. Extraordinary.

We then came to the church. After St. Peter's Basilica and the others yesterday, this just seemed like a quaint little chapel.

But there was of course a pretty neat relic there, just to the right of the altar.

When St. Peter was escaping with his life out of Rome, he had a vision of Jesus Christ on the Appian Way.

He said to his buddy, Christ, "Quo vadis?" ("Where are you going?")

Christ said, "I am going back to Rome, to be crucified a second time."

Peter heard this and knew what he was supposed to do. He flipped a U-turn and returned to Rome to offer to be crucified himself. (I'd seen the results at the Basilica di San Pietro in Vincoli, earlier).

I had earlier passed the Chiesa del Domine Quo Vadis church, on the exact site where the meeting took place. But here, in this church, hanging next to the altar, were the foot imprints, in marble, of the feet of Christ where he stood that day as he talked to St. Peter.

I guess the power of God made the imprints in the solid rock?

Faith.

Believe it or not, it was still a cool story.

I took a picture and split.

As I was getting ready to get on the bus, I realized I had lost my ticket, which was the equivalent of seventy-five cents. Of course, I bought another one, so I didn't have to make that loathsome and dangerous trek a second time.

I met an American girl on the bus, and we chatted. She was studying in Florence but knew the Roman bus system well. She helped me out by telling me which bus I needed to transfer to once we returned to the city.

I got off and thanked her for her help.

With her great advice, I got on the correct bus, aiming to transfer to the Metro (my intent was to go to the train station to check on tomorrow's departure to Pompeii via Naples).

Of course, I missed the transfer.

I got off at the next bus stop and had to double back to get to the Metro station transfer.

I made it to Termini and confirmed my train.

Just when I got back to my hotel, the thunder rolled.

The skies opened.

But I was safely cloistered in my new, smaller, but cheaper, room. Time to relax.

October 24

I set my alarm, and it surprisingly did its job, going off nice and early. I showered and then gluttonized breakfast.

I was off to Termini to catch a three-hour train south to Naples and then Pompeii. On a side note, I believe that Naples was the birthplace of one of the greatest creations of humanity, the pizza.

I was excited.

Before I got on the train, I picked up a *USA Today*, opting to leave the heavy, brick-sized *War and Peace* in the room. I read the newspaper the whole way, every damn article.

Ciao, Napoli!

It was a big town, shockingly with skyscrapers, a rarity for European cities. It was also not as I expected. After reading so much about it, I'd half expected a dreary, smoggy, run-down dump reminiscent of Gary, Indiana. But it seemed fine. I only explored it briefly, though—I needed to catch a train even further south to Pompeii.

I returned to the station and searched for my track. I saw a conductor and asked directions.

Whew, I asked the right guy. My train was not in the station proper but in a satellite area accessible through an underground tunnel.

Once I got to the proper area, I found myself at a gate with a turnstile and another conductor. He told me I needed a supplemental ticket for this local train to Pompeii.

What?!

He then looked at the ticket line.

He looked at his watch.

He looked at me and said, "Forget it, you don't have enough time." This hero then let me through the turnstile with no charge.

What a guy. Did I say I loved Naples? Well, I do.

I got on the train to Pompeii, which that shithead Frommer said took twenty minutes.

Of course, it took more than twice that.

But I was fine as the train raced first high and then low around the Bay of Naples and the Amalfi Coast.

The Isle of Capri.

The beauty was astounding. Goddamn, Italy, hogging all that natural beauty is just unfair.

The train arrived in Pompeii, and, for what I hoped would be the last time, I consulted Frommer's. (Einstein said insanity is doing the same thing over and over and expecting a different result—that was me and that Frommer book) The guidebook said to turn right out of the station. I did, but it was the wrong way; I should have turned left.

I was briefly lost because of that.

I quickly navigated through the small city of Pompeii (the modern-day city, not the one buried in lava—yet). The town square and the stores were crowded; there was a celebration for a big race. I fought through, eventually getting directions to the ancient site.

Before I went in, I needed film, so I went into a little shop where a nice old man helped me. He even gave me a free bottle of water. As I was paying, I looked through a partially drawn curtain in the back of the store and saw where he lived with the rest of his extended family.

I left and crossed the unattended finish line of the race on my way to old Pompeii. Sadly, I was not recognized as the winner of the race even though I obviously passed through the finish line before anyone else.

Anti-Americans.

I saw the gates of ancient Pompeii, the city leveled in 79 AD by nearby Mount Vesuvius. I picked up a ticket, a Coke, and a smile at a little store at the entrance.

My first destination was the amphitheater. Tourists were allowed to climb around anywhere inside. It also, unlike the Roman Colosseum, had its floor intact. It was considerably smaller than Rome's Colosseum—it only seated twenty thousand. Still an insanely high capacity for a place built two thousand years ago.

From there, I rambled on, often referring to my newly purchased Pompeii guidebook.

I have to say, the roads back then were terrible. Huge, uneven stones. Every step I took, I was afraid I would sprain an ankle. Those Romans must have been very nimble or had great high-top sneakers.

The dwellings on those roads were quite humble, close to the size of studio apartments in a modern big city.

The bars/take out restaurants were great to experience. One had its counter still intact, with a mosaic on the back wall. There were also women's names etched throughout, surely written by the creepy men they rejected. I took a few pictures of those.

Throughout the city, glass shields protected this graffiti of the ancient Romans. Some of it was light-hearted, like the women's names, while some was political propaganda aimed at the ancient residents when time stopped for them in 79 AD.

Onto the larger dwellings. The original art from many of those homes was taken to the Naples National Archaeological Museum to keep it safe from tourists and the elements. In order to preserve the interior design, the art that was discovered there was replaced by reproductions. A great example of this was at the House of the Fawn.

The main element that stood out in Pompeii was the commonness of it all. Usually, history is concerned with the great events, the great people, the great achievements. Here in Pompeii, the greatness of the site was just the opposite of "usual" history.

We, the modern visitors, could see how the Romans lived—how we would have lived if we had been alive in 79 AD. The narrow streets we would have navigated; the bars at which we would have eaten and drank; the political signs spreading their propaganda; the bouldered streets where we would have broken our ankles.

That is what was so great about the place. It was a time capsule; a moment, long ago, captured in time. A photograph, a painting that you could visit. You could enter the dwellings of those unfortunate Romans just as they were two thousand years ago. Seeing the mosaics where they were intended to be, rather than in the sterility of some museum, made them seem more authentic. There was not a lot of need even for imagination. The sites and objects were still there, in the private homes, open to explore. The experience was real, for the most part, not reproductions or museum pieces.

If you could get away from the crowds (there were a lot of English, American, Australian, and Japanese tourists there) and find a quiet side street on which to be alone, you could really feel the energy of the ancients.

I did that and lost myself in the moment so much that I scared myself. I was down a very quiet side street, a desolate row of stone structures. I could hear no other tourists.

Then I thought, "Uh-oh, I'm going to see a riot squad of Roman toughs in togas turn the corner."

"Quo vadis," I would say, as that was the only Latin I knew.

I would then run like Scooby Doo from the ghostly crew.

Well, after that self-inflicted mind game, I hightailed it out of there and back to reality, surrounding myself with a group of modern-day, elderly Japanese tourists.

I only briefly stayed with that group as I was sensing some glances aimed my way.

I followed my Pompeii guidebook to the forum. It was quite small, about a tenth the size of Rome's, but much more intact. The buildings were still erect, so I could get a grasp of the spatial features. I could see the stores and the temples as they really were.

I walked all through the forum, eventually looping around its perimeter. I noticed a sort of gated-off storage area nearby. It was filled with a lot of found pottery jugs which were probably a dime a dozen to the ancients.

But some other objects stored there caught my eye. Those brought me back to the gruesomeness and tragedy that befell the sorrowful inhabitants of this ancient town—plastic casts of humans who were caught in the violence of Vesuvius. One man was shielding his face from the hideous eruption.

Those ghastly sculptures were created by careful archaeologists who would shave off small layers of lava from areas of the site. Once they uncovered a hole, they knew that organic matter had been there and had decomposed. They poured plaster-of-Paris into the hole and continued their scraping. Once they reached the bottom, they pulled out what the plaster had formed. Occasionally they would find human remains set in the plaster. Quite an amazing feat of simple, patient science that aided in the remembrance of those that died there.

I continued my exploration through a garden which led to the city theater. This was much smaller than the amphitheater but much better preserved. Its style was reminiscent of the ancient Greeks. I was sure the crowds heard the croaking chorus there many times.

From there I ventured outside of the city walls and found the patrician necropolis. I wished I knew Latin, as there were many varied inscriptions on those tombs.

It did not look like there had been a lot of excavation work done, as there was a lot of overgrowth. Bushes and unkempt trees were abundant.

There was no one else around, so my imagination went off again. Shit, it was an ancient cemetery. I had good reason to be freaked out!

I wandered a bit, careful to look behind me but praying I would not see anything. Just before I took off like Shaggy, I found a little road and eased out of the necropolis.

I walked the narrow, walled-in road for a time and eventually found the main gate, where I'd entered the ancient city a few hours previous.

I left the first-century world and return to the twentieth.

I headed to the train station and caught the train back to Naples. This one was much faster than the first, but I was able to enjoy the Amalfi Coast once again.

In Naples I immediately hopped on a train to Rome, forgetting that I was going to get a pizza in town. Damn it!

On the train I didn't have much to do. Also, I was still quite disappointed in myself because of the pizza failure.

I did notice that there was a young couple in the car with me. Unfortunately, for me, they did their best to recreate the "El" train scene from *Risky Business*. He wasn't Tom Cruise, and she sure as shit wasn't Rebecca De Mornay. More like Tootie's friend Natalie from *The Facts of Life*.

Rome—was I happy to be there and out of that car.

I confirmed my train track and travel time for tomorrow's departure to Venice. Then I headed back to my hotel.

Once I returned, I decided to pay my bill so I wouldn't be delayed in the morning. When I got my bill, I saw that the clerk had added a phone charge of twenty-four hundred lire to it.

I protested, as the phone that I had been using was the pay phone in the hall. I had not used the room phone once.

He erased the charge without an accusation or apology.

Vultures, vultures everywhere.

Fucking Italy. Scamming folks at every goddamn turn. What a country of good Catholics.

October 25

Today, I woke up at six and showered again. With all of that cleanliness, I was fearful my skin would fall off. But it did not.

I gorged again and said toodle-oo to the Romans.

I hustled to the train station to catch my 7:45 train. I boarded without a problem, choosing a car with an older guy and a younger guy. They conversed, with no breaks, for two and a half hours. How was that possible?

Do Italians breathe like other mammals?

Those two didn't even know each other; God only knows what they discussed.

"Look at that American fool."

"I bet he's an imbecile."

"He is very clean."

After a few stops, the loquacious old guy left and a few more people entered the car. In time, the car was filled with a middle-aged man, another younger man, and a woman with her one-year-old baby.

Everyone except the first talkative guy was smitten with the little baby. Watching the tiny girl be amused was a nice way for all of us (minus one grump) to pass the time.

After playing with the little girl for a time, everyone reverted back to themselves. I read *War and Peace* and chatted about nothing with a couple of people in the car.

I noticed that we'd all been lucky; the train was crowded with people standing in the hallway.

We made it to Mestre, where I was to change trains for the ten-minute jolt to Venice. For a laugh I took a look at Frommer to see what was suggested. If I had solely taken advice from the Frommer's book and not consulted with the desk in Rome, I would have stayed on the train. Frommer's said that that train would go directly to Venice, no transfer needed. But if I had listened, I would now be on my way to fucking *Vienna, Austria.*

Butthole Frommer.

As I was prone to do in new cities, I went directly to the Venice tourist office to book a room. I got a nice, cheap place, left the station, and then immediately got lost. I was able to find two different pairs of girls that spoke English and asked them for directions. They both pointed me the same way, and I found my hotel.

I checked in to my one-star accommodations and went to my room. Every room in Italy must post their maximum room rates, so I was shocked when I read theirs—they were not charging me their high-end rate of forty-nine thousand lire but the discounted rate of forty-five thousand lire.

I was saving about four dollars!

With the money I had saved, I planned to buy a fur vest and bottle of expensive champagne. I would order truffles and tiramisu from the best chef in the lagoon. I would lease a gondola with a singing pilot for the entire evening.

Nah, I'd just buy an extra water bottle or two.

I left the hotel and immediately saw a strange sight—a Venetian beer distributor delivering kegs of beer via gondola. I quickly took a picture.

Venice was like no other city I had ever been to. There were canals in Amsterdam, but they were a sidenote; cars and trams dominated the city. In Venice, the main thoroughfare was the lagoon. The landed walkways seemed secondary, as there were, of course, no cars. Stranger yet, especially in Italy, there were no mopeds. (Thank God!)

Adding to the *bellezza* of Venice was the sun. I hadn't seen it much since I crossed into the Italian peninsula, so it was a welcome sight.

I liked Venice.

I tried to follow my map, but getting lost in Venice was a given, so I felt right at home. I worked my way to Piazza San Marcos, where there was an American Express office. I had a large transaction to carry out.

I would be accessing the first of the two $5,000 accounts here in Venice. I'd be changing this set of funds into American currency to give to Jovo. The other set I would access in Vienna and get in Deutsche Marks. If it was deemed too dangerous for me to go into Yugoslavia, I could just give it to him in Budapest. I also exchanged some of my own money to give to Jovo. I would be reimbursed by my extended family once I returned to the United States.

In the AmEx office, I got the dollars in denominations of fifty and one hundred. (I did exchange some traveler's checks for lire so I had some spending money in Venice.) I figured I could spread the dollars throughout my person so that if I got robbed, they hopefully wouldn't find it all.

I took the bills and went into the restroom of the American Express establishment. In a stall, I stowed the bills, some in my money pouch (secured around my neck), some in my socks, under my feet (I hoped those would not disintegrate from the jungle rot) and the rest in my pants pockets.

Now I was off to shop. I am not really a shopper, more of a buyer, so this activity did not take long. In Piazza San Marcos I found an area that was quiet and seemed almost elegant. There were a few lace shops, where I picked up a couple of items including a pair of eight-setting tablecloth and napkin sets. I also bought some lace decorations to give to relatives back home.

I figured those pieces would be easy to carry as I could keep them wrapped in their plastic, shove them to the bottom of my backpack, and then forget about them until the trip was over.

I was relatively confident that was it for my shopping (buying) in Venice. If I decided that I needed more gifts, I would pick them up later, in Vienna or Budapest.

Next, on schedule, I got hopelessly lost. But, as I had already recognized, travelers were supposed to get lost in Venice.

There was a problem: I really needed to use the facilities, but I was so lost that finding a public toilet seemed impossible. I tried to follow the map to the train station but ran into sidewalks that ended in the lagoon. I approached a few other tourists, and they all basically said the same thing: it's an island; you won't stray too far.

Straying too far was the least of my worries. My main concern was wetting myself. At one point, I seriously considered just adding to the water in the lagoon.

Relief. I finally found the train station and used the bathroom there.

Since I was there, I decided to check out my train's daily departure time for Vienna. I would not be catching it for two days, but the departure time was always the same. After I verified the time, I found a gelato stand and then went back to my hotel.

In my room, I shoved the newly acquired fabrics into my pack. It was tight. I realized that I would not have room for much more unless I jettisoned some of my property. That would be a last resort—deciding what to discard was too much of a Sophie's choice to be made at that time.

As I wrote this, I sat in a chair next to my bed. My other journal and camera were next to me. My shorts and shirt were airing near the window. On my bed was my swollen pack and money pouch. I had unloaded my pockets and shoes, so I had a couple of piles of fifty- and one-hundred-dollar bills arranged on it as well.

It looked like the room of a very filthy smuggler.

Next, I figured out the finances for the rest of the trip. After I was reimbursed for the extra money that I would give to Jovo, I was sure that I would still be under budget.

It was time to plan the next day's goings-on. There was not a lot more that I wanted to do, so it would be a day of relaxing. I would not be busting my jaded ass to see a lot of sights, and I was very happy about that.

Bedtime. I had been up and traveling since six thirty that morning.

October 26

A slow and easy day was in store for me, and I needed one. But I began to feel guilty about taking it easy. Was I just going through the motions? Was I not experiencing Venice as I should? Had I become the beefy American girl I'd met in Gimmelwald?

I decided that it did not matter; I only needed what was commonly referred to as a mental health day. A day to rejuvenate the mind, body, and soul. I may be beefy and American, but I was certainly not anything like that girl.

As it was, I ended up sleeping in. Then I had a nice continental breakfast of bread and strong coffee. As I sat, enjoying my cup of caffeine, I realized that I never really drank coffee much before this trip, even in college. In Europe, it was everywhere, and I was beginning to like it.

I also noticed that I had begun ordering anchovy pizza. I never did that before—I'd regarded that topping as an abomination. But I learned that I loved those salty little fish. I wondered if that would stay with me after I returned.

After breakfast I decided that I was just not quite ready to hit the road, so I went back to my room. I lay back down on my lumpy, uncomfortable mattress and took a short nap.

I awoke at eleven and figured it was time to finally seize the day. I had packed all the currency in my neck pouch, where it actually fit with room to spare. I was relieved that it did; I did not want to keep it in my easy-to-steal bag. If someone wanted it, I guessed they'd have to cut my head off to get it.

Despite my earlier thoughts of having completed my consumerism, I was strangely drawn in by more stores. I was convinced I was under an alien's brain control; I normally hated shopping. But before I could analyze this alien invasion anymore and construct a tin foil hat for myself, I headed into another lace store and picked up four small pieces. I was confident they would fit in my bag without my having to surrender any property.

After spending so much money buying trinkets, I felt I was now an official tourist of Venice. So, I fought the crowds and did more window-shopping.

I did that all the way to Piazza San Marcos. From there, I walked and walked and walked. I walked down large tourist filled avenues, down small desolate side paths—I took in the city. I saw laundry hanging out of medieval windows, and I saw flood-scarred buildings. I walked over odd canals and tiny bridges. I saw red and white poles measuring the depth of the water, and gondolas and scows racing about the lagoon.

I finally got it. *This* was what it meant to be lost in Venice. Not when you had to use the bathroom, but when you wanted to feel the city—to experience every last nook and dead end.

It was beautiful not to be in a rush.

I discovered that there was a Salvador Dalí exhibit, so I began a slow stroll there.

It was an interesting exhibit, filled with marvelous prints and several originals. I must say that I did not know a lot about Dalí. I reminded myself to do a little research on him after I returned to the States.

From there, I decided it was time to eat. I found a nice cheap restaurant and ate quite a bit, as I had been walking most of the day.

I didn't mind the extra calories; I had lost a lot of weight on this trip, although that was certainly not the goal. I didn't know exactly what I weighed as I hadn't been on a scale in a month and a half. But earlier, as I was deciding what to wear, I grabbed a pair of long pants. I had not worn that particular pair in about a month because they had been a bit tight at the waist. I tried them on, and not only did they fit, but I had about two inches of room to spare!

Either the pants got larger, or I got smaller.

After my meal I decided to walk and window-shop, eventually making it to the Piazzale Roma. This was where cars and tourist buses could park, there being no way to drive into the city itself. At that piazzale, a pedestrian bridge connected the old city with the mainland. I also noticed a man playing an organ grinder, soliciting for tips. But, sadly, no monkey on a chain. Talk about a stereotype.

I did not stay there long; I liked the illusion of old Venice, and I had seen too many large cities already on this tour.

I was near the train station, so I went to make a reservation for my trip to Vienna for the next day. I estimated that it would be the equivalent of four dollars to do so. But the clerk told me that it would be much more. I had recognized a few scams in Italy already, so I simply didn't believe him. We started to argue. I told him he was trying to work me, and he got feisty right back. I didn't want to be arrested in Venice (especially with five thousand dollars around my neck), so I told him to fuck-off and left.

Keep in touch.

The incident passed through me surprisingly well. I was not upset at all. I guess fighting scammers in Italy had become second nature.

I did some more window shopping, and then I headed back to the hotel.

Once there, I hopped on my lumpy bed and read my book.

Good night to day forty-eight of tourism and adventure.

October 27

Yesterday, I woke up early and ate three pieces of bread with a couple of cups of coffee. I went to the desk and spoke to the clerk. He told me that checkout was at eleven, but I could leave my (heavy) backpack there, as I had a few hours to kill before my train to Vienna.

I once again hit the paths of Venice. I'd done a lot of walking, but I did have one last place that I wanted to see, the Peggy Guggenheim Collection. Earlier that year I had visited the circular Guggenheim Museum in New York City and loved it. I was expecting nothing less today.

I found it without much difficulty. Was I getting to know this town or what?

The Peggy Guggenheim Collection was housed in a former eighteenth-century palace that the American heiress lived in seasonally for nearly thirty years. The classic, white square building housed her collections from the early twentieth century.

That is my favorite artistic period, and I will never tire of viewing the works that came from it. During that era, all the globe was in flux, not just the art world. The old ways were collapsing, and new ways were emerging. Cubism, fauvism, and futurism were developing, as were their new masters, Picasso, Braque, Matisse, and Boccioni.

This museum did not disappoint—all of my favorites were represented. I even noted a great new piece that I had never seen, *The Regular*, a cubist portrait of a saloon patron. I have to admit, I forgot who painted it. Something else to research when I can.

From the galleries I went out the back door of Peg's old house and into the gardens. Nice digs. I saw that the patio overlooked the Grand Canal and the Accademia Bridge for a world-stopping view. I strolled through the garden and stumbled upon the heiress's grave. Next to hers there were about fourteen other graves. "My babies," it said; her dogs were buried there.

I saw another building on the grounds and ventured inside. This was a workshop and a gallery filled with photographs. Some were violent scenes of the Mafia. Some were of celebrities, including Federico Fellini, Anouk Aimée, and Marcello Mastroianni, screwing around. Some were of people actually screwing. The whole story of modern photography contained in one of Peggy's sheds.

I left there and explored deeper in the garden. I discovered a curious, square little robot sculpture by Ernst. It was one of my favorites, as it seemed so odd to be in such a place.

A stranger in a strange land.

I decided it was time to leave, but I'd really enjoyed this stop. The Guggenheim's, Solomon and Peggy, were two for two. Too bad Benjamin met such a horrible end.

I still had a couple of hours to wait before my train departed so I bought some fruit, headed to Piazza San Marcos, found a seat, and read *War and Peace*.

I read for a time and then decided that it was time for a real meal. I found an out-of-the-way restaurant but, oh-no, it was just after three, and nearly all the eateries closed midday from three to six. I was about to leave when the fantastic owner waved me in.

"I'll serve you," he said in English with a smile.

After this delicious meal, I strolled back to my old hotel to retrieve my pack and then headed to the station.

Once there I bought a *USA Today* and entered the waiting area. Inside there were three obnoxious Australians arguing, joking, basically being loud and annoying.

The country founded by criminals.

It was finally time to board my northbound train. For the first hour, I had a car to myself. Then an elderly couple joined me, but they stayed only for a few stops. I was helping them with their bags as three middle-aged people entered the car. They did not stay very long either, as they all got off two towns down the line.

I was relieved to be by myself again in the car. However, it did not last. Just as I lay down and began to relax for the overnight trip, the glass doors jolted open, and a well-dressed man entered.

Shit. As he was situating himself, I shot him some sneers and evil looks. My spoiled self wanted this car to myself, *wah, wah!*

After I came to terms with the fact that that this big baby, me, would not get his way, the man and I began to chat. He was a very genial, intelligent person. He knew many languages, but not very much English. He certainly knew more English than I knew Italian, which was none.

After some time, we secured our bags and doused the lights. Then the passport check. All was in order, so I fell asleep.

12

Austria, Hungary (part I)

Vienna, Budapest

October 28

I did not sleep very well. When I awoke for good, my travel-mate was already gone. It was six thirty in the morning, and the train was slowing down, braking. We were at the outskirts of overcast Vienna.

Ah Austria, the homeland of Hitler.

Once I deboarded, I, as was par for me, immediately went the wrong way. I straightened myself and found the exit to the streets of this old Hapsburg capital.

For some reason, and going against all that I had learned, I thought that I would not get lost and would be able to find a hotel without a lot of guidance. Also, since I'd added the merchandise and the five thousand dollars in Italy, my bag and body seemed a lot heavier. Finally, I was extremely tired. I had not slept well on the clattering train.

So, against all logic, I began my plod through the city. I had no map and had no idea where to go, so I made wrong turn after wrong turn onto desolate streets and into industrial zones for over two hours.

It was a horrible walk with a heavy—almost painfully heavy pack—yoked to my bent and near broken back. At a few points I caught myself talking to myself, alternating from encouragement to scolding.

I felt my face contorting into scowls.

I had gone mad in Vienna. I would be placed in the sanitorium that housed Dr. Caligari. I would befriend a somnambulist who lived in a cabinet. My world would consist of odd-angled doors and hallways.

Just as I was about to give up and wait for the men in white suits, I saw civilization. I saw a woman walking and grunted, "Hotels?"

She told me, in broken English, that I could find them in the "ring," and she pointed me the way.

In my near-animal devolution, I offered her no thanks; I just snorted and knuckle-walked down the *strasse*.

I was able to follow her directions and headed the way she gestured. I discovered that the "Ring," short for *Ringstrasse*, was a series of avenues that encircled central Vienna. It was also the central tourist section of the city.

Thank God.

I desperately needed a room, so I only ventured to a couple of hotels before taking the cheapest one at the equivalent of seventy American dollars. However, it was en suite and in the center of everything in the Ring.

But, of course, it was not my time to rest. The room would not be ready for four hours.

Time for *tourismus*!

The very pretty desk clerk handed me a map and suggested an itinerary to get the best experience of her city during my short stay.

I realized that I was not too filthy, but I was very tired and hungry, so the first thing I did was sit and eat some delicious pastries at a nearby café. I had strong coffee as well, but that did not bring me out of my daze.

I then wearily hit the streets of another city.

I passed St. Stephen's Cathedral. "Big," was the only thought my shattered brain could come up with.

I walked past memorials, ancient walkways, and palaces, and then I stumbled across a set of grand horses yoked to ornate carriages. They were there, proudly, patiently waiting for their charges in the early morning fog. It was a sublime sight. I took a picture.

"Damn, it is a beautiful, magnificent city," I thought, finally coming to my senses.

I suddenly got a second wind and hopped on the subway. I took a trip to the train station I would be using tomorrow when I ventured east to Budapest.

At the station I got my travel information to Hungary. I also found out how often trains left for Amsterdam as I would need one in a week. That is, if all went well and I was able to spend that week in Yugoslavia.

From there I found the American Express office, where I repeated what I'd done at the Venetian money exchange. The only difference was that I took the second five-thousand-dollar installment in the largest possible denominations of Deutsche Marks. Jovo had told my aunt and uncle that Marks were a widely accepted currency in Yugoslavia, so that would work fine.

From the exchange window I headed to the bathroom and stowed the money in my money pouch. I was shocked that it all fit. But then I remembered that I had gone through a ton of traveler's checks on the trip, which had opened up a lot of room in the pouch.

Even with the dollars and Deutsche Marks as insulation, it was quite cold in Austria. There were actual kiosks with chestnuts roasting on open fires throughout the city. It seemed like Christmas.

But instead of carols running through my head, I began to daydream—maybe I would run in to a prancing and dancing Burgermeitser Meisterburger. If so, I would be sure to lend him a hand in stealing gifts from all the local children.

My next destination was the Schönbrunn Palace, the home of the Hapsburgs and the birthplace of Marie Antoinette. It was colossal. Glenn, the fifty-foot man, could comfortably live there.

I did not feel like paying the fee and going inside, so I walked the grounds. The gardens were massive, like nothing I had ever seen, so I guess I got my no-money's worth.

I passed the Angel Fountain and the statues. I strolled up a giant hill to a memorial.

I spent about an hour and a half exploring this site and taking pictures. It was impressive. I also had time and film to burn.

At that point I was spent. I decided that it was time to return to the hotel; my room would certainly be ready. Back I went and into my exceptionally clean, very white room. I turned on the radio (a radio? How affluent I had become!) and cleaned up.

After washing and scouring myself, I lay down for just a bit.

After a quick nap, I remembered Berlin. I worried that, if I fell back asleep, I might doze through the night. There were a few more sites I wanted to see, so I forced myself up and exited the hotel.

It was off to Mozart's house. It was incredible to think that he lived and loafed there, probably sporting fancy, colorful clothing. He gazed out those same windows to view Vienna while he composed some six hundred pieces of near-perfect music. I tried to imagine him in those rooms, young and fancy, an incredible genius penning the greatest music ever.

The displays there were a disappointment, though. They were only photocopies, no original manuscripts or compositions. I was sure those had been hoarded away to larger institutions.

Next it was a twenty-minute walk to Sigmund Freud's place. I found it without any issues, maternal or otherwise. I did not go into the museum. Since I didn't read German, I suspected there wasn't much I would understand. I just checked out the street and the exterior of the house where he invented psychoanalysis. I took a picture and then scanned the area for any inspirational phalluses. None, so I went on my way.

I had an urge to call my mother but did not.

It was time to return to the Ring.

I found a great restaurant across the street from my hotel where I had some incredible German food.

I went back to my clean, white room, where I read just for a bit. I got to page one thousand of the mammoth *War and Peace*, which is when I decided to call it a day. It had been nearly twenty-nine hours since I began the jaunt from Venice. Good-bye windows, I was done— enough writing as well!

October 29

Like in Berlin, I got a marathon sleep, but this time it was planned. After twelve hours I woke, took a shower in my room—feeling like the king of the castle—then ate my stale bread.

I checked out of the hotel, found the subway, and got to the station with no problems. My bag didn't feel nearly as heavy as it did yesterday, probably because I was not a walking zombie today.

I checked the departure board to find my track. There it was, Budapest, a 10:05 departure on Track Eight. All seemed correct. But then I saw the *Notes* posted on the board. This particular run had a name. I would be boarding the *Orient Express*!

From Paris to Istanbul, this was the legendary and dangerous run from literature and film. Dangerous, as seemingly everyone on it would be a murderer. They all took their best shot in the book at least. I decided that, if I saw a crazy looking dame in a fur hat, I would jump off.

Then I started to think about the reality of the entire run. Paris to Istanbul. France to fucking Turkey? Are you kidding me? Three goddamn days on a fucking train? What a horrible endurance test. In this day and age, who the fuck would willingly do this run? A masochist? An imbecile? Just the fetid body stench of those enclosed cars would kill a person in half a day, let alone three!

Thankfully, I would only be on the thing for three and a half hours, and, so far, it didn't smell that bad.

So far.

Just after I boarded, I realized that I'd entered the wrong part of the train, a sleeping car. Yikes, those were for the long haulers. I quickly moved to a regular second-class car.

In my little six seat cabin, there was an English-speaking guy (who departed after only forty-five minutes), a French *fille*, and two Serbian (or Croatian) *muskarci*.

The ride was boring; there was no romance to be had with the French girl; she was not my type.

There was no intrigue from the Balkan men; they just slept.

The constant fog did murder any chance of enjoying the scenery, so I guess there was that.

I just read my USA Today and tried to stay awake. Once we crossed the Hungarian frontier, there were two separate passport checks. I wondered if they realized that the Cold War had ended.

We pulled in to Keleti Station, where I planned to rendezvous with my cousin Jovo.

I checked out track one, where I'd told him I would meet him in two days. However, I chose that track for the meeting without knowing the layout of the place. Track one was removed from the main terminal and was lousy with former communist galoots. It seemed to be dedicated to heavy industry, not tourism.

I decided to run with the plan; it was too late for changes.

I returned to the main terminal and was immediately approached by hostel runners. (I had learned that was the title of the people that worked as barkers for the hostels.)

"No, thanks."

"I'm fine."

I refused them all, as the city, which had only been recently behind the Iron Curtain, was way too inexpensive to use a hostel. Also, I simply could not imagine what the conditions of a (former) communist hostel would be. I wasn't even going to speculate.

I finally got approached by someone I could work with, an old woman. As she spoke a small amount of English, we haggled.

She would drive me to her building, where I would get my own apartment, with a bathroom, sitting room, etc., for twenty dollars a night. I got her down to fifteen, but I wanted it for ten. Little did this old lady know but I was now playing hardball.

At ten she balked, and I walked.

Next, I was approached by another septuagenarian woman and her thirty-something son, who was acting as her English interpreter. She, through him, offered essentially the same deal, minus the personal chauffeur. But to balance it out, the location was better. It was near Parliament and the Danube. I questioned them about the cleanliness (I had the Selecty Home Pension on my mind), and I was reassured that all was in order; they stressed that the shower was especially clean.

Had there been problems with grimy showers in this town?

We haggled a bit, and I got them down to ten dollars a night.

So, unlike in Vienna where I had to walk for two fucking hours in the morning rain, in Budapest I had two solid room offers before I was even out the station doors.

I love (former) communism.

Before we left the station, we stopped and bought ten Budapest Metro tickets. The lady handed them all to me. Then, my new friends (and temporary landlords) and I strolled out into the cold early-morning air of Budapest.

The son and I chatted a bit, but he had somewhere to go, so he left me with his very capable mother.

I had to walk quite fast to keep up with her as I followed her into a Metro tunnel. Once there I began to dig in my pocket to get out two tickets for the ride. She saw what I was doing and said, "No, no."

She whispered something to me in Hungarian. I realized I was abetting an outlaw. A turnstile jumper.

But I then saw how easy it was to bypass the gates. There was nothing that I recognized as security around any of the entrances.

We boarded what was undoubtedly the fastest, steepest escalator I had ever ridden in my life. It seemed like it ran straight down—it actually felt as if I was falling. Not only that, but it was long, maybe an eighth of a mile into the earth. It was also crowded. For the first time since I was a little tiny kid, I was terrified to be on an escalator. I would now pay for the sin of jumping the turnstile.

My Budapest buddy had absolutely no problem. She seemed to be daydreaming during the ride into the pit of hell itself.

Once we reached the bottom, I was shocked that Ol' Pitch wasn't waiting to sentence me to an excruciating eternity of sodomy. Instead, there was only a common Metro train waiting for us.

We boarded a packed car, and I grabbed a strap for stability. Just as the doors were about to shut, an early-morning, already very inebriated Hungarian stumbled in and lumbered toward us. The car jerked and the drunk pitched forward, stabilized himself, and then crashed headfirst at my feet.

Hooray!

I did a quick dance as he just missed me and my bag. No one in the car reacted. No expressions changed. No one checked his condition. All were concerned only with their final destination.

Was Machiavelli a Hungarian?

But I soon found myself thinking like those around me.

"Great," I reasoned, "I will have a lot more room in this car with this guy as my buffer. No one is going to come near me with this gin-soaked moron at my feet."

Just as I was getting comfortable with the paralyzed wreck protecting me, my Budapest buddy jostled my arm. It was our stop.

One fucking stop? About half a minute of travel?

She'd sent me down into the pit of Hades, thrust me into a sardine can, and had a sloshed Magyar nearly assault me for *one stop*?

It was fine. I liked her and her delinquent ways.

We exited the train and took another excruciatingly steep escalator up to the surface. At the top, there were no Eloi there to greet us, only a bright blue sky.

I told her that I needed to exchange money, so she led me to a bank, which was unfortunately closed.

Next, we headed to her flat. My accommodations were on the second floor, through a kitchen and a then a side room. My quarters were a long, narrow, and exceptionally clean space. The bedroom had two single beds made up with very puffy white comforters.

I paid her twenty American dollars, and we took a seat in her kitchen and tried to have a conversation. I was able to tell her that I was there, in Budapest, with my family in 1985. She got extremely excited at that and rubbed my face, laughing.

My outlaw friend was very sweet.

We talked a little bit more, and then I said farewell and hit the streets of the Hungarian capital.

Before I left, I was sure to get directions to another bank to exchange some currency. The place she'd sent me had excellent rates.

I headed to the city center of Pest. Budapest is a city divided into three parts, primarily by the Danube River. One side (where I was staying) is Pest, while the other is Buda. The third section is Óbuda. But the city is not called Budobuda or Óbudapest, so fuck that area.

The city was much different from what I remembered only eight years prior. The end of Communism occurred during that period, and the changes were stark and real. I remembered it being dreary and oppressive, with machine gun-toting military patrolling the street. We were warned not to take pictures, as those troops would confiscate the film, the camera, and maybe the photographer.

I then recalled the extraordinary passport checks from earlier that morning. But that seemed in the distant past, as Hungary, or at least the city of Budapest, seemed open and progressive. The people seemed happier as well. The city seemed prettier.

There were all types of shops filled with consumer goods that were just not there in 1985. There were modern sporting goods shops as well as fashion boutiques, book dealers, and appliance stores. You name it, and it was there.

I also noted another inevitable result of freedom: sex. Topless bars and sex shops dotted the cityscape. There didn't seem to be a seedy red-light district yet, so those establishments were scattered throughout the city.

Corporate capitalism had reared its head there as well, I saw Burger King, Pizza Hut, and McDonald's.

Budapest was like the proverbial butterfly, free after forty-five-years in its iron chrysalis.

I found the shopping district and began a leisurely stroll. I did some more window-shopping. I had been out of practice since Venice.

I then found a Hungarian fast-food joint. I had made a conscious effort to avoid fast food for this entire trip. But I broke my rule. I wanted to see what an "authentic" Hungarian fast-food restaurant was like.

Rather tasty, with nearly standard-fare cheeseburgers. The only difference was the coleslaw covering the patties.

It had been a long day, and the sun was getting low. I had decided to head back to the flat when I passed a small market that caught my eye. It was not a tourist shop, just a store for locals to pick up incidental food items and small wares.

As I had intended on picking up some paprika in Hungary, I figured this was a fine place to do so. After all, this was where the average Hungarian found theirs. As my money situation was so good, I bought three top-of-the-line containers of the spice.

I exited the store and easily found the street my accommodations were on. As I was walking back to the flat, I noticed, through the dusk, that the Danube was right in front of me, about a hundred feet away. In the now-dark city, I headed to the massive river.

The Danube was wide. It put the Tiber and the Seine to shame. It was fast as well. I could see how it had become the dominant waterway for Central Europe for thousands of years.

Strauss filled my mind.

The river ran and rolled to the rhythm of a waltz.

However, I only watched and did not dance in three-quarter or any time. So, I was quite able to stand still and snap a picture of the stunning view of the castle in Buda, on the other side of the majestic river.

Back to the flat, which I found without getting lost! Once there, I took a stroll around the complex. It was of classic communist design, square and utilitarian, with concrete buildings overlooking a dirt-covered middle courtyard. It was grotesque but efficient.

At the flat, I had a bit of trouble getting the exotic European key to work. Why are the keys in Europe, one, never the same, and two, so fucking strange?

My partner in crime heard me and opened the door. Thankfully, it was not too late. She just laughed at me and then showed me the idiosyncrasies of getting her key to work.

There was no time for chatter; I was beat. I retired to my ten-dollar-a-night pad, took out my contacts, filled up my water bottle, and prepared my calendar for the next day. I was so tired that I did not even read *War and Peace* despite being near the end of the mammoth tome.

I'm feeling alright. But I am feeling too good myself. Sorry for the change, Joe Cocker.

Good night.

OCTOBER 30

I awoke at eight and took an Irish shower. While I was doing that, and before I put in my contacts, I heard the bathroom door open and then shut very quickly. I thought I'd locked it. In fact, I know I did; I'd checked. The lock must not have engaged on the other side.

Tomorrow I have a full schedule, so I plan on showering. Too bad I am not an exhibitionist as I'd be looking forward to that gratification.

I exited the flat and walked along the Danube to the central area of Pest. I spent a considerable amount of time strolling about, sitting on park benches, and people-watching.

It was nearly lunchtime, so I took off in search of a place to eat. No Hungarian fast food today though, as I would be looking for a decent restaurant.

I found a place with fine white tablecloths and a salad bar. Being an American, I thought it was all-you-can-eat. So, I loaded up three separate times, trying to fill up so I could buy only one meal throughout the day.

Uh-oh. It was not all-you-can-eat for one price. I was charged for each trip I made to the salad bar. Thankfully I was in Budapest and not Stockholm, so each trip was only the equivalent of $2.50.

Lesson learned. I would no longer make assumptions on the road.

But my plan did work, as I did not eat for the rest of the day.

After my lunch fiasco, it was time for actual shopping—I needed to get something for my girlfriend, Carly. For her, I intended to buy something genuine, not fake jewelry off a street vendor (as I had been known to do in the past).

I found a quiet, reputable jewelry store and went to the counter. I actually shopped, looking at an array of pieces. I finally decided on a silver necklace and a matching pair of earrings. As it was a respectable place, I got a receipt and everything for the purchase.

I was astonished by my mature fanciness. I would adorn Carly and myself in the finest of jewels. We would flaunt our matching tongue and navel studs. Each of our toes would sport custom platinum rings. Our wrists would be draped in turquoise bangles.

Later, though.

I also ventured to several nearby stores to buy a few cheap trinkets for people in Seattle. I then picked up two rolls of thirty-six exposure film.

I was the Hungarian handler; the Magyar master of merchandise.

After my spending spree, it was time to head to the Széchenyi Chain Bridge, the mile-long main bridge connecting Buda and Pest.

I remembered this site from the 1985 trip because it was the bridge that housed a memorial honoring the Soviet soldiers that put down the pro-West forces during the 1956 Hungarian Revolution.

My whole family, Tati (my father), my mother, my sister, and my cousins David and Jovo all walked this bridge. I, however, being sixteen and too tired, did not.

Today, unlike in 1985, I walked to the middle of the bridge and stopped. I took in the sights. Pest with its new modernity behind me; Buda and its ancient grand castle in front; the cascading Danube below.

Stunning.

I also caught a glimpse of the Forum Hotel, where we had a grand lunch eight years ago. Then, the communists loved to put it to the Westerners, charging them prime prices whenever they could. I realized that my father must have spent a small fortune on that trip, especially in Budapest.

I continued on my way into Buda, heading toward Buda Castle. It was much quieter on that side of the city. There were more silent parks and graceful fountains than on the other side. Since I was there and I had some time, I decided to find a comfortable seat in the early autumn air and just idly watch the city pass by.

I really enjoyed getting away from all the tourists on the other side of the Danube. They could truly be pests in Pest. (I could not resist that.)

From my serene seat, I decided to move on and up the grand hill to the Castle, where I found another seat. This one was next to a man with a little dachshund. The little wiener-dog disobeyed every command that his laughing owner could throw at him. He and I laughed as the tiny dog kept us entertained for a good twenty minutes.

After the little dog and pony show, I delved deeper into Buda. I explored much more than we had in 1985. There were not a lot of tourist sites. It was just a quiet section of Hungary, readying itself for the twenty-first century.

I did get lost a few times, but I always had the Danube as a marker. I made my way back to the old bridge and took some more pictures. I crossed back over to Pest and my nearby flat. There, I dumped out the goods I had picked up earlier. The bathroom was occupied, so I just stretched out on my puffy, comfy bed.

After I completed all I needed to do, I headed back out into the early dusk to take one last walk around my neighborhood in Budapest.

I headed straight to the Danube and took some more pictures. From there I strolled around the Parliament building.

I then got lost as usual while looking for a pay phone to call my mom. I found a phone, but it didn't work. But luckily, in finding the phone I was able to get a handle on where I was. I remembered, like so many before me, to just follow the Danube.

After a couple of hours or so of walking through the quiet Saturday night of the capital, I decided it was time to call it a day. I made a mental note of which way Keleti Station was and headed back to the flat.

Right now, I have my glasses on and I am very tired. I must get up early. Tomorrow is a big day.

13

Yugoslavia (Serbia)

Sombor, Subotica

OCTOBER 31

I t is the next morning, so I will be catching up on yesterday.
I actually got up a bit too early, so I had time to do some reading.
I was still quite tired, so I was lucky I did not fall back asleep. After half
an hour or so, I showered with no interruptions, dressed, and then
tied, shoved, and stowed the ten thousand dollars and Marks all over
my body and backpack.

The flat-owner's son then knocked on my door and asked if he
could change the sheets. I took that as my cue to beat it out of there.
They were probably ready to head to the station to find another traveler
to scare the hell out of.

As I still had the Metro tickets from the landlord, I decided that,
damn-it, I would venture back down into that coal mine of a subway.
But, to my surprise, after the hellish descent, it was quite fast and
convenient. I got on and off with absolutely no issues (and no early-
morning drunks).

When I arrived at Keleti, it was close to ten in the morning. I was
to meet Jovo at eleven at track one. I had scouted it two days earlier, so
I knew which way to go.

After I ran a gauntlet of five *babas* (old women) trying to get me
to rent their rooms, I made it to track one and took a seat at around
ten thirty.

I waited there a bit, but no one showed. As I was getting up to look around, I spotted a man in the distance with a mouthful of bread, walking with a young woman. As we approached, I thought that he looked a bit like Jovo, but I was not sure. As we passed, we snuck a glance at each other, but neither said a thing.

After I'd walked about twenty feet, I turned back and headed their way.

"Jovo," I yelled three times.

"Mike," he finally responded.

I had found him. The first part of my goal was complete. I now had just a couple of objectives left to realize on the trip.

Jovo and I hugged, generally happy to see one another but both still in mourning for my father.

I saw that there were two adults with him. The first, the man, was obviously his son, Dusan. Dusan had been a thirteen-year-old kid when I had seen him last. Now he was a tall, sturdy-looking adult. He was recently discharged from the military after serving his two-year compulsory service. He still had the same shy and quiet demeanor that I remembered.

The woman was Jovo's daughter, Mirjana. The last time I saw her, she was an adorable, itty-bitty, tiny little girl with puffy jet-black hair who we nicknamed, *Kiki-Riki* (Peanut). She looked so different grown up that Jovo had to tell me who she was.

We all hugged as I fought back tears, so happy to see such grand, wonderful faces.

After this reunion in this most industrial, rough area, we worked our way through the main station and into the parking lot. We headed to their car, a new red model, not the white death trap Yugo Jovo drove us around in in 1985.

Mirjana and I hopped in the back, and Jovo sat in front so he could navigate for Dusan.

Jovo grabbed the unyielding city map and got us out of the parking lot. Job one was complete.

After some confusion in the city, we finally reached the highway and headed south. Any navigational confusion was lost on me—I couldn't stop smiling. I was with family again. I was also quite happy to be away from trains and timetables, hotels and hostels, cities and crowds.

Despite the language barrier, we talked the whole time. I was sure I understood less than they did, as Dusan had a decent grasp of English. Mirjana, not so much; she had taken French in school. Jovo, like me, was unilingual. I had a bit of regret that I never learned Serbo-Croatian, but at that moment I was too content to worry about it.

As we chatted, the radio played the all-too-familiar Balkan music that I grew up listening to at the Serbian hall and picnic grounds in Gary, Indiana. It awakened memories of the old days, and I was surprised that I did not become depressed thinking of those bygone times. But just then I was too exhilarated to be beaten down.

After an hour and a half, we stopped at a town on a river near the Hungary-Yugoslav border. It looked like the same town we'd stopped at in 1985 when we were returning from our trip to Budapest. I asked Jovo, but he said no, as he remembered the stop as well.

We walked around the small town square. Not many people and not many businesses were open. So we headed to the Duna Hotel to eat.

Just like in 1985 at the other small border town, I ordered a nice big, deep-fried fish. To drink, unlike the 1985 trip (when I'd been sixteen), I ordered a beer. Great meal.

I was still riding high.

We hopped back in the car and made our way to the border. I began to see the effect that the Western (American) embargo was having on the region. The lines at the border with Yugoslavia were extensive, maybe four miles in length, because the embargo had cut off most oil to the country and people were forced to go to Hungary to buy gasoline. The line on this side was the Yugoslavs returning with full tanks of gas. I could not fathom what the line looked like on the other side.

We pulled to the back of the line and waited for about a half an hour. Then Jovo, as impatient as I remembered, jumped out of the car. He told Dusan to drive around the line as he walked outside, shotgun. After some time and some angry honks and cursing from those we passed, we arrived at the border checkpoint. We were now second in line as the car in front of us was just completing entry through passport control.

Jovo was still outside the car when a group of well-armed Yugo-slavian border guards surrounded the vehicle. They first questioned

Jovo, who kept his calm. I found out later that they asked him why he cut in front of the miles-long line. He told them that he had an American in the car. This seemed to satisfy them, and they did not send us to the back of the line like castigated schoolchildren.

The group of guards began to inspect the car. They held mirrors underneath and popped the hood and trunk. However, they did not order the rest of us out. They were satisfied with three guards individually aiming rifles at us.

The only thing that I thought about was the money that was strapped all over my body. If they decided to search us and do anything but a cursory pat-down, they would certainly find it.

Well, I began to think, "I sure am glad that my last few hours on Earth were filled with such familial exuberance."

But, to my relief, all was in order, and we passed that inspection.

Jovo hopped into the driver's seat, and I thought we were about to put the experience behind us. Instead, he gathered all of our passports and told us they would need to inspect the American's a bit more closely.

One of the border guards directed us away from the line and into a parking space. Jovo then let me know I needed a visa to enter Yugoslavia.

This I did not have. The American embassy in Dublin had said I did not need one. Goddamn bureaucracy. I remembered that the informational documents they gave to me were quite old, but I had been assured that they were accurate.

You would think the most powerful country on Earth—the winners of the Cold War, the defenders of democracy—would have up-to-date information for its citizens, especially about entering one of the most dangerous places in the world.

Fuck. I had bet my life and ten thousand dollars on that old information!

I quickly forgot about the inadequacies of the American State Department; the sequence of events that happened next would stay in my mind forever.

The three guards that had held their guns on us returned and again took position, now aiming their rifles at our heads.

They allowed Jovo to get out of the tiny car with all four of our passports. He headed into the small building—the defending fortress at the Yugoslavian/Hungarian frontier. As he walked in, I saw Jovo wave at a smallish, bespectacled woman dressed in military fatigues.

She did not wave back.

He entered the building and headed directly to her. She displayed no affection; she seemed as stern as a dominatrix. It was hard to discern what was transpiring, but I saw him wildly gesticulating and pointing to the car, speaking not just to her but to all the guards.

The woman, obviously the boss, stood there, still, listening intently as this crazy man nearly hyperventilated.

Jovo and the woman disappeared from my sight. It ran through my mind that they had had enough of him: time for torture at the Yugoslav border.

Then, after a few harrowing minutes of worry, I saw Jovo near the door. He made one last innocuous gesture, and then he exited. As he walked to the car, his expression divulged no emotion.

He motioned for Dusan to get into the driver's seat, which he quickly did.

Jovo, with a guard now following him, opened the passenger-side door, got in, and lowered the window. The guard that was behind him approached and quietly said something meant only for Jovo.

They both laughed their Serbian asses off and shook hands.

Then Jovo rolled up the window and said in English, "All OK. Let's go." It was the most English I had ever heard him speak.

As Dusan put the car in gear, I still couldn't believe it. I thought it was a joke. I saw Jovo smile and wave as a slew of guards came out to bid farewell to the crazy man.

I hesitantly waved with my left hand as my right kept my heart from pounding out of my chest—and gripped the currency-filled neck pouch.

Jovo handed me my passport. He explained, through his son's interpretation, that the woman was an old friend of his. They went to her back office, dug up an old stamp, and created a visa for me. She forged the appropriate signature. Then they had a shot of slivovitz (plum brandy) and Jovo went on his way.

What the fuck?!

Jovo never told us what the guard said at the window. He never even told his kids. I like to think it was a dirty joke, *Srpski* style.

We were back on the road, and I was in Yugoslavia, still with five thousand dollars and five thousand Deutsche Marks hidden throughout my clothing and pack.

From that side of the border, I got to see much more of the embargo's effect. The lines to get into Hungary for precious gasoline (petrol) were twice, maybe three times as long as the lines to enter. Nearly all of the cars were out of fuel. Their drivers and passengers sporadically pushed them as the line advanced at the speed of a glacier.

As we passed out of the border region, I began to remember this area of old growth oaks, well-kept farms and small rivers slicing through the northern region of Serbia (Yugoslavia). The comfort I felt in Hungary was beginning to return as I stared out the window and took in the crisp autumn air.

Just as I was becoming fully relaxed, I saw a uniformed man waving his arms at the side of the road.

Did the border patrol set us up? Was this a sting? Was I going to a Yugoslav prison? So much for the ten grand now, I thought.

Dusan slowed the car down and brought it to a stop. The man approached the car and said, "Mike?"

Shit. The border guards did call ahead, and they told this guy to be looking out for this car and only pick-up the guy named Mike. I was sure of it.

I was wrong. It was Dusan's friend Bogdan, a person I had met in 1985. He was now a federal police officer.

Bogdan, all smiles, was just getting off patrol. He evidently knew we would be passing this way, so he just waited patiently by the roadside for a ride to town.

He wedged his way into the now overloaded Eastern European car.

As we got nearer to the town of Sombor, we passed a man on a bicycle. This one was Jovo's friend. Dusan slowed the car to a crawl so his dad could speak to his pal. I didn't understand much of the brief conversation, just a lot of "*Jebi se*" and "*Jebi ga*" yelled with smiles to each other.

Good friends for sure.

We passed him and then approached a car on a long, straight stretch of road. Everyone in the car (except me, of course) knew those folks. One and all began yelling at each other. Dusan and the other driver slowed down and pulled over to the shoulder. Dusan hopped out and got in the other car, leaving his dad, sister, buddy, and me behind. I didn't blame him. I would have done the same and joined my rowdy friends.

With our driver gone, we all changed seats. I found myself in the front seat with Jovo driving. I remembered what a completely aggressive, dangerous driver he was eight years ago, when I'd shouted, "Oh no, Jovo!" a few times as he narrowly avoided a number of collisions. Collisions he would have been the sole creator of. But today he seemed to have mellowed with age. Sitting in the front seat was not the nightmare it once was.

He got us the short distance to his house, a place I fondly remembered from 1985.

Everything still looked about the same.

Anja, Jovo's wife, was waiting for us at the door. Bogdan took off, and the three of us went inside. I hugged Anja as she motioned to the table, where three shots of rakija and three cups of strong Turkish coffee waited for her, Jovo, and me—none for Mirjana, as she was still a teenager.

Yum. It hit all of the perfect spots as we then took a seat at the kitchen table.

I noticed that the place was a bit different. In the kitchen, there was a wood-burning stove where the couch had been. That was because of the embargo. They needed the stove to heat the entire house because there was no heating oil for residential customers.

We did our best to catch up, but the most I got out of the conversation was the constant lament from Anja, "embargo, embargo, embargo."

As we talked, the slivovitz came out, and we took a few shots. That certainly warmed up the body—the embargo and the loss of heating oil be damned!

I asked Jovo and Anja if there had been fighting in Sombor. They both, thankfully, said no.

I then asked if Serbs hated Americans. They both found this amusing and laughed it off.

"Serbians tough," Jovo proudly exclaimed.

At that point I asked Jovo to call Uncle Nick (Nicola) and Teta Jean (Yagoda). I wanted them to tell him about the money I had for him. I was concerned that I would not be able to explain to him who exactly was responsible for the windfall. But they were not home, so I had to improvise.

I was not quite sure the subtleties of smuggling currency, so I grabbed my pack and asked Jovo to come to a back room to speak with me in private. Once we were alone, I emptied out about two hundred dollars from the money belt around my neck. I told him there was more, much more.

As at the border, his expression did not change.

I gestured around myself, telling him with body language that I had money located all up and down my person. He nodded his head and waved his hand to say "OK, OK," then left me alone in the dimly lit room.

I took my time as I dug out the dollars and Marks that I had so carefully hidden throughout my clothing and bag. As I removed each bundle, I threw it onto the bed—creating a significant pile of American and German cash.

Once I'd organized the bills and then myself, I called Jovo to come back into the room.

He came in, and then he closed and locked the door behind him. At that point I was confident that I'd made the correct decision in keeping this handover quiet.

I handed him all of the money and said the names of our family: my mother, uncle, aunt, sister, cousin and the others. That was all I said as he counted the money.

Again, his damned expression never changed.

Coolness personified.

I had handed him ten thousand dollars. That was more than ten years' worth of wages for Jovo, a middle-class citizen of Yugoslavia.

He nodded his head as he went through the money. I could tell the wheels were turning. He was formulating a plan to distribute this illegal windfall to close family and friends throughout the country.

When he finished his count, he looked at me with his same serious expression and again said, "OK, OK." But this time, he tousled my hair as we walked out of the room and back to the kitchen.

Now—to my relief—it was time to eat. After having such a large load lifted off of me, literally and figuratively, I ate a lot. I was sure that they thought I was an animal as I ate plate after plate of the delicious home-cooked food.

So much for a diet in Yugoslavia.

After dinner, we headed to the family room and turned on the TV. First, we watched a French cartoon, *Lucky Luke* or something like that.

Next was a Fellini film in the original Italian (I believe Fellini died either that day or the day before). I did my best to follow it, but I knew less Italian than I knew Serbo-Croatian.

And it was Fellini, for God's sake.

That was followed by an unforgettable *Popeye the Sailor Man* cartoon. It was so noteworthy because its voice dub seemed to have been done live, right off the cuff— no rehearsal, and for that matter, no script. The voice actor would stumble on lines and interject "uhs" and "ohs" while he was thinking of something to say. Brilliant unintentional comedy.

I tried to contain my laughter (there was no way I could explain ironic humor in a language I did not speak) but did crack up a few times.

I ended up falling asleep on the couch in the living room. After half an hour or so, Jovo woke me up and showed me the sleeping quarters they had prepared for me. They had set me up in the warmest room of the house.

I slept the best I had in months.

November 1

W*hen I awoke today*, Anja and Mirjana were in the kitchen preparing breakfast. Soon Anja left for work, while Mirjana continued with breakfast. I offered to help, but she waved me off. So I went back to the TV room and turned on the Serbian news.

Dusan came into the room and told me that the food was ready. He and I gorged on breakfast. Again, with all the food I had been eating, they must have thought I was an animal.

When Dusan and I finished our meal, we discussed some of his money-making endeavors. The capitalist in the making had been going up to Budapest every few months with a couple of his friends and buying thick winter coats.

The embargo had stopped virtually all imports, so there was a shortage of everything. Winter coats were, and would continue to be, a necessity; the weather was already chilly. He told me that they sold them for more than twice what they paid.

I then had Dusan call my mom. But she was not home, so I could only leave a message.

After the failed call, Dusan had to run an errand, and Mirjana had disappeared. They left me alone, so I watched MTV. It was Beatles Day or something, so the channel was playing only the Fab Four's videos. All great. I especially liked the one for "Hello, Goodbye."

As I watched the Beatles, I began to reflect.

I had no intention of contemplating my travels while I was still living them. But self-reflection is impossible to control—it can spring up at any time. It is simply not a planned construct.

If someone had asked me on June 1 where I would be or what I would have seen by November 1, I would have answered, Merrillville, Gary, Valparaiso, Crown Point, Munster, and maybe Chicago.

But things had changed, and I struggled to believe it. I could not believe that I had been traveling one hundred out of the last one hundred and fifty days. The only time I hadn't been traveling was while I was finishing my final summer session of graduate school. I had gone from the East Coast of America to the West Coast. I had traveled solo through Europe—from Amsterdam to Ireland to Yugoslavia. I had experienced what I had only imagined through twenty years of school.

The reverie ended as Dusan and Mirjana returned along with some of their friends to show off their American sideshow cousin/eating-machine.

I greeted them all as they practiced their best English on me. I did the same with Serbo-Croatian, but they were much better speakers of my language than I was of theirs.

One of Dusan's friends, Vlado, spoke the best English and was quite easy to understand. Of course, he was the one most embarrassed about his English-speaking ability. He had to close the door and would not allow anyone else to hear him and I converse.

Vlado was definitely young, and definitely a partisan Serb and proud communist. He spoke of the prowess and power of the Serbian leaders, Milosevic in particular. He lauded the former Soviet Union's power and might in spite of their recent Cold War defeat and ensuing systemic collapse. Traitors were to blame, he calmly assured me. The Soviets would rise again.

As I did not want to get in any political conversations (it was my country creating this crippling embargo after all), I told him we should go out back and find the rest of the group.

We found Dusan and his other buddies in the garage, fucking around with a car battery. I did not ask and did not want to know what they were planning to do with it.

In the garage, we all did our best to converse. After that, I took a picture of the boys and then told them that I was off to see the city center.

As I was walking, I made sure to note landmarks so I did not get lost. But it was a relatively straight shot. I went quickly, trying to get some exercise, as it was only about a twenty-minute stroll.

The city center was nearly the same as I remembered. However, the central park had a large pile of coal that was used to heat the nearby church.

I looked into the shops and saw those were quite different from what I remembered. There was virtually nothing on the shelves. They were bare from the embargo.

Now I saw the reasons for the lament, "embargo, embargo, embargo." The austerity measures had taken hold of nearly every aspect of daily life.

But just as I was beginning to feel disgusted by this economic blackmail, I realized that I'd forgotten my passport at the house. This was the first time on the trip that I had done such a thing. It was also the worst possible location to do it. I was an American, here illegally, with absolutely no papers to vouch for who I was.

I began to get rightfully fearful that something was going to happen. So, I quickly made a one hundred-eighty-degree pivot and headed back down the path I had so recently memorized.

Every time I saw a police officer or a person in military clothing, my paranoia grew. Frankly, it was not paranoia. If one of those officers had decided to stop and question me, I would be done for.

I made the twenty-minute walk in ten, and I was back at home base.

It was perfect timing as Jovo was home, dealing with a large supply of seed bundles that had just been delivered. Everyone, the family and Dusan's friends, was helping load them onto a trailer attached to Jovo's Yugo.

After we loaded it up, Anja fixed us lunch.

Next, Jovo and I hopped in his car and towed the seeds down the road ten to fifteen miles. We stopped to pick up Jovo's friend, and then we drove down a dirt path and into a farm field.

There, in the open area, we stopped in front of a tractor. The embargo had cut off innumerable food imports, so most citizens had been forced to plant and cultivate their own food. Jovo had to lease this farmland from a friend who would do most of the actual farming for a set price.

Well, I was going to be a farmhand today. I was more than happy to help wherever I could.

We got out of the car, and the three of us began to unload the seeds. Soon another of their friends moseyed up and lent us a hand.

After we unloaded the trailer, the first friend hopped onto the tractor and started to drive it—I guess he was now farming?

Jovo and the second buddy chatted as I looked around, happy to be out in the open, country air.

But, before I could relax, I looked up and saw an ominous sight: a never-ending line of planes overhead. Sometimes as many as five filled the airspace. The field I was standing in was under the air corridor between Germany and Bosnia. Those were the American and Western allies' cargo planes flying aid over the embargoed state of Serbia. It was very creepy to realize that as I watched the air traffic for half an hour.

I was shaken back to reality as the tractor came roaring back and stopped just in front of us. I found out later that, because of the gasoline shortage, this farming usually took hours, as it had to be completed by a horse and plow. Today, though, they were able to use the gasoline-powered tractor.

With the farming completed, we all piled in the small car and drove back to the "farmhouse," which was in a suburban neighborhood.

The four of us headed inside and met up with some more of Jovo's pals, two women, two other men and a kid.

After such a long, arduous day of farming(!), it was time for more drinks and snacks. Brandy, coffee, and pastries for all (just soda for the little kid of course).

I was beginning to like being a farmer.

After a few rounds, Jovo became the center of attention. He filled the house with life, just generally fucking around, teasing and joking—no one was safe.

Everyone was laughing at his—obviously filthy—jokes. That included me, even though I couldn't understand a word being said. He was just such a high-spirited, positive guy that you could not help but laugh and smile while he was on. I was convinced that if he had made the move to America, he would have been a fucking star.

As the sun began to set, the star and I left. We got back to Jovo's, had another drink, and ate a second dinner.

After dinner, Jovo, Anja, and I watched TV (*The Indiana Jones Chronicles*) and talked with the aid of our respective phrase books. Vlado and Dusan showed up not long after, which made the conversation much easier as both acted as interpreters.

After a time, my stomach got upset; I was not used to so much booze mixed with strong coffee and rich food.

Time for bed.

November 2

A much quieter start to today. No one was home, so I was able to catch a movie in English, *On Golden Pond,* as I was lying in bed.

At eleven thirty I received an unexpected call from my mom, who was returning my call from yesterday. Not a lot of news, just reassuring her that all was well.

Around noon, folks started to arrive back home. First Vlado and Dusan and then Jovo.

Jovo seemed to be in a serious mood, and I asked the boys why. I was told that he would be heading south to Lika tonight or early tomorrow morning. That was what he was formulating when I gave him the money the other day. He planned on distributing the money to relatives located all over Yugoslavia.

He laid out the plan to me via Vlado. He believed it would take about two days to get everything done. It would normally be a two-hundred-kilometer trip, but with the war, the occupation, the closed roads, etc., the trip would take about four hundred circuitous kilometers to complete.

At that point I told him that I wanted to go with him. I wanted to help out more. I wanted to see the war.

Jovo, speaking quickly and still through Vlado, curtly said, "No, Mike."

He explained that there were over ten military posts throughout the trip. I assumed those checkpoints were manned by troops he would not be able to sweet-talk. But he was greatly confident that he would be able to get through without much of a problem.

But not me.

He told me, quite frankly, that I would most likely be shot over my forged papers by the second or third post.

Well, that was an easy decision.

Godspeed, good sir! I will enjoy your home and your brandy.

Before he was set to leave, Jovo told me that we might be able to go to the Danube later in the week. I told him that was a great plan.

Jovo left the house just as Bogdan, the hitchhiking police officer from a few days prior, stopped by.

Dusan had to finish some work around the house, so Vlado, Bogdan, and I hit the town of Sombor.

Our first stop was the police station.

Fantastic.

But we were in and out. Bogdan just needed to pick up his paycheck.

Our next stop was the video store, which was stocked with American films. I recommended *Goodfellas*, but they had seen it. They opted for two Serbian films I had never heard of, and we headed to the door. Just as we were about to exit, Vlado stopped and pointed at two large, puffy winter coats hanging on the wall.

"Those are coats that Dusan and I brought back from Budapest last month."

He explained that most items now on sale in the country were via the black market. The video store was no exception. There was no market regulation, so everyone could skirt taxes and procedural checks. It was a free-for-all for those willing to take a chance.

After that we just walked around Sombor. There was not a lot to see in this sleepy Eastern European town. We stopped at a sort of ice cream parlor where we got a dish of whipped cream and wheat paste that was surprisingly good.

We went into some of the other stores. The shelves were bare in the government-owned shops, and the prices were too high in the privately owned ones. I took a picture in a government-run one and was promptly yelled at and thrown out by the manager. Oops. The guys just laughed while the manager hustled us out.

Next, they took me to a pharmacy. Bare. No drugs on any of the back shelves. I took pictures there as well, but the employees were so beaten and depressed that they just didn't care.

During our trek, Vlado mentioned that he would be heading to his university in Subotica tomorrow to pick up a few things and visit his girlfriend. As Jovo would be out on his adventure all day, I decided to ask to tag along.

Vlado was up for it.

The three of us went back to the house, and Vlado and I finalized plans for the trip. As the day was ended, the boys left, and the family got ready for bed. I set my alarm for seven and quickly fell asleep.

November 3

At six thirty Jovo woke me.

He was undeniably a unique guy. At that time of day, he was already restless, bouncing off the walls, full of crazy. *Jebi se* this *jebi ga* that, and constantly on the move. He was like a hurricane, filled with kinetic energy, affecting everything around him. But there was not a whiff of put-on with this guy—his craziness seemed so sincere.

I like him.

At around half past seven, Vlado arrived. Jovo and I went outside, ready for our separate journeys.

"Mike, Mike. Good boy," Jovo said as he tousled my hair once again.

We said good-bye, and Vlado and I headed to the train station by foot. It was a long walk. I had no clue as to how far and long it was taking, only that the sun began to rise.

At the final kilometer or so, Vlado asked me the time. I told him, and he said, "Now we must run." Which of course we did.

We made the train just as it started to slowly move out of the station.

The train was unlike any of the others that I had experienced on this trip. It was only two passenger cars and an engine. The inside looked like a school bus. This train certainly reaffirmed to me that I was in Eastern Europe.

After about an hour on the "school bus," we arrived in Subotica. Judging by the train station and the buildings, Subotica was a larger, more affluent town than Sombor.

As we walked to the university, we passed shops that actually had a few goods stocked at reasonable prices. That was a welcome sight; it meant that the war had not fully engulfed the entire country.

Not yet, at least.

It was about a half an hour's walk to get to Vlado's dormitory building. Once inside I discovered that it was small, dirty, and stunk of human urine.

It was an all-male dorm after all.

We climbed the four flights of stairs to his floor. We got to his room, which had three beds and a wood burning stove in the middle. It was very cramped.

He handed me some of his books and notebooks. As they were written in Cyrillic, I had absolutely no clue what subject they were for. I just nodded knowingly and gave them back to him.

After a time, we left, through the city once again.

This time, we were headed through the center of Subotica. Just at the outskirts of the town square, we saw the black-market denizens: truly shady men with Russian hats and trench coats, selling black market currency. These guys were the stereotypical Eastern European gangster, bad guys out of a James Bond film.

As we passed through the gauntlet of ten to fifteen racketeers, I realized there was a lot of paper floating around the city. I didn't think anything of it and kept following Vlado.

We arrived at the university proper. It looked like a mid-sized American school as we ventured into the student affairs building. We left after Vlado filled out a few forms.

After that, we went into a few classroom buildings and a few of their lecture halls—very old and stale lecture halls.

From there, we went to the cafeteria of a dorm next door. We ate a tasty cheese with a name that I forgot. To drink, I got water and Vlado got a yogurt. He chugged the plain yogurt as if it were a beer.

Finally, we headed upstairs to meet his girlfriend. The hallways there, thankfully, didn't smell like urine. More like a hostel, but I didn't really mind.

He introduced me to Ruza as she took a drag on her cigarette. She was very polite to me but immediately started to chide Vlado.

"You haven't been here in three days! What is wrong?" She said to him in English, obviously intended for my ears.

Vlado stammered a bit but recovered with a smooth hug and kiss.

With that, I began to get a bit homesick. I hadn't seen my girlfriend, Carly, in three months. And, like Vlado, that was my choice.

We all took a seat as Ruza offered us loads of food. They explained to me that, because she was a Muslim, she was considered a refugee, so she got aid packages from the United Nations to counteract the embargo. In addition to the aid packs, she was allotted more space at the university. Her room had three beds like Vlado's, but she was the only student assigned to it.

With all this room, we spread out, each laying on our own bed, eating, drinking, and chatting into the late afternoon.

As the day progressed, people popped in and out, eager to see Vlado and meet the freak show American. It really wasn't that bad, as everyone that came by, although curious to meet me, was also very nice.

Finally, it was time to eat. We headed out, first stopping by the black-market crew of shady characters near the town square. I gave Vlado some American dollars so he could buy black-market dinars to pay for dinner.

On the way, he explained that inflation in Yugoslavia was out of control. Bills that were valued at one billion dinars two hours ago had been devalued down to one thousand. If one wanted to buy anything, they needed to have the most current paper currency which you bought on the black market and then spent immediately. If you did not, the bills became worthless.

As he was telling me that, I realized that the pieces of paper that were everywhere were old dinar notes, discarded after the money was devalued. There were virtually millions of billions of dinar notes flying everywhere. They were just trash, litter, at that point, so I picked up a few, to the bewilderment of Vlado and his girlfriend.

"Souvenirs," I told them.

They smiled and nodded.

Vlado, an old pro by then at dealing with the black market, finished his transaction quickly and returned to us with a stack of current dinars.

To my utter delight, we went to a pizzeria. A genuinely nice, swanky pizzeria that was playing nonstop songs from 1983—"Der Kommissar" and the like.

Any order we placed, we immediately paid for so we could use the current currency. After an hour of doing our best to spend the dinars, which by then had all been devalued, we bid farewell to Vlado's girlfriend and walked to the train station.

Once there, Vlado's face dropped. There was an inordinately long line.

He motioned for me to follow him, and I did, straight to the beginning of the queue. Once there, he glanced at me again, and I realized we were going to cut the line.

He hopped on. I hopped on. The train began to roll. Perfect timing: the crowd on the platform had no time to sling their anger (or fists) at us.

Again, the quintessential Eastern European ride. It was smoky, dirty, and stinky. People were passed out on each other in the dark of the slow-moving train.

Well, we didn't have to worry about anyone sleeping on us; we didn't have seats. So we stood in the dark, depressed car, counting the seconds until Sombor.

Once we got back to town, we ran into two more of Vlado's friends at the station. The four of us walked in the darkness back to Jovo's house. They warned me to walk on the grass, as people had been stealing the metal manhole covers in the street to sell on the black market.

What a fun country.

We made it back without anyone falling into any punji traps.

Back at Jovo and Anja's, everyone was home, including Dusan and Mirjana. I gave everyone a hug, happy because, at the very least, I had survived the walk home.

Jovo, again through Vlado, told me that all went well with the delivery of the currency. He had no problems and completed his task much more quickly than anticipated. Although his papers were checked at every stop.

But now the bad news: The trip took him a bit farther out of the way than he had anticipated, using more gasoline than budgeted. So, if we planned to take the car to Budapest, even to the border, we would not be able to go to the Danube.

I told him that was absolutely fine. I was honestly relieved, as I was a bit worried about traveling deeper into the country the more I thought about the checkpoints and forged visa. And the firing squads and the death and everything.

Win for me, I guess.

As we were discussing gasoline and the embargo, Dusan told me there was a local entrepreneur who bought two gas stations some time ago. Since the war began, he rebranded them as "Embargo 1" and "Embargo 2." He got gasoline somehow (black market) and charged ridiculous prices for it. The "Embargo(s)" had made him rich.

November 4

After such a long one yesterday, I took it extremely easy throughout most of the day.

I grabbed my passport and headed out the door after breakfast. I walked into the city again and found an open-air market that was quite depressing. Unlike farmers' markets in America (or the Pike Place Market in Seattle), where goods were plentiful, this one had barely anything. Each seller's setup was basically a card table with a few assorted gloomy goods in front of them. Nothing consistent: some people had a few electronic gadgets with some extension cords and other assorted objects. Others had a few books mixed with packs of toilet paper.

I quietly walked through the whole market and did not buy a thing.

After some time exploring more of the city of Sombor, always careful to note my direction, I headed back to Jovo and Anja's.

I watched a bad soap opera on TV because it was in English. I watched the whole hour-long mess starring some actor named Clive Longbody or something like that, and then read *War and Peace.*

I hoped to finish the behemoth before the flight, as I only had two hundred and thirty pages left.

How the fuck did Tolstoy write a book that long? How was he able to keep all of the goddamn characters straight? Napoleon, a fucking minor character?!

People were in and out the whole day, although none stayed very long, so I got a lot of reading done. At eight, Vlado and Dusan showed up and told me it was time to go out. Time to shoot some pool.

I was up for that as I had done nothing all day. After we ate a quick meal, we hit the road, walking back to the city to a nice little bar/billiard hall.

After sloppily playing three games, we didn't know how much we had spent—the tables were charged by the hour. So Dusan asked the bartender what our bill was up to that point. With a look of shock, Dusan told Vlado, who looked genuinely disturbed—I guess the price went up during the embargo.

The boys paid and we left before there were any problems.

We didn't go far. There was another pool hall across the street. It was a bit rougher, but the pool tables were much cheaper. The boys told me this was the place they normally went early in the evening to catch a buzz, as drinks were cheap as well.

But, what? They were out of beer? No *pivo*? After the bartender assured us that beer was on the way (black market again), we ordered juice and sat at a table to play dominoes.

After two hard-fought games (matches? contests? bouts?) of dominoes, the beer arrived. Good, strong Yugoslavian *pivo*, Jelena Pivo, I believe. Whatever it was, it hit the spot as we delved even deeper into our domino tournament (bowl? meet? derby?).

Once the dominoes had worn out their welcome, we started to shoot pool on an absolutely shitty miniature pool table.

After we played five more games of pool, I began to talk to the bartender. First, I told him that I was an American.

"Nirvana?" he asked.

How was one to answer that unusual question if one did not know he was talking about a band?

Yes, Yugoslavia is nirvana; it is heaven on earth, my good sir.

I just nodded and told him I was from Seattle (despite having lived there for only three weeks).

Hearing that, he got excited and beamed. He bought us a round. But, as it was past one in the morning, we only drank a bit of it. We took a picture with the odd little man (who smelled like Teen Spirit) and then hit the road, bound for home.

November 5

Today, Friday, I had yet to shower as I woke up late. I took it easy again through most of the day, exploring the neighborhood and then briefly going into town.

Around three in the afternoon, Cousin Mirko called the house. Mirko was Jovo's late sister Mira's only child. I think that made him my first cousin once removed.

When I was in Sombor in 1985, Mirko was around nineteen and still a conscript in the Yugoslav People's Army. He was a quiet but very considerate person who I got along with very well. In fact, my entire family got along with Mirko very well. He was a genuinely kind person.

Mirko told Anja that he, along with his wife and two daughters, Katarina, age four years, and Mimi, age four months, were on their way to see me.

When they arrived, it was great to see my cousin and to meet his family. However, I noticed, and mentioned, that he had lost a lot of weight. He explained to me (in exceptionally good English) not to worry, as his health was fine. When he was in the army, he had to bulk up to keep up with everyone else in his platoon. These days he could relax.

When he relaxed, he lost weight? And this guy had some of the same genes as me?

Mirko and his wife wanted to take me to the house they were building in a new neighborhood of Sombor. So, the five of us piled into his Yugo and hit the road. We didn't have to go very far, as the new development was near Jovo's house.

The site, although unfinished and in the middle of construction, was impressive. A large, three-floor home with two bedrooms, a large living room, a dining room, and even a built-in bar room. It seemed very American.

After checking out the whole construction site, we piled back into the car and headed to his parent's old apartment, the same one we'd visited in 1985.

Once there, we talked about our family, his late mother and father (who had recently passed away after living for decades with Parkinson's) and my dad. There was sadness, but we did our best to reminisce about only the good times.

Grief is love with nowhere to go.

I knew then that I had succeeded in completing my self-imposed covenant.

Vichnaya Pamyat.

Early in our conversation, as his wife and kids played around the apartment, Mirko got up and headed to a cupboard. He grabbed a beautiful bottle of French whiskey, peeled off the seal and poured us each a glass, neat.

His wife joined us after a time, and he poured her a glass as well. They turned on their wedding video, and we watched the ceremony as we polished off more of the tasty spirits.

The wedding was like a Serbian American wedding in Gary, Indiana, except the people were not as dressed up, and the ceremony was civil. The video evoked my childhood and the good times I'd had with my family. Tears welled, but I did not break.

Next, we looked at pictures, including those taken of our families together in 1985. It was nice to see those pictures. They were new to me, as I was used to the ones that my family took of that trip.

After some time lost in the past, Mirko's mother-in-law came by as well as her neighbor. They were both very nice and shared a bit more of the whiskey with us as we talked some more.

After three hours and a spent bottle of French whiskey, it was time to head back to Jovo and Anja's. Once we got back, I gave the little girls five American dollars each and said good-bye to my cousin Mirko and his wife. It was bittersweet; I wished that I could have spent more time with them. Maybe I will the next time I am in Yugoslavia.

As it was my final night in Sombor, and in Yugoslavia for that matter, a few more people came by to meet me, including a distant relative named Jovan. His grandfather was brothers with either my grandmother (Baba) Yeka or her husband, my grandfather who passed away before I was born. I really did not understand when they explained the lineage.

He laughingly gave me a handful of worthless dinars to take home as souvenirs.

Hvala, pal.

Jovan had just left, and I was getting ready for bed, when Vlado and Bogdan barged into the house. They were ready and raring to go out drinking once again, despite the plan for the four of us (including Dusan) to leave for Budapest at four the next morning.

I took a hard pass, but Dusan readily accepted. Those youngsters were two years my junior, so I let the young bucks have their fun.

After they left, Jovo, Anja, and I talked some more. As we chatted, I wrote down several friends and relative's addresses and phone numbers in America. They in turn did the same.

Next, to bed for this old man.

14

Hungary (part II), The Netherlands (part II)

Budapest, Amsterdam

November 6

A lright, time to catch up once again.
Today, I awoke at three in the morning and began an adventure that did not stop for thirty-one hours.

I cleaned up (but did not take a shower), got dressed, and then saw that Jovo and Anja were already awake and had made coffee. Dusan was awake as well, but he was outside getting the Yugo ready for our trip.

I said my good-byes to Jovo and Anja, genuinely happy that I could see them and help them out in any way I could. As I was giving them one final hug, Dusan pulled the car around to the front of the house. I headed outside into the darkness and made out the other two friends heading up the street.

But Bogdan was missing. Vlado had brought his college roommate, whom I had not yet met, instead. It seemed the police officer had a bit too much to drink last night and bailed out at the last second. Apparently, they needed three guys to accomplish their mission of buying black market winter coats, so Vlado had hastily recruited his roommate that morning.

We hit the desolate, empty roads around four o'clock in the morning, Dusan and I in front and Vlado and his roommate in back.

We listened to Freddie Mercury's song "Living on My Own" a number of times on the tape deck as we raced through the cold air of Serbia.

As we neared the border, Dusan began to tell me the plan. It was nearly the same one as coming into Serbia. However, there was one large difference. My fraudulent passport would not matter. Hungary did not require a visa, so those guards wouldn't care how I'd gotten into Yugoslavia.

I was relieved.

Dusan continued. We would bypass the long line and get to the front of it at the border control checkpoint. There, they would present my passport and me. This would, hopefully, compel the border guards to let us through as we would not simply be there for gasoline or embargo supplies like the rest of the crowd. And, I guess, they won't want to stir up an international incident by messing with the sovereignty of an American citizen.

The plan sounded good, and it had sort of worked once already, so I signed on.

After an hour or so of driving, we got to the end of the border line. This queue was about five miles deep of out-of-fuel Yugos. The air was tense but had a party atmosphere. I was sure the slivovitz was flowing freely down this entire five-mile line.

Dusan slowed down and eventually came to a full stop. He spoke to his friends in Serbian, and then he slowly started to accelerate, barely missing a couple of pedestrians.

He then swung the wheel right and gunned it onto the small sidewalk. At first, people jumped out of the way, barely avoiding getting hit. He then swung around a sidewalk barricade (others must have tried this) and into a few front yards.

At that point, someone had had enough and kicked the car. I mean really laid a soccer foot into the metal—it rattled us all.

Dusan immediately stopped the car in the middle of the yard. The doors flew open, and my three Serbian comrades rushed out into the crowd.

I stayed put, at first just sitting in my seat with my door being the only one still closed and locked. However, I heard what I could only identify as gunshots.

Pop, pop, pop. Three times for three short-tempered guys.

Three times was enough for me. I fell to the floor of the tiny car. I threw my backpack on top of myself and hid the best I could. I felt my body trying to flatten itself, instinctively trying to make myself less of a target than I was.

My fat body betrayed me as I could only shrink so much.

I then started to curse myself. I was going to be home in two days. Fuck, I survived fifty-eight goddamn days only to be shot in Serbia by a mob because a car door got kicked.

Fuck.

I was mad, sad, and scared.

Before I could freak out anymore, the boys returned. They were laughing; they'd only argued with a few people down the road.

The *pop, pop, pop*? Fireworks. The boys told me that people set those off all the time to kill their boredom at the border.

Well, I hadn't soiled my pants, so all was not lost. I regained what was left of my tough-guy composure, and we continued the last unaccosted mile or so down the sidewalk to the border station.

Once we got to the booth, the guard looked at the Yugoslavian plate and lazily shook his head *no*.

No one gets through until the border opened at eight, he told us.

Who knew that the nation of Hungary had store hours?

Dusan started up, just like his old man.

"*Amerikansi, Amerikansi!*" he yelled, and then he literally threw the guard my passport.

The guard, still seated, caught it, looked at it, and then looked at Dusan, who was pointing at me. He then raised his ass, oh, maybe two to three inches from his seat to get a better view of me. He handed Dusan my passport, wearily nodded his head, and waved us through.

Living on my own. Thank you Der Kommissar.

Down the road, we yelled and celebrated as we stopped for precious gasoline and bottles of juice all around.

The hour-long ride from the Hungarian border to Budapest was desolate. There was absolutely no one on the road, so we made excellent time.

We got to the capital at around eight o'clock in the morning. Our first stop: a street bazaar that was just opening. As we couldn't find a parking spot, Vlado and his pal hopped out, and Dusan and I stayed in the car. After a short time, the boys returned empty-handed. They had hoped to pick up a few extra items to sell on the black market, but there was nothing worthy that early in the day.

From there it was on to the train station. We arrived extremely early, so we had about three hours to kill before my train to Vienna was set to depart. Even though it was raining rather hard, the boys decided to hang out for a time and explore Budapest. They knew where they would pick up their coats to sell, so they didn't really worry about finding a shop.

As the day was young and we had not eaten breakfast, that was next on our agenda. The boys wanted pizza. I, surprisingly, did not, as I wanted morning food.

The four of us were arguing about where to eat when I offhandedly said, "I saw a McDonald's down that road."

Oh shit—they got wildly excited.

"McDonald's is *super*," Dusan exclaimed, a great big smile on his face.

Vlado, the guy who looked down on America and held everything Soviet in the highest regard, beamed at the thought of this craven, capitalist institution of bad nutrition.

Off to McDonald's.

When we got there, it became apparent that this was the first visit to McDonald's for all of the boys, as they immediately headed to a table.

Nope, no servers here in this wonderland. You ordered at the harsh, brown and yellow counter.

As I was leading them to the cashier, Vlado grabbed four trays, one for each of us, from a nearby rack.

The cashier tried to tell him that they would supply the trays to him, but he was insistent on bringing them to the register.

Nope, this isn't a grade school cafeteria. In this culinary paradise, they give the trays to you, filled with "food."

I stepped up and placed my order. The boys then followed my lead, and each of them ordered exactly what I did.

I guess the boys recognized a developed palate for shitty food when they saw one.

We got our food on individual trays(!), took a seat, and gorged ourselves.

After that, we waded through the pouring rain and returned to Keleti Station. I got my pack from the car, and the four of us walked to my train.

The boys boarded with me. I don't think they had ever been on a train of that type and size. We looked for a suitable car.

Second-class, my friends. Only the second-best for me.

In my car, the boys were amazed by all of the buttons and knobs, and they pushed and pulled at every one of them. As they were fiddling with the simple switches, a couple of girls passed by on the platform. Vlado made an extremely offensive, sexist comment that thankfully they did not hear.

With that, I was ready for those Eastern European knuckleheads to hit the road, which they did in short time.

From war to peace.

Time to relax and read my nearly completed Russian novel. Back to Pierre and Natasha and Nikolai.

As I waited for the train to leave, two Austrian couples joined me in my car. The four of them were quite nice, apart from one man's obnoxious laugh.

Oh well. At least he wasn't yelling horrible things to women passing by. I would be fine dealing with a weird laugh for a few hours, I told myself. In fact, as time passed, the laugh actually grew on me. It turned out that I was weird as well.

Who knew?

Besides the odd laugh, it was a fully uneventful three-hour trip. I was awestruck at its unexceptionalism.

In Vienna. First, I found an exchange to change four dollars in order to get cheese, bread, water, and a *USA Today*. I stowed those in my pack and looked for a WC.

The WC I found was a pay toilet. I'd just spent the last of my money, so I decided to hold it for three hours and go on the train.

From there, I went to the warm waiting room and read the paper. At last, there was nothing in the news to pique my anxiety.

The train arrived, and I hopped on for the fourteen-hour trip from Vienna to Amsterdam. I was amazed at my luck. No one, not a soul (except for the conductor and the passport checker) bothered me during the entire trip through central Europe.

During the first part of the run, from seven in the evening to ten, I read *War and Peace*. I then slept from ten to six in the morning. I watched the scenery for a while and then read for the last portion of the trip.

With about thirty minutes left of travel before reaching Amsterdam, I did something I'd thought that I would never do. Something that even a year ago I would have deemed impossible—laughable—to even consider: I finished *War and Peace*. All 1,455 fucking pages, consumed by my brain. Prince Andrei, Boris and Natasha (not Bullwinkle's nemeses), Nikolai, Petya, Kuragin, Denis, Sonya, Lisa, and goddamn Napoleon would be in my head forever.

Fucking Russians (and French).

November 7

I arrived again, after two months, in Amsterdam. This time, I pulled into the train station on a cold, rainy early Sunday morning. There were not a lot of people, but I was approached by a couple of hostel hawkers almost immediately.

No thanks, I politely said to them as I walked to the tourist information booth.

After I passed the ubiquitous Amsterdam junkies, I got to the booth located just outside the station. At that moment I realized that I must look like a junkie myself. I was tired and dirty, with filthy, stinking clothes plastered to my body.

When I entered the small building, I was the only tourist inside, so I headed to the first window.

"Good morning."

"Goedemorgen," the polished and pretty Dutch girl repeated to me with a smile.

"I would like an *en suite* room, preferably in a hotel with a fine dining restaurant, near Schiphol."

"Are you sure you would not like a hostel? There are many fine ones in the city for very low prices."

"No, thank-you. I would like an *en suite* room, preferably in a hotel with a fine dining restaurant, near Schiphol."

"For such a place, I will need a credit card for prepay," she said, expecting me to balk.

"That's fine. Will Visa work?"

With my hotel paid for, the little Dutch girl then told me how to get there. I would have to take a train to the airport and then double back on another track to get to the hotel.

No problem. I could navigate that. I was now a major league, world-class fucking traveler.

I arrived at the airport and just got a five-guilder taxi to my hotel, which was only four kilometers away.

At the hotel desk, I saw some dismay on the very clean and clear face of the Dutch woman who was checking me in. She asked for and studied my passport before she finalized the room for me.

I passed by the lovely little restaurant, rode the elevator, and arrived at my room.

What a room! *En suite*, TV, radio, phone, bar. The fucking works, for the equivalent of fifty-eight dollars!

I put down my bag, turned on a cartoon and assessed my situation.

I had gone eight days without a shower, as I did not want to waste anything in Yugoslavia. I had had my striped shirt on for eight days. My underwear had remained unchanged for eight days as well. My socks were relatively clean, as they had only been on for seven days. That brought me to the pants. *The pants.* Eleven days straight they had been on me. They had been on me since Venice fucking Italy. I had to peel them off, as they were stuck to my unclean flesh.

I am a monster.

So I took a shower. Well, not a shower but a pair of showers. Once I finished the first one, I decided that I was just not clean enough, so I repeated the whole process. I shaved my face and combed my hair for the first time in almost a month. I ventured back downstairs to the lobby in my fresh clothes.

At the desk I asked the same clerk who checked me in if the restaurant was open. As she was answering me, she suddenly realized I was the "junkie" who she'd checked-in an hour before. She laughed in relief and then complimented me that I looked a whole better.

"*Bedankt*" I thought, as I only smiled.

She showed me to the restaurant, where, for the second time on this trek, I ordered and ate two meals.

After that, fat and happy, I retired to my room and actually took one more shower. I then turned on the TV to watch Mentos commercials interrupted by cartoons. I fell asleep early.

Epilogue

This is my tribute to 1970s detective shows that always ended with an epilogue.

I am finishing this journal one month after I arrived back in the United States. I am in a Highland, Indiana middle school, where I'm about to give a presentation on the trip.

After getting up at dawn in the fancy Dutch hotel, I took one more shower, the fourth in that room in one day. I then left for the airport via taxi and then train, ready to board my 9:00-a.m. flight direct to Seattle.

It would end up being literally the longest travel day of my life. The previous record had been set only one day before, when I traveled for (only) thirty-one hours straight from Sombor to Amsterdam.

Arriving at Schiphol, I was a bit late for boarding, so I ran to the United Airlines counter. But once I got there, I found out that the flight I was scheduled for, the flight whose paper ticket I had held in my neck pouch for sixty days, had been canceled. Not delayed, but canceled—nearly one and a half fucking months ago!

After a few nail-biting moments, the airline was able to book me on a flight to Seattle via a stop at Dulles in Washington D.C. But it would not be departing for five hours.

I had time to kill in Holland, so I picked up two magazines and read most of them. I also walked. I walked and walked. My body was accustomed to it.

When I was finally able to board the plane, I was happy to see that I had two seats to myself in the sparsely sold flight. On the boring eleven-hour Atlantic crossing, they showed an equally boring Olympia Dukakis film, so I read anything and everything they had onboard. But, thankfully, unlike my crossing to Europe, I was able to catch a bit of sleep.

In Dulles, I had to pass through customs.

"Did you go to Amsterdam?" was the first question from the American officer.

"Yes, two months ago," I answered. A bit of a lie, but I was only in the city for a few minutes yesterday. (Or was it two days ago? Who the hell knew anymore.)

He then asked if I had any knives.

What? No, I told him.

"Not even a Swiss Army Knife?"

OK, you got me.

"Oh, yes, I do."

He was just fucking with me, looking to get a rise from a kid. He didn't care about the knife, as he just waved me through.

From there, I easily found and boarded my connection to Seattle, where I discovered I had the whole back row to myself. I didn't care that I couldn't recline as I stretched out for the six-hour flight and watched *The Fugitive*, happy not to be one.

The plane touched down around eight at night. Thirty-four hours of travel to end the longest day and the longest trip of my life.

Also, the end to the most important journey I had ever undertaken.

Not a real profound ending, but there will be more journals of future trips.

Until then....

Appendix I
Daily Cities

September 8: Seattle, London
September 9: Amsterdam
September 10: Amsterdam
September 11: Cologne, Berlin
September 12: Berlin
September 13: Berlin, Dresden, Prague
September 14: Prague
September 15: Prague
September 16: Prague, Kraków
September 17: Kraków, Oświęcim
September 18: Kraków, Frankfurt
September 19: Frankfurt
September 20: Luxembourg, Brussels
September 21: Paris
September 22: Paris
September 23: Paris
September 24: Paris
September 25: Cherbourg
September 26: Rosslare
September 27: Dublin
September 28: Galway
September 29: Galway
September 30: Dublin
October 1: Rosslare
October 2: Cherbourg, Bayeux
October 3: Bayeux
October 4: Bayeux
October 5: Bayeux, Irun, Madrid
October 6: Madrid

October 7: Madrid
October 8: Barcelona
October 9: Barcelona, Cerbère , Nice
October 10: Nice
October 11: Nice
October 12: Nice
October 13: Nice, Geneva
October 14: Geneva, Gimmelwald
October 15: Gimmelwald
October 16: Gimmelwald, Florence
October 17: Florence
October 18: Florence, Pisa
October 19: Florence
October 20: Orvieto, Bagnoregio, Civita di Bagnoregio
October 21: Rome
October 22: Rome
October 23: Rome
October 24: Rome, Naples, Pompeii
October 25: Venice
October 26: Venice
October 27: Venice
October 28: Vienna
October 29: Budapest
October 30: Budapest
October 31: Budapest, Sombor
November 1: Sombor
November 2: Sombor
November 3: Sombor
November 4: Sombor
November 5: Sombor
November 6: Sombor, Budapest, Vienna
November 7: Amsterdam
November 8: Washington, D.C.; Seattle

Appendix II
Transportation

Amsterdam to Cologne: 3 hours
Cologne to Berlin: 8 hours (couchette)
Berlin to Dresden: 3 hours
Dresden to Prague: 2 hours
Prague to Kraków: 8 hours
Kraków to Oświęcim: 1 hour (automobile)
Kraków to Frankfurt: 18 hours
Frankfurt to Luxembourg: 3 hours
Luxembourg to Brussels: 3 hours
Brussels to Paris: 3 hours
Paris to Cherbourg: 3 hours
Cherbourg to Rosslare: 20 hours (ferry)
Rosslare to Dublin: 3 hours
Dublin to Galway: 3 hours
Galway to Dublin: 3 hours
Dublin to Rosslare: 3 hours
Rosslare to Cherbourg: 20 hours (ferry)
Cherbourg to Bayeux: 1 hour
Bayeux to Paris: 3 hours
Paris to Irun: 6 hours (TGV)
Irun to Madrid: 9 hours
Madrid to Barcelona: 7 hours
Barcelona to Cerbère: 3 hours
Cerbère to Nice: 8 hours (couchette)
Nice to Monaco: 1 hour
Nice to Geneva, 11 hours (couchette)
Geneva to Interlaken: 3 hours
Interlaken to Lauterbrunnen: Less than an hour (non-Eurail)
Lauterbrunnen to Stechelberg: Less than an hour (bus)

Stechelberg to Gimmelwald: Less than an hour (funicular)
Gimmelwald to Mürren: Less than an hour (funicular)
Mürren to Stechelberg: 1 hour (funicular)
Stechelberg to Lauterbrunnen: Less than an hour (bus)
Lauterbrunnen to Interlaken: Less than an hour (non-Eurail)
Interlaken to Brig: 3 hours
Brig to Milan: 2 .5 hours
Milan to Florence: 3 hours (no seat)
Florence to Pisa: 1 hour
Pisa to Florence: 1 hour
Florence to Orvieto: 2 hours
Orvieto to Bagnoregio: 1 hour (bus)
Bagnoregio to Orvieto: 1 hour (bus)
Civita di Orvieto to Orvieto: Less than an hour (funicular)
Orvieto to Rome: 1 hour
Rome to Naples: 3 hours
Naples to Pompeii: 1 hour
Pompeii to Naples: 1 hour
Naples to Rome: 3 hours
Rome to Venice: 5 hours
Venice to Vienna: 10 hours
Vienna to Budapest: 3.5 hours (the Orient Express)
Budapest to Sombor: 4 hours (automobile)
Sombor to Subotica: 1 hour
Subotica to Sombor: 1 hour
Sombor to Budapest: 4 hours (automobile)
Budapest to Vienna: 3.5 hours
Vienna to Amsterdam: 14 hours
Amsterdam to Hoofddorp (Schiphol Airport): 1 hour

Appendix III
Accommodations

Amsterdam: Anna Hostel, 1 star
Amsterdam: Hotel Van Oona, 3 stars
Germany: Couchette, 2 stars
Berlin: Tourist Hotel, 2 stars
Prague: Jana's Flat, 4 nights, 4 stars
Poland: Train, 1 star
Kraków: Hotel Pod Rosa, 4 stars
Germany: Train, 1 star
Frankfurt: Hotel Westfalinger, 3 stars
Brussels: Hostel Sleepwell, 2 stars
Paris: Hostel, 2 stars
Paris: Hotel du Prince Eugene, 3 stars
Paris: Hotel Excelsior, 2 nights, 3 stars
Ferry: Hallway, 1 star
Rosslare: Farmhouse Bed and Breakfast, 4 stars
Dublin: Isaacs Hostel, 2 stars
Galway: Hollywood Bed and Breakfast, 2 nights, 3 stars
Dublin: Isaacs Hostel, 1 star
Ferry: Couchette, 3 stars
Bayeux: Hotel de la Gare, 3 stars
Bayeux: Hotel Notre Dame, 2 nights, 4 stars
Spain: Train, 1 star
Madrid: Concha Hostela, 2 nights, 2 stars
Barcelona: Hostel Kabul, 1 star
France: Couchette, 2 stars
Nice: Selecty Home Pension, 3 nights, 3 stars
France: Couchette, 1 star
Gimmelwald: Mountain Hostel, 2 nights, 3 stars
Florence: Franco Bucherelli Hotel, 2 nights, 2 stars

Florence: Hotel Pina, 2 nights, 2 stars
Orvieto: Hotel Centrale, 4 stars
Rome: ISA Hotel (en suite), 2 nights, 5 stars
Rome: ISA Hotel, 2 nights, 4 stars
Venice: Hotel Villa Rosa, 2 nights, 3 stars
Austria: Train, 1 star
Vienna: Hotel Zur Wiener Staatsoper, 5 stars
Budapest: Private home at Falk Mika Utica II-4, 2 nights, 4 stars
Sombor: Jovo's home, 6 nights, 5 stars
Germany: Train, 2 stars
Amsterdam: Hotel Bastion (en suite), 5 stars

Acknowledgments

Ava Sever
J. Scott Codespoti
Dan Glumac
Gry Løklingholm
Erin MacCoy
Jenny Ling
Jason Johnson
Cheryl Bond
Bryan Tomasovich
Caroline Lebedoff
Michael Harrington
Nancy Cauley
Darlene Sever
Andrea Evanich

CPSIA information can be obtained
at www.ICGtesting.com
Printed in the USA
LVHW090917011221
703726LV00006B/5/J